SOPHOCLES: THE THEBAN PLAYS

ANTIGONE
KING OIDIPOUS
OIDIPOUS AT COLONUS

The Focus Classical Library

Aristophanes: Acharnians • Jeffrey Henderson
Aristophanes: The Birds • Jeffrey Henderson
Aristophanes: Clouds • Jeffrey Henderson
Aristophanes: Frogs • Jeffrey Henderson
Aristophanes: Lysistrata • Jeffrey Henderson
Aristophanes: Three Comedies: Acharnians, Lysistrata, Clouds • Jeffrey Henderson
Euripides: The Bacchae • Stephen Esposito
Euripides: Four Plays: Medea, Hippolytus, Heracles, Bacchae • Stephen Esposito
Euripides: Hecuba • Robin Mitchell-Boyask
Euripides: Heracles • Michael R. Halleran
Euripides: Hippolytus • Michael R. Halleran
Euripides: Medea • Anthony Podlecki
Euripides: The Trojan Women • Diskin Clay
Golden Verses: Poetry of the Augustan Age • Paul T. Alessi
Golden Prose in the Age of Augustus • Paul T. Alessi
Hesiod: Theogony • Richard Caldwell
Hesiod: Theogony & Works and Days • Stephanie Nelson
The Homeric Hymns • Susan Shelmerdine
Ovid: Metamorphoses • Z. Philip Ambrose
Plautus: Captivi, Amphitryon, Casina, Pseudolus • David Christenson
Roman Comedy: Five Plays by Plautus and Terence • David Christenson
Roman Lives • Brian K. Harvey
Sophocles: Antigone • Ruby Blondell
Sophocles: Electra • Hanna M. Roisman
Sophocles: King Oidipous • Ruby Blondell
Sophocles: Oidipous at Colonus • Ruby Blondell
Sophocles: Philoktetes • Seth Schein
Sophocles: The Theban Plays • Ruby Blondell
Terence: Brothers (Adelphoe) • Charles Mercier
Vergil: The Aeneid • Richard Caldwell

Copyright © 2002, 2004 Ruby Blondell.

Cover: Apulian jug (Oinochoe) by the Darius Painter showing Teiresias led into the presence of Oidipous, c. 340/330 B.C. Courtesy: Antikenmuseum Basel und Sammlung Ludwig, Inv. BS 473. Photo: Claire Niggli.

ISBN 13: 978-1-58510-037-8

This book is published by Focus Publishing, R. Pullins & Company, Inc., PO Box 369, Newburyport MA 01950. All rights are reserved. No part of this publication may be reproduced, stored in a retrieval system, or transmitted in any form or by any means, electronic, mechanical, by photocopying, recording, or by any other means, without the prior written permission of the publisher.

If you have received this material as an examination copy free of charge, Focus Publishing/R. Pullins Company retains the title to the material and it may not be resold. Resale of any examination copies of Focus Publishing/R. Pullins materials is strictly prohibited.

Printed in the United States of America

11 10 9 8 7 6 5 4

1011TS

SOPHOCLES: THE THEBAN PLAYS

ANTIGONE
KING OIDIPOUS
OIDIPOUS AT COLONUS

TRANSLATION WITH NOTES AND INTRODUCTION

RUBY BLONDELL
UNIVERSITY OF WASHINGTON

Focus Classical Library
Focus Publishing
R. Pullins Company
Newburyport MA

To Douglas

ἀνδρῶν πρῶτον ἔν τε συμφοραῖς βίου
ἔν τε δαιμόνων συναλλαγαῖς

Table of Contents

Preface vii

Introduction 1
    Sophocles 1
    Theater and Performance 6
    Mythic Background 16
    Religious Background 20

Antigone 33

King Oidipous 91

Oidipous at Colonus 155

Map 1: Mainland Greece 228

Map 2: Attica and Environs 229

Suggestions for Further Reading 230

Preface

This volume combines updated versions of my translations of Sophocles' three Theban plays, which have already been published as separate volumes.[1] *Oidipous at Colonus* appears in its second edition, which was heavily revised from the first. *Antigone* and *King Oidipous* have been corrected and more lightly revised, with an eye to consistency for this volume as a whole. The notes have been trimmed, and the interpretive essays at the ends of the individual volumes have been sacrificed, in order to keep the volume from becoming too large. The Introduction recapitulates those of all three earlier volumes, but also includes an expanded section on religion, in order to include some essential background material that originally appeared in the essays.

The translations are aimed at readers, especially students and teachers, who wish to work with a version that is close to the Greek. I have tried as far as possible to remain faithful to Greek idiom and metaphor, to translate words important for the meaning of the play consistently, and sometimes to retain the original word order, verse and sentence structure. This approach sometimes leads to awkwardness, but I hope this will be outweighed by its benefits. Though many aspects of the poetry have inevitably been lost, as they must be in any translation, I believe, and hope the reader will discover, that much of the poetry of meaning is best communicated in such a way.

The original meters have inevitably been sacrificed, but I have used a kind of six-beat iambic line for the iambic (spoken) portions of the drama, and tried to retain an approximately anapestic rhythm for Sophocles' anapests (which are printed in italics). I have not used any formal metrical scheme for the lyrics, or sung portions of the text, which are simply rendered in short lines and indented. (In order to avoid confusing the reader, in some lyric passages I have increased the number of lines so that they match the marginal line numbers, which are the same as in the Greek text.) Despite this attempt to retain some of the rhythmic sense of the original, my first priorities have

---

[1] M.W. Blundell, *Sophocles' Antigone, Translated with Introduction, Notes and Interpretive Essay* (Focus Classical Library, Newburyport MA 1998); R. Blondell, *Sophocles' King Oidipous, Translated with Introduction, Notes and Interpretive Essay* (Focus Classical Library, Newburyport MA 2002); R. Blondell, *Sophocles' Oidipous at Colonus, Translated with Introduction, Notes and Interpretive Essay*, revised edn. 2002 (Focus Classical Library, Newburyport MA).

usually been accuracy and consistency.

The spellings of Greek names represent an attempt to reap some of the benefits of both comfort and defamiliarization. For the most part I have used traditional English spelling for the names of historical persons and places (e.g. Aeschylus, Athens), but transliterated mythological names in so far as this accords with modern English pronunciation (e.g. Kreon, Polyneices). In the case of Oidipous, there are further reasons for preferring this spelling over "Oedipus," since it not only captures more effectively the many puns upon this name in *King Oidipous*, but encourages the reader to resist the anachronistic Freudian associations of the traditional spelling.

The explanatory notes are aimed at those approaching this play, and perhaps all ancient Greek literature, for the first time. They provide factual information on such matters as mythology, geography and unfamiliar customs, together with clarification of obscure phrases and a few interpretive pointers. There are no stage directions in ancient Greek texts. Those provided in the translation are based on indications in the script, and are intended to clarify the stage action for the modern reader.

The translations of *Antigone* and *OT* were based on Hugh Lloyd-Jones and Nigel Wilson's Oxford Classical Text (Oxford 1990), but I have departed from their text on occasion. In places I followed the text of Mark Griffith's edition of *Antigone* (Cambridge 1999). I also found his notes extremely valuable. My original translation of *Oidipous at Colonus* followed A.C. Pearson's Oxford Classical Text (Oxford 1924), with some departures. For the revised edition, I also consulted Lloyd-Jones and Wilson's OCT and followed their text in numerous places. The translation and notes for all three plays are indebted to Jebb's great work,[2] and to a lesser extent to Kamerbeek's more recent commentaries.[3] I also consulted Dawe's edition of *OT* (Cambridge 1982), and benefited from felicitious phrasing in Hugh Lloyd-Jones' translations for the Loeb Classical Library (Cambridge, MA 1994).

It remains to reiterate my thanks to friends, students and colleagues who assisted me in various ways with the individual translations: James Clauss, Ann Cumming, Alain Gowing, Mark Griffith, David Guichard, Michael Halleran, Yurie Hong, John Kirby and his students, Brady Mechley, Pauline Ripat, Douglas Roach, Stephen Sharpe, and the students in my Sophocles class in the Autumn of 2001.

UNIVERSITY OF WASHINGTON
SEATTLE

---

[2]   R.C. Jebb, *Sophocles, the Plays and Fragments. Part I: The Oedipus Tyrannus* (2nd edn. Cambridge 1887); *Part II: The Oedipus Coloneus* (3rd edn. Cambridge 1900); *Part III: The Antigone* (3rd edn. Cambridge 1900).

[3]   J.C. Kamerbeek, *The Plays of Sophocles. Commentaries Part II: The Oedipus Coloneus* (Leiden 1984); *Part III: The Antigone* (Leiden 1978); *Part IV: The Oedipus Tyrannus* (Leiden 1967).

Introduction

SOPHOCLES

Of the hundreds of tragedies produced in fifth-century BCE Athens, only a handful of works, by just three dramatists, have survived to the present day. Seven of these plays are by the poet Sophocles, who was born at Colonus, the rural village near Athens where *Oidipous at Colonus* is set, in about 495 BCE. This makes him a generation younger than his great predecessor Aeschylus (c. 525-456), and ten or fifteen years older than Euripides (c. 480-406). But the relationship between the three tragedians and their works is not strictly linear. The first dozen years of Sophocles' career overlapped with Aeschylus' final years, and for the rest of his long life Euripides was his rival. Aeschylus made use of Sophocles' theatrical innovations (discussed below), and Sophocles in turn was influenced by Euripides. It is said that when Euripides died in 406 BCE, Sophocles dressed his chorus in mourning at a public ceremony that preceded the dramatic festival (the *proagōn*). He himself was to die later the same year, or early in the next. In the fourth century and beyond, these three men rapidly became canonized as the great figures of the Athenian tragic theater, which led to the survival of some of their works when the entire output of the other tragic playwrights was lost. As with all ancient texts, the survival of these particular plays depended not only on the vagaries of taste, but on the chancy process of hand-copying and recopying manuscripts, until the advent of printing nearly two thousand years later.

Sophocles lived a long and active life, spanning almost the whole of the fifth century BCE, which saw a great many political and cultural achievements at Athens. We know almost nothing of his background (except that his father, Sophillus, is said to have owned a weapons factory), but the evidence of his career suggests a well-connected family. Like any Athenian boy whose father could afford it, he will have received the customary education in music, poetry and athletics. The mainstay of this education was Homer, especially the *Iliad*, which was thought to embody not just literary excellence but traditional cultural and moral values. As a child, Sophocles will have learned to recite large quantities of the epic from memory. This must have been especially significant for the future playwright whom later writers were to describe as "most Homeric" of the tragedians.

1

The poet's childhood coincided with the Persian Wars, in which the Greeks, largely under the leadership of Athens, foiled repeated Persian attempts to invade the Greek mainland. Sophocles was about five years old when the Athenians won their first great victory over the Persians at the battle of Marathon (490 BCE). When the Persians were defeated again, in a sea-battle off the island of Salamis in 480 BCE, the young Sophocles is said to have led the dance in celebration of the victory. If true, this was a significant honor, as well as a tribute to the youth's good looks and physical grace. He grew to maturity in the years that followed the Persian Wars, when the power and influence of Athens were on the rise. After their victory, the city founded the Delian League, an alliance of Greek states for mutual defense against the Persians. But as the fifth century progressed Athens took increasing control of the League, until it grew to resemble an Athenian empire more than an alliance of free states. The so-called allies were soon required to pay Athens large amounts of annual tribute in the form of ships or money. This period of Athenian history is marked by the leadership of Pericles, who was born around the same time as Sophocles and dominated public life from about 460 BCE until his death from the plague in 429. He both strengthened democracy at home and expanded Athenian influence abroad, in large part by exploiting Athenian leadership of the Delian League.

One of Pericles' most ambitious enterprises was the public building pro-gram that culminated in the construction of the Parthenon—the great temple of Athena, the city's patron goddess, on the Acropolis. Like other such projects, this temple, with its magnificent architecture and sculptural decoration, was partly financed by taxes from members of the Delian League. Besides sup-porting the visual arts, Pericles was a patron of writers and thinkers, helping to promote the extraordinary artistic and intellectual accomplishments of fifth-century Athens. Literary excellence was also fostered by the generally open and tolerant nature of Athenian democratic society, which placed a high value on artistic achievement and freedom of expression. (The notoriously provocative philosopher Socrates was active as a "gadfly" throughout most of this period, and was not prosecuted until 399 BCE, after Athens had become demoralized by defeat and less tolerant of public criticism.) But the cultural achievements of Periclean Athens meant little to the oppressed members of its empire or to its rivals, headed by Sparta. In 431 BCE, when Sophocles was in his sixties, the resentment aroused by Athenian expansion culminated in the outbreak of the Peloponnesian War, between Athens with its allies on one side and Sparta with its allies on the other. This long and draining war dominated the last twenty-five years of the poet's life, and he was to die before it finally ended with the defeat of Athens in 404 BCE.

Sophocles began his dramatic career in 468 BCE, when with his first set of plays (which have not survived) he defeated Aeschylus to win first prize in the tragic competition (discussed further below). By this time tragedy in Athens had already developed into a mature art form. But the conventions of the genre were not static, and Sophocles earned a reputation as a theatri-cal innovator. Aristotle tells us in his treatise on drama, the *Poetics*, that he increased the number of actors from two to three, and introduced the practice of scene-painting. He is also said to have enlarged the size of the chorus from twelve to fifteen, written a book on dramaturgy, and founded an artistic society dedicated to the Muses (the patron goddesses of music and the arts). In the course of his long career he wrote more than a hundred and twenty dramas—about ninety tragedies and thirty satyr plays (a kind of mythological burlesque). Of this enormous output we have only seven tragedies, significant parts of two satyr plays and some scattered fragments. The survival of these particular plays was not random, but probably results from their conscious selection as Sophocles' "best" plays, in somebody's opinion, at some point in the process of transmission.

Of the surviving tragedies we have secure production dates for only two, which also happen to be the last of the seven: *Philoktetes*, produced in 409 BCE, and *Oidipous at Colonus*, produced posthumously in 401. The dating of *Ajax*, *Elektra* and *Women of Trachis* is highly speculative. *Antigone* may have been produced about 442 BCE. The evidence for this is insecure, however. An ancient commentator tells us that Sophocles was elected general for the Samian War because of the admiration aroused by this play. We know from other evidence that Sophocles did indeed hold such a post, serving alongside Pericles during the Samian revolt of 441/440. The idea that he was elected on the strength of *Antigone* is thought by most scholars to be dubious, like many stories concerning the lives of ancient poets; but it is not impossible, given the ancient Athenians' belief in the educational value of poetry, and this play's explicitly political subject matter. (A fourth-century orator was to quote Kreon's opening speech with approval for its patriotic content.) Even if the story is untrue, however, its existence suggests that the play came before the generalship rather closely. *Antigone* could not have been produced in 441, since the election came before the dramatic festival. So a hypothetical date, usually accepted for lack of any other evidence, is 442. *King Oidipous* was probably produced somewhere between 430 and 425, but once again the evidence is tenuous. For example, the description of the plague that opens the play is often thought to have been influenced by the terrible plague that devastated Athens at the outset of the Peloponnesian War, in which Pericles died, along with a quarter of the Athenian population. But although this *may* be true, it is by no means certain, especially since there is a literary tradition of plague-descriptions going back hundred of years earlier, to the opening of Homer's *Iliad*. Accordingly, some scholars have dated the play before the beginning of the war.

Whether or not we believe that *Antigone* secured Sophocles' election as general, the story does suggest both the high regard in which a popular poet might be held, and the lack of a sharp dichotomy between artistic and political life. Despite the modern connotations of the title, Athenian "generalship" was not exclusively, or even primarily, a military position, but an elected political office. Sophocles' service as general thus shows him taking an active part in the political as well as the military life of Athens, in line with cultural expectations for male citizens of the leisured classes. An anecdote about the

Samian campaign helps bring him to life for us. A contemporary writer reports that one day when the two men were dining together, Pericles remarked that Sophocles was a good poet but a bad strategist; in response, the poet displayed his "strategic" expertise by craftily stealing a kiss from a handsome boy who was pouring the wine. Another story, from Plato, recounts that Sophocles was relieved to be freed by old age from the tyranny of sexual desire for women (*Republic* 329bc). Such anecdotes suggest an urbane and passionate man who participated in the wide range of activities—political, social, erotic—expected of his gender, class and culture.

Besides serving as a general, Sophocles held the important office of public treasurer in 443/2. Late in life he was again chosen for significant public office. In 413 BCE Athens suffered a crushing defeat in Sicily, and the poet (now more than eighty years old) was one of ten commissioners appointed to reorganize Athenian affairs after the crisis. Another incident shows him participating in a different area of public life. In 420 BCE the cult of Asklepios, god of medicine, was formally introduced into Athens. The god, who took the form of a snake, remained in the house of Sophocles until his official residence could be prepared. For this service the poet was honored after his death as a cult hero, under the name of Dexion ("Receiver").[1]

Sophocles was probably acquainted with many of the most important cultural figures of his day. Besides the association we have already seen with Pericles, his name is connected with such people as the philosopher Archelaus (a teacher of Socrates), and the historian Herodotus. Both *Antigone* and *OC* provide evidence for his familiarity with Herodotus' work.[2] When Oidipous compares his sons to the Egyptians, whose customs are said to be the opposite of the Greeks', he is probably drawing on the colorful account in the second book of Herodotus' *Histories* (see n. on *OC* 338). And when Antigone explains that she buried her brother because, unlike a child or husband, he is irreplaceable, she too is echoing an argument from Herodotus (see n. on *Ant.* 908).

The plays of Sophocles also show an unmistakable familiarity with the rhetorical techniques popularized by the contemporary thinkers known as "sophists." These itinerant intellectuals offered instruction in many subjects, and were associated with moral relativism and other intellectual challenges to traditional ethical and religious values. Their principle subject, however, was rhetoric, for which they found a ready audience at Athens, where public life was pervaded by debate and persuasive speaking was the key to political success. In democratic Athens, public policy was decided by an assembly open to all adult male citizens, who voted on each issue after extensive debate. Athenian society was also highly litigious, and a citizen had to plead his own case in court before a jury of several hundred of his peers. It is therefore not surprising that the dramatists and their audience had a highly developed appreciation

---

[1] On hero cult see below, pp. 29-30.
[2] I use the standard abbreviations *OT* (= *Oidipous Tyrannos*) to refer to *King Oidipous*, *Ant.* for *Antigone*, and *OC* for *Oidipous at Colonus*.

for oratory. Though Sophocles' style may seem less self-consciously rhetorical than that of Euripides, the influence of public oratory can be seen clearly, especially in the long and formal speeches with which his characters often debate each other. The influence of legal language is also apparent, notably in *OT*, which in some respects evokes a murder trial.

Sophocles lived to an age of about ninety. The story goes that in his advanced old age he quarreled with his son Iophon, who then sued him for senility under a law allowing a son to take control of an incompetent father's property. In his own defense, Sophocles read aloud in court from the play he was working on at the time: the opening lines of the song in praise of the Athenian land in *OC* (668-93). Naturally he was acquitted. Like most such stories, this one is unlikely to be true. (It is probably derived from a contemporary comedy, lampooning the poet and his son.) But it tells us something about the image of Sophocles that was constructed even at an early date. He did not inspire such colorful anecdotes as many others, including the other two major tragedians. (Aeschylus was supposedly killed by a tortoise dropped on his head by an eagle, and Euripides was said to be a misanthropic cave-dwelling vegetarian who was torn apart by hunting dogs.) This accords with the way he is presented by the comic playwright Aristophanes. In Aristophanes' play *Clouds*, Aeschylus and Euripides are used to embody stuffy traditionalism and new-fangled immorality respectively, with no mention at all of Sophocles (*Clouds* 1364-72). Likewise in Aristophanes' *Frogs*, Aeschylus and Euripides are polarized and pilloried as exemplars of extreme styles of drama—the old-fashioned and the new-fangled—while Sophocles is said to have been a good-tempered man in life and death (*Frogs* 82). We may also note that his style is much harder to parody than that of either of the other two dramatists. All this suggests that Sophocles was elided from the competition of *Frogs* in part because of his apparently "moderate" qualities, both personal and poetic. The fact that the year of his birth falls between the other two poets has further encouraged this picture of him as a kind of "mean" between the other two tragedians.

From earliest times, then, Sophocles has been constructed as the most "serene" and "ideal" of the dramatists, the one who aimed at and achieved alleged classical canons of moderation and harmony. This idealization of Sophocles as the quintessential classical Greek tragedian has continued to the present day. *Antigone* and *OT*, in particular, are among the most canonical works of the entire European literary and cultural tradition. In some ways, this reverence has damaged the study of Sophocles, by casting an aura of sanctity or dusty respectability over his works, enshrining them as "classical" and therefore unexciting or impervious to criticism. Yet these plays retain their power to be reimagined anew by successive generations. *OC* is one of Sophocles' less well-known plays, yet it has been transformed into one of the most successful of all modern reinterpretations of an ancient drama, Lee Breuer and Bob Telson's Gospel musical, *The Gospel at Colonus*. And *Antigone* continues to serve as a locus for philosophical inquiry, from the influential interpretation of the nineteenth-century German philosopher Hegel, to the explorations of the contemporary theorist Judith Butler.[3] Through countless appropriations and re-stagings its heroine has become a patron saint of civil disobedience, free speech, and resistance to oppression.

As for *OT*, it too occupies an extraordinary place in the modern imagination, thanks in large part to two men: Aristotle and Freud. The former's use of Sophocles' play in the *Poetics*—whose influence on literary criticism would be hard to exaggerate—made this drama exemplary, enshrining it for many later readers as the pinnacle of classical Greek tragic art. And Freud's thinking has so permeated contemporary culture that the name of Oidipous is, for many readers, more strongly associated with him than with Sophocles.[4] Thanks to his incalculable influence, Oidipous has become synonymous with the deepest and most terrible fears and desires of the unconscious. Indeed, one of our more challenging tasks as readers of these plays is to remember that they preceded the birth of Freud by thousands of years. Their persistent cultural significance inevitably informs and enriches our own encounters with Sophocles' text. Nonetheless, we should try, in the first instance, to focus on the texts themselves and their original contexts, remaining alert to the biases introduced, whether consciously or otherwise, by our own cultural accretions.

THEATER AND PERFORMANCE[5]

The form of drama that we call "Greek" tragedy was in fact a peculiarly Athenian art form, closely associated with the life of Athens in the fifth century BCE. The theater was enormously popular in Athens, in a way that may be hard to grasp today since there is no direct modern equivalent. Athenian dramatic performances combined the official status of a public institution (both civic and religious), the broad popularity of a Hollywood blockbuster, the emotional and competitive appeal of a major sporting event, and the artistic and cultural pre-eminence of Shakespeare. The theater was so far from being reserved for a culturally elite minority that a fund was instituted to enable poor citizens to buy tickets. Audiences were as large as 15,000-20,000, out of a population of only about 300,000 men, women and children (including slaves and resident aliens).

The exact composition of the audience is, however, a matter of controversy. In particular, scholars are not entirely agreed on whether women were permitted to attend. The traditional assumption that they could not is based on the exclusion of women from most public arenas of Athenian life. But there were exceptions to this exclusion. Women were able, and indeed required,

---

3   *Antigone's Claim: Kinship between Life and Death* (Columbia UP, New York 2000).
4   For a brief introductory account of Freud's use of Sophocles' play see Segal 2001: 39-42.
5   A fuller version of this section appears in the general introduction to *Women on the Edge: Four Plays by Euripides*, translated with introductions and commentary by R. Blondell, M.-K. Gamel, N.S. Rabinowitz and B. Zweig (Routledge: New York 1999). For a thorough discussion, with ancient sources translated into English, see Csapo and Slater 1995.

to go out in public for such events as religious festivals and funerals. And drama at Athens was produced only at public festivals of this kind, held in honor of Dionysos, god of the theater. Moreover Dionysos was a god whose myths embraced all kinds of outsiders. Women played an important part in his cult, in contrast to those of most other major male divinities. This fact reinforces the slight concrete evidence we have, which suggests that women, along with other socially marginal groups, including even slaves, were indeed permitted to attend the theater. It seems likely, however, that these socially inferior groups would have been present in much smaller numbers than the male citizens who were the dramatists' primary audience.

Dionysos is associated with song and dance, masking and shifting identities. He is thus an apt patron for an art form that celebrates the crossing of boundaries and the playing of roles. It was at his principal Athenian festival, the City Dionysia, that most of the great tragedians' works were first performed. At the beginning of this festival, a statue of the god was carried in a torchlight procession to the theater, and it remained present throughout the dramas. When the chorus of Thebans in *Antigone* sing and dance to Dionysos as their patron god, invoking him as a chorus-leader (*Ant.* 1146), the Athenian citizens performing in that chorus are singing and dancing for Dionysos as the god of theater (cf. also *OT* 896). Yet the plays were not religious rituals in any modern sense. Drama may have arisen from ritual, and often makes use of ritual forms such as sacrifice, wedding and funeral rites; but drama was not *itself* a ritual. Playwrights and performers were honoring the gods by their work, but there is no suggestion in our sources that the dramas were composed, produced, or evaluated using religious criteria.

The festival of Dionysos, which lasted several days, included processions, sacrifices, and musical and dramatic performances of various kinds. It was a major civic as well as religious celebration, an occasion for public festivity and civic pride, and an opportunity for Athens to display itself and its cultural achievements to the world. The City Dionysia took place in the spring, when the sailing season had begun and visitors from all over the Greek world might be in town, including the members of the Delian League, who brought their tribute to Athens at this time of year. This tribute was displayed in the theater during the festival. Other related ceremonies included the awarding of golden crowns to public benefactors, and the presentation of sets of armor to young men whose fathers had been killed in battle. All this offers striking testimony to the political context in which Athenian drama was originally performed. We should bear this in mind when seeking to understand plays like those in this volume, whose central themes include the relationship of the individual to society and the proper conduct of a ruler. The primary subject matter of tragedy is traditional mythology, but this material is used to scrutinize the political and cultural ideology of the poets' own time, including democracy, gender norms, and Athenian identity.

The tragedies at the City Dionysia were produced as part of a competition. Greek culture generally was highly competitive, and religious festivals often involved various kinds of contest. The Olympic games are one prominent example, and the City Dionysia itself included contests in comedy and choral song as well as tragedy. The tragic competition lasted for three days, with three poets each producing four dramas (three tragedies followed by a satyr play) in the course of a single day. The five judges who decided the contest were carefully selected by an elaborate procedure designed to prevent undue influence and bribes, and their decision was made under pressure from a rambunctious crowd. The winning playwright and *chorēgos* or chorus-director were publicly announced and crowned with ivy (a plant sacred to Dionysos), and had their names inscribed on a marble monument. Sophocles was extremely successful, winning at least eighteen victories and never coming third out of three in the competition.

Sometimes the three tragedies offered by a single playwright would constitute a connected trilogy, like Aeschylus' *Oresteia*, and even the satyr play might be on a related theme. But Sophocles seems to have preferred individual, self-contained dramas. Like the *Oresteia*, his three "Theban plays"—*Antigone*, *OT*, and *OC*—focus on the doings and sufferings of a single royal family over more than one generation. Unlike the *Oresteia*, however, they are not a trilogy. The plays of the *Oresteia* (the only trilogy that survives) were composed to be produced together in a single performance, following the fortunes of the house of Atreus in chronological sequence. But Sophocles' three plays were written at wide intervals, without following the legendary order of events. *Antigone* was probably the earliest of the these plays to be produced, yet it is the last in mythological sequence. Conversely, *OT* dramatizes the earliest part of the mythological sequence, but was probably the second to be written (above, p. 3). Each stands alone as a dramatic unity, and they were never intended to be performed together.

It is therefore not surprising that the three plays are inconsistent with each other in various ways. Oidipous' death, for example, is described quite differently in *Antigone* and *OC*. In the earlier play, Ismene says their father died "hated and in ill-repute" (50), Antigone laid him out for burial, presumably at Thebes (897-902), and there is no trace of the miraculous death dramatized in *OC*. Similarly the character of Kreon—the only character with a speaking part in all three plays—fluctuates from one drama to the next. Yet allusions in the two later plays show that Sophocles had not forgotten the thematic threads connecting his Theban dramas, and may have hoped that his audience would remember them too.

Certainly, awareness of such connections may enrich our understanding of the plays. Thus when Oidipous entrusts his daughters to Kreon's care at the end of *OT*, the audience would presumably remember that Kreon had in fact killed Antigone in Sophocles' earlier play (*OT* 1503-10). *OC* echoes—and reverses—the structure of *OT*, and repeatedly recalls it, especially by Oidipous' reiterated self-defense for the terrible deeds of his past (*OC* 265-74, 521-48, 960-1002). Even though Antigone's role in this play is relatively minor, her impetuous, transgressive behavior at the end recalls her portrayal in her eponymous drama, in contrast to her "good girl" sister Ismene (cf. esp. *OC* 1724-36). And when Polyneices begs his sisters to be sure to bury him (*OC*

1405-13, 1435), the audience would naturally remember what happened to Antigone when she carried out his wish. At such moments Sophocles seems to invite us to read the plays together, despite the fact that they were composed for performances many years apart.

Since only three playwrights were allowed to stage their work at each festival, even having one's plays produced was a competitive challenge. In keeping with the public nature of the event, a city official was in charge of "granting a chorus" to three finalists out of those who applied (how he reached his decision is unknown). A wealthy citizen (the *chorēgos*) was appointed to bear most of the production costs, as a kind of prestigious extra taxation. Chief among these costs was the considerable expense of training and costuming the chorus. The poet was his own producer, and originally acted as well, or employed professional actors (Sophocles is said to have been the first to stop acting in his own plays). But around the middle of the fifth century the state

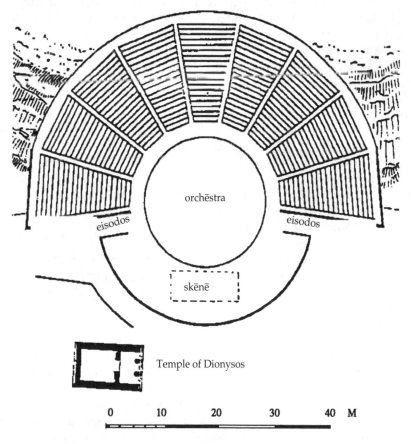

A reconstruction of the theater of Dionysos in Athens during the second half of the fifth century BCE. (Based on the sketch by J. Travlos, Pictorial Dictionary of Ancient Athens [London 1971] 540.)

also assumed control of allocating a principal actor to each production, and began awarding a prize for the best actor.

The plays were performed in the open-air theater of Dionysos on the southeastern slope of the Acropolis, where an impressive view of the mountains and coastline of southern Attica stretched behind the theatrical scene. Performances began at dawn and lasted all day. The action of some plays, such as *Antigone*, begins at dawn, which may be an allusion to daybreak in the actual theater. Once the sun had risen, the size and openness of the theater were enhanced by the bright daylight enveloping performers and audience alike. This generated a very different and specifically more public atmosphere than the darkened theaters and artificial lighting of today. The audience must have been very conscious of one another as well as of the play, and thus aware of their collective engagement in a public civic and cultural event. They sat crowded together, expressed their opinions, sometimes vociferously, and ate and drank during the performances, especially if they did not approve of the acting. They responded to the plays with visceral emotion, judging them not as aesthetic artefacts remote from real life, but as contributions to the discussion of contemporary political, moral and social concerns. The theater was an extension of their world, not an escape from it.

In size and shape the theater of Dionysos resembled one end of a large football stadium (see diagram, p. 9). The judges sat in carved stone seats at the front, along with the priests of Dionysos and other religious figures, public benefactors, high-ranking officials and important foreign visitors. Most of the audience probably sat on the ground, on the sloping sides of the Acropolis hill above the theater. Foreigners, women, children and slaves were probably seated at the back and sides of the seating area. The performance space was dominated by a large dancing floor, the *orchēstra*, which was about seventy feet across. Contemporary scholars are divided over the shape of the *orchēstra* in Sophocles' time. (It may have been round or rectangular.) Behind it was a wooden stage-building, the *skēnē* (literally "tent" or "hut") which served as a set. Whether or not there was a raised stage in the fifth century is also a matter of controversy. If so, it was merely a low, narrow platform in front of the stage-building.[6] The *skēnē* had one or more doors through which characters could enter and exit, and was also used by the actors as a changing-room.

In performance, the *skēnē* usually represents a house or other structure, but may also serve, for example, as a cave (as in Sophocles' *Philoktetes*). In both *OT* and *Antigone* it stands for the palace of the Theban royal family. In *OC*, however, it represents a sacred grove at the village of Colonus. To judge from Antigone's description (16-18), this was an impressive and picturesque spot. Bearing in mind Sophocles' supposed introduction of scene-painting (above, p. 3), it is plausible to assume that the building was appropriately decorated. We do not know to what extent specific locations were indicated through painting and props. But any such indicators were probably stylized and minimal,

---

6   For convenience, it is usual in discussing Greek drama to use the word "stage" to refer to the entire performance area, and I have followed that practice.

since the theater was so large that detailed scenery would not be easily visible to the audience. The grove was therefore probably indicated simply, leaving the imaginative appeal of poetic description to fill in the details. But however the *skēnē* was decorated, the action of the play requires a large rock, located in front of it but within the sacred area, for Oedipus to sit on (19). The low ledge further forward, where he sits later (192-6), may also have been part of the set, unless it was represented by the edge of the stage. *OT* and *Antigone* require a less elaborate set, but *OT* calls for an altar in front of the house, where the initial group of suppliants is gathered.

The main action of a Greek play always takes place outside the stage-building, though interior scenes and scenes from distant locations are often described by the players. The dominant presence of the *skēnē* at the center may be dramatically powerful, as when Oidipous emerges blinded from the palace (*OT* 1298). Occasionally an interior scene is revealed through the *skēnē* door, usually at a climactic moment, as when Eurydike's corpse is revealed at the end of *Antigone* (1293). Sometimes this was accomplished in performance by means of a device called the *ekkyklēma*, a low wheeled platform that could be rolled out of the *skēnē* to display a tableau from within. This device may have been used at the end of *Antigone*.

Entrances and exits not involving the *skēnē*, including the entry and departure of the chorus, were made along the side-entrances—two long ramps, one on each side of the *orchēstra*, called *eisodoi* (the singular is *eisodos*; these ramps are also sometimes called *parodoi*). The same *eisodos* is used consistently throughout the play to represent a particular locale. Thus in *Antigone*, one of them represents the path to the upland plain where the battle took place and Polyneices' body lies, and the other the road from the city of Thebes proper. In *OT*, similarly, one leads to the countryside (and thence to Corinth and Delphi), the other to the city. In *OC* all visitors from Thebes arrive from the same side, and those from Athens and the village of Colonus from the other.

The structure of the tragic stage, with its central doorway flanked by two side entrances, may itself be used to dramatic effect. In OT, it evokes the fatal fork in the road where the hero meets and kills his father. Like Oidipous at the crossroads, the palace stands between the world outside Thebes and the city itself, between civilization and wilderness. And in *OC*, it is dramatically effective for the two sides of the stage to represent Oidipous' friends and foes, while he remains at the center of the conflict. The length of the side-entrances could also be exploited for dramatic purposes, as when Kreon is sighted in the distance in *OT* (78-86), Antigone excitedly watches the approach of Ismene in *OC* (310-323), or the guard in *Antigone* draws attention to his own leisurely progress (231-2).

The entire "production team" of Athenian tragedy (playwrights, producers, dancers, musicians, chorus and actors) was male. This extends to the numerous female roles, all of which were played by adult men (not boys, as in Shakespearean drama). The sex, age and status of each character were indicated in a formal, stylized way by costumes and masks. The masks were bold in design—as they had to be if they were to be visible to spectators seated at the far edge of the theater—but naturalistic in manner. They covered the whole head, including the ears, and had wigs attached. The lavish costumes included long, colorfully decorated robes, and sometimes tall, thin-soled boots. (Grotesquely exaggerated masks and thick-soled "buskins" came later.)

Details of costume and props made clear the status of each character and might also reflect familiar Athenian activities. In *Antigone*, the two sisters may be dressed in mourning for their dead brothers. In *OT*, the opening tableau displays the tokens of supplication (below, p. 21), and Kreon arrives wearing a laurel wreath (82-3). In *OC*, Ismene is dressed for traveling, and wears a distinctive hat (313-4). The shocked exclamations of Oidipous' visitors indicate that his clothing is filthy and his hair unkempt, he carries a beggar's wallet, and the scars where he put out his eyes are plainly visible (see esp. *OC* 551-6, 1256-63). A king would probably carry a scepter or staff of office, and helpless old men like the blind old Oidipous and Teiresias would also lean on a staff.

Such props might be exploited by the playwright to serve dramatically significant functions. Thus in *OT*, Oidipous bears the staff with which, unbeknownst to him, he assaulted his own father (810-11). He will lean on it when he returns, blind, at the end of the play. Teiresias, by contrast, enters leaning on the blind man's staff, which signifies physical fraility but also the insight betokened by his blindness. In *OC* the staff has a different kind of significance. Since a scepter is in origin a staff or walking-stick, the same word is used in Greek for both. Sophocles exploits this ambiguity to create a pathetic contrast between Oidipous' helplessness (848-9, 1109) and his sons' bid for the royal scepter of Thebes (425, 449, 1354).

The standard number of speaking actors in a given production, apart from the chorus, was three, though there were usually several non-speaking extras playing silent parts such as guards, attendants, and young children. The reasons for this restriction are unknown. But it helps to account for some apparent peculiarities. Ismene, for example, is silent for nearly 500 lines from *OC* 1096 to 1555. After she exits through the grove at 509, the actor who plays her must return to play Theseus at 1096-1210, Polyneices at 1249-1446 and Theseus again at 1500-1555. Meanwhile Ismene herself is played by a silent extra, until another speaking actor is released by Oidipous' departure. As this example shows, the restriction to three speaking actors means that where, as in this play, there are more than three speaking characters, at least one actor would have to play more than one part. Sometimes, too, a single role had to be split between two or more actors. The latter practice was facilitated by the fact that the actors were all male, and wore not only distinctive costumes but rigid masks identifying each character clearly. Moreover the acting was highly stylized, and did not rely on subtle body movements or facial expressions (which were ruled out by the masks). In such a large theater the actors must have delivered their lines loudly and emphatically, and used broad, clear gestures, in order to be seen and heard.

A central feature of all Athenian tragedies is the chorus, a group of fifteen performers representing local citizens or other concerned persons, who normally remain present from their entrance until the end of the play. Its members are masked and dressed in character like the main actors. They are not the "voice of the poet" in the abstract, but a character in the drama with a clearly defined identity, a specific gender and social status, which befit the particular segment of society they embody. Though played by men, they are generally of the same sex as the central figure of the drama, with whom they enjoy a certain solidarity. In *OC*, the chorus' age also gives them a special sympathy with Oidipous (cf. 1239). *Antigone* is unusual in this regard, if we regard Antigone herself as the central character, since the male gender and advanced age of the chorus give them more in common with Kreon. The most obvious effect of this is to enhance the heroine's isolation. (Contrast Aeschylus' use of a young female chorus for his telling of the story [below, p. 20].) As this example illustrates, the chorus' status and relationship to the main characters give them a specific point of view. They thus do not represent an "objective" or "true" view of events. Indeed, their judgment of the situation as it unfolds is often quite mistaken. It is characteristic of Sophocles to give his choruses songs of misplaced rejoicing just before disaster strikes—songs that show clearly the limitations in their understanding (e.g. *Ant.* 1115-54, *OT* 1086-1109).

The choral identity is a collective one. In contrast to the heroic individuality of the actors, the chorus-members are numerous, anonymous, and almost always unanimous. They have no individual names, and they speak of themselves, and are addressed, indiscriminately in the singular or plural. They therefore represent, to a certain extent, the group, as opposed to the individual, showing the effects of the main actors' words and deeds on the larger human community. As a group, they are in a sense continuous with the audience whose fellow-citizens they are. The actors who performed in the chorus were all male Athenian citizens—indeed, participation in dramatic choruses was an important civic duty. The audience, itself dominated by such citizens, would presumably identify to some extent with their peers portraying non-royal members of the civic body, as opposed to the extreme, heroic characters who dominate the story.

But we should not exaggerate the extent to which the chorus embodies "the community." Whether we view them as actors or citizens, they form only one segment of society as a whole. As citizens, they are free adult male Athenians playing a role in the theater. In their dramatic persona, however, they represent, remarkably often, a socially marginal segment of society—women, old men, foreigners, underlings or even slaves. They are thus far from being an embodiment of the Athenian *polis* or of "society" in the abstract. The "Theban plays" are somewhat unusual in this respect, since all three of their choruses represent elite males. But in *Antigone* they are explicitly distinguished from the city as a whole, since they have been hand-picked by Kreon as supporters of the royal house (164-6). And in all three dramas they are old men, whose frailty is often emphasized. This helps to render plausible their frequent failures to affect the action. Although some tragic choruses play an active role in the story (as in Aeschylus' *Eumenides*), more usually they play the part of bystanders. Sometimes the chorus-members seem to participate quite vigorously in the stage action, as in *OC* when they try to stop Kreon from kidnapping Antigone (829-43). But their dramatic effectiveness is usually quite limited: the attempt to save Antigone is unsuccessful. We do not know how much physical contact took place between chorus and actors during such scenes, or to what extent they shared the same performance spaces.

The primary dramatic medium of the chorus is lyric song and dance, performed in the *orchēstra*, or "dancing area." At intervals throughout the drama they perform a song, singing and dancing in unison. Although we know little about the choreography, it certainly included a strong mimetic element and drew on the rich living tradition of public choral dance, which was an integral part of many ritual, competitive and festal occasions in Greek life. The accompanying music was simple and did not interfere with comprehension of the words, which are always significant for the drama and sometimes of the highest poetic complexity. Such profundity may at times seem inappropriate to the chorus when viewed in character, e.g. as a group of sailors or slave women. But choral lyrics give the poet a different dramatic idiom in which to explore the themes of the play, and should not be tied too closely to the specific character of the chorus that gives them utterance. Though the sentiments are those of the choral character, the richness and complexity with which they are expressed often open up wider horizons and more diverse points of view than one might expect of this particular social group. In general, the chorus' "personality" is both blander than that of the main characters, and more fluid as it is refracted through their reactions to unfolding events. The old men of *Antigone* are exceptionally wishy-washy, even by the standards of tragic choruses. But their vagueness makes them an apt mouthpiece for the songs in this play, which are exceptionally complex, opaque and suggestive.

Choral song serves other functions as well. It may be used for the impressionistic or imaginative reporting of off-stage events, such as the assault on Thebes in the opening song of *Antigone*, or the rescue of the kidnapped girls in *OC* (1044-95). In the latter case, song provides a dramatic substitute for the direct reporting of the battle, enabling the poet both to compress this stage of the plot and to reserve the climactic device of a messenger speech for the end of the play. Choral song is often used like this to manipulate dramatic time. The shift of focus to the song and dance of choral performance, together with the accompanying pause in the stage action, makes it easy for the audience to accept that a considerable period of time has passed. Similarly, the *parodos* of Antigone marks the passage of sufficient time for Antigone to bury Poly-neices' corpse—something she could not have done by then in "real time." This technique is often used before a messenger arrives to tell us of extensive off-stage events (e.g. *Ant.* 1115-1154, *OT* 1186-1223, *OC* 1556-78).

Athenian tragedy is structured around the alternation of speech and song. Most plays open with a spoken monologue or dialogue by the actors (the prologue), which sets the scene and provides the audience with any necessary background information. Sophocles characteristically accomplishes this exposition through conversation, which simultaneously introduces important characters. This opening scene is followed by the arrival of the chorus, who enter singing the *parodos* or "entry song." They normally remain in the *orchēs-tra* for the rest of the play, performing further songs with dancing (known as *stasima*, which means "songs in position") between the scenes of the drama. This alternation of actors' speech and choral song is a fluid form rather than a rigid structure. Actors will sometimes shift into lyric meters, or converse with the chorus in a sung dialogue, especially at moments of high emotion, such as the entrance of the blinded Oidipous, or the departure of Antigone to her death. In *OC* the chorus' entry song takes the unusual form of an extended lyric dialogue (117-253). Such a dialogue may also play the scene-dividing role of a choral ode, or serve to vary the tone of a long scene. Conversely the chorus have a leader (the *koryphaios*), who not only leads the dancing but exchanges a few spoken lines with the actors, serving as the mouthpiece of the chorus as a whole.[7]

Both the spoken and the sung portions of Athenian drama are composed in verse. Greek poetry is not structured through rhyme, but depends on rhythmic patterns (meters) to create poetic form. The lyric songs are composed in highly varied and elaborate meters, which are unique to each song. A typical choral ode consists of a series of paired stanzas called the strophe and antistrophe. Each strophe has its own complex rhythmic structure, which is repeated precisely in the antistrophe. There may be several such strophic pairs, each metrically unique. Occasionally the strophe and antistrophe will echo each other thematically or structurally as well as metrically (cf. e.g. *Ant.* 359/370, 614/625; *OT* 168/178, 872/882, 895-6/909-10; *OC* 693/706, 1456/1471). The strophic pair or pairs may be followed by an epode—an additional single stanza sometimes found at the end of a lyric song, which has its own unique metrical pattern (as at *Ant.* 876-82, *OC* 208-54 and 1239-48). Though the spoken portions of Greek drama may be highly emotional—for example in the rhetorical expression of anger—lyrics are most often the vehicle for intense emotions such as grief or pity, which they convey in a more impressionistic, less rational style than spoken dialogue.

The actors' spoken lines, by contrast, are in iambic trimeters, a regular six-beat meter approximating the flow of natural speech (rather like Shakespearean blank verse). Other meters are occasionally used, especially anapests, a regular "marching" rhythm often associated with entrances and exits. (These are printed in italics in the translations.) Anapests were probably chanted rather than spoken or sung, and may have had a musical accompaniment. In *Antigone* they are used unusually often for the announcement of a character's entrance (cf. 376-83, 526-30, 626-30, 801-5). They are also used to accompany Antigone's final exit to her death (929-43). The concluding scene of *OC* is in this meter, which is often used for the final lines of a tragedy, though not usually as extensively as here.

The actors' spoken speeches range in length from the long rhetorical ora-

---

7 Since it is not always clear exactly when the *koryphaios* is speaking for the chorus, in most translations, including this one, all choral passages are attributed simply to the chorus.

tion, or *rhēsis*, to *stichomythia*, a formal kind of dialogue in which the characters exchange single alternating lines (or occasionally two lines apiece). *OT* has many long stretches of stichomythia, a mode well suited to the gradual—and suspenseful—disclosure of information. Stichomythia is also highly effective for crystalizing divergent values and points of view, as at *Antigone* 508-25. In this exchange, the two characters' differences are sharpened by the verbal echoes between their lines. This kind of echoing is a frequent feature of sticho-mythia, with rhetorical victory going to the speaker who caps the other's lines (cf. e.g. *Ant.* 726-57, *OT* 543-52). Such modes of speech—like many other aspects of Greek tragedy—may strike the modern audience as artificial. But every kind of drama relies on its own formal conventions. We tend not to notice the artificiality of our own standard theatrical modes (including film), because familiarity makes their conventions seem natural to us.

MYTHIC BACKGROUND

Athenian tragedians nearly always drew their material from traditional Greek mythology. But there was no official canon or approved version of such tales, and no requirement that various versions should be consistent with each other. The dramatists and their audiences were exposed to many versions of the myths, oral and written, traditional and innovative, in varying contexts that affected their mode of presentation and their meanings (epic recitation, theatrical performance, religious ritual, songs at parties, children's stories, oral tale-telling, and so on). Our own knowledge of these rich and varied traditions is scanty. It is helpful for our understanding of the plays to reconstruct, as best we can, any versions that we know to have been current in the poet's own day. Yet we must bear in mind that countless stories unknown to us undoubtedly influenced the dramatists' practice and helped to shape the plays' meanings for their original audience.

Like other writers, the tragedians were free not only to select or vary the legendary details of these stories for their own dramatic purposes, but also to create their own innovations. Some central features of the myths may have been unchangeable (the Greeks always win the Trojan War), but the degree of possible variation that remains may surprise the modern reader (Helen does not necessarily go to Troy; Medea does not always kill her children). A dramatist could vary the character traits even of well-known figures, for example by making a traditional personality more or less sympathetic. Mythology was thus a highly flexible medium for the ancient dramatists, enabling them to draw on past traditions and present expectations while adding their own developments to the future store of tales.

The three plays in this volume all focus on the terrible events surrounding the family history of Oidipous, which formed the subject of several lost epic poems and was an extremely popular subject in poetry and art, both before and during Sophocles' lifetime. Oidipous was the most famous mythic king of Thebes, a very ancient city some thirty miles northwest of Athens (see Map 2). Both *OT* and *Antigone* are set there, exemplifying the tendency of Athenian tragedy to locate disturbing mythological events beyond the territory of Athens itself. Thebes, in particular—a historical enemy of Athens—serves as a kind of ideological alter ego or "anti-Athens," used to embody and explore cultural tensions that might be highly disturbing to the audience if dramatized in an Athenian setting.[8] Athens and Athenians, by contrast, usually behave impeccably in tragedy. Thus in *OC*, Athens under its idealized king Theseus serves as an enlightened and generous haven of refuge for the exiled Oidipous. In the best-known tradition, Theseus is also instrumental in securing the burial of Polyneices and his allies (below, p. 20).

OT opens upon Oidipous at the pinnacle of his greatness, as a king beloved by his people, an intelligent, confident and compassionate man in the prime of life. We learn in the course of the play that he was raised in Corinth, but left that city to consult Apollo's oracle at Delphi about his parentage.[9] The oracle does not answer his question directly, but instead predicts that he will kill his father and marry his mother. In order to prevent the prophecy from coming true, he travels away from his "parents" in Corinth in the direction of Thebes. On his way, he is provoked by an unknown man at a fork in the road, and kills him.

Proceeding on to Thebes, he finds the city terrorized by the Sphinx, a winged monster with a lion's body and a woman's head and breasts. The Sphinx had entered Greek mythology from Egyptian tradition by the Bronze Age, and is a popular theme in Greek art, especially on tombstones. She is first mentioned in literature by Hesiod (*Theog.* 326-32). Unlike the Egyptian Sphinx (but like some near-eastern equivalents), she is both female and winged. Like many other such figures in mythology (Sirens, Gorgons, Furies, Keres etc.), she is a bringer of death, who binds and entraps men. She is often eroticized, as a monstrous female who preys on youths on the verge of manhood, whom she carries off and kills. In the Oidipous myth, she kills anyone who cannot answer a riddle. Her name may mean "strangler," and the riddle is an intellectual form of weaving or entrapment (cf. *OT* 130, 391).

One version of the Sphinx's famous riddle, which may derive from a lost tragedy, runs: "Two-footed and four-footed and three-footed upon the earth, it has a single voice, and alone of all those on land or in the air or sea it changes form. And when it goes supported on three feet, then the speed of its limbs is weakest."[10] The answer is, "a human being," whose lifetime is often likened in Greek imagery to the passage of a day (e.g. *Ant.* 788-9). In the course of that "day," we go first on four feet (a crawling baby), then on two (an adult) and finally on three (two legs and a walking-stick). Like the enigmatic Sphinx herself, who is made up of human, bird and beast, the human creature's identity is made up of a complex fusion of roles whose meaning must be deciphered. With her riddling speech delivered in hexameter verse,

---

[8] On this issue see Zeitlin 1990, Blundell 1993. The only surviving drama in which an Athenian king behaves dubiously is Euripides' *Hippolytos*, which is not set in Athens itself.

[9] For the locations of Thebes, Corinth and Delphi see Map 2.

[10] This translation is taken from Gantz 1993: 496.

the Sphinx is also a kind of malevolent counterpart to Apollo, god of prophecy, whose oracles—likewise delivered in hexameters—were typically riddling in their language and easily misunderstood.

Oidipous solves the riddle, thus causing the Sphinx's death and saving the city from her depredations. In gratitude, the Thebans give him the crown of their recently murdered king, Laios, and the hand of the queen in marriage. This pattern of events is familiar from many myths and folktales. But Oidipous' story inverts the usual happy ending. In the course of Sophocles' drama he discovers that he is actually the son of Laios, who was the unknown man at the crossroads, and Jokasta, who is now his own wife. When Oidipous discovers the dreadful truth, he puts out his eyes in horror and longs only to go into exile from Thebes. But at the end of the play his fate is left uncertain, since Kreon, his brother-in-law, uncle, and successor as king, will not allow him to go into exile without first—once again—consulting Apollo's oracle at Delphi.

The influence of Sophocles' play has been such that this is the figure of Oidipous most familiar to the modern mind: the hero who falls from the pinnacle of human accomplishment to the depths of an excruciating self-awareness, becoming a universal symbol of the tragic blindness of the human condition. The earliest myth of Oidipous, however, makes him no such figure of doom, despite the parricide and incest that are part of his story from the beginning. There was an epic on the subject that is now lost, but the very little we know of it suggests that it diverged considerably from the accounts in tragedy. In the *Odyssey* we hear that though Oidipous was distressed at the discovery of his deeds, he went on ruling at Thebes (11.271-80). There is no mention of oracles or of Oidipous' self-blinding, though his mother/wife does hang herself. The *Iliad* mentions that he died violently—perhaps in battle or a fight—and was honored at Thebes with funeral games (23.679-80). Other treatments prior to that of Sophocles included a tragedy by Aeschylus. Though this too is lost, we know that it included the Sphinx and Oidipous' self-blinding, as well as his curse upon his sons, and probably focussed more on the family curse than Sophocles' play (cf. below, p. 27).

Some twenty years after *OT* was first produced, Sophocles, by now an old man himself, returned to complete the story of Oidipous in his last tragedy, *Oidipous at Colonus*. At the end of *OT*, his two daughters, Antigone and Ismene, appeared on the stage as young children. His sons, Eteokles and Polyneices, were also mentioned as being at the point of manhood (*OT* 1460-61). According to *OC*, Oidipous was expelled from Thebes some time later. By this time, the boys were old enough to speak up on his behalf (427-30), and his daughters to assist him to the best of their ability. When *OC* opens, he has been wandering in exile for many years, with only Antigone as his guide, companion, and protector. Ismene has been supporting them with visits and news from Thebes. Meanwhile his sons have come to blows over the right to rule in Thebes, and a great battle is impending. Oidipous is furiously angry with his sons, because, by contrast with his daughters, they permitted his exile (427-30) and then did nothing to alleviate it (337-56). But an oracle has decreed that whoever has his support will win the throne of Thebes. Polyneices, who has assembled an army of six allies (known, along with him, as the "Seven against Thebes"), visits his father to beg for such support. But Oidipous is unrelenting. He curses both his sons with a terrible fate: they will die at each other's hand in a battle over the throne of Thebes. At the end of the play, he proceeds to an awe-inspiring and uniquely miraculous death, which establishes him as an Athenian cult hero (below, p. 30-31).

Sophocles introduces a number of apparent innovations in this treatment of the myth of Oidipous and his sons. One small but interesting variation from other versions known to us is that he makes Polyneices the elder son (*OC* 374-6, 1292-8, 1422-3). Euripides makes him younger than Eteokles, and nowhere else does either brother's claim to the throne depend on primogeniture. Instead the two brothers are usually said to have agreed to rule alternately. Eteokles is first, but refuses to surrender the throne at the end of his allotted time, giving Polyneices a legitimate grievance against him. Since primogeniture was not the custom in classical Athens, Sophocles' innovation is likely to have reduced the audience's sympathy for Polyneices. It also gives Oidipous a further reproach to hurl against the son who appears before him, for as the first to rule he was also the first who might have recalled his father (cf. *OC* 1354-9). Sophocles has adapted a detail of the myth to prevent us from choosing sides between the brothers. Both are equally guilty, and equally damned.

Another variation in Sophocles' treatment of the myth is more substantial. In earlier accounts known to us, Oidipous' curse upon his sons is delivered at Thebes, and *causes* the strife between them. An epic fragment tells us that he cursed them for setting on his table the wine-cups of Laios (thus presumably reminding him of his parricide). The Erinys—a goddess of revenge—heard his curse that his sons should be at strife forever.[11] In *OC*, however, the curse occurs years later, and is a *consequence* of the brothers' strife. This enables the poet to exploit Oidipous' curse for maximum dramatic impact within his play. It also makes the curse more justifiable, since Oidipous does not utter it until his sons have come to blows, after already neglecting him for many years. Yet Polyneices seems to know already about his father's avenging spirit or Erinys (1298-9), and Oidipous himself mentions earlier curses (1375). Though the latter could simply refer to his previous imprecations within the play (421-7), it is certainly not difficult to imagine the irascible Oidipous cursing his sons repeatedly over the years. But we need not insist on perfect clarity. The important point for the drama is that the curse we witness is the decisive one, uttered as Oidipous is rapidly acquiring the cult hero's special powers.

The latest of the three dramas points back to the events of *OT*, but also forward (in mythic time) to the earliest to be produced, *Antigone* (see above, pp. 8-9). When this play opens, the great battle between the Thebans, led by Eteokles, against Polyneices and his many allies has just ended in victory for the Thebans. The two brothers are dead at each other's hand, and Kreon, their uncle, is in power. As Antigone reveals in the prologue, Kreon has commanded an honorific funeral for Eteokles, the defender, but forbidden burial entirely

---

[11] On the Erinys (plural Erinyes) see below, p. 23.

to Polyneices—a prohibition she defies, at the cost of her own life. In earlier versions of the story that we know of, there is virtually no mention either of Kreon's specific prohibition or of Antigone's defiance. In most accounts, Kreon forbids burial to Polyneices' entire army, and eventually backs down under the beneficent influence of Theseus. Sophocles may have been the first to shift the emphasis away from the unburied Argive army (merely touched on at *Ant.* 1080-84) towards the special case of Polyneices.

There is one possible exception to this. At the end of Aeschylus' tragedy, *Seven Against Thebes* (produced in 467 BCE), the corpses of both brothers are brought in, and both Antigone and Ismene are in attendance as mourners. A herald proclaims Kreon's edict forbidding Polyneices' burial, and Antigone declares her intention to defy it, alone if necessary. This scene is extremely close to Sophocles' play, but there are some interesting differences as well. In the Aeschylean version, the punishment for disobedience is not specified as death, nor is Antigone as isolated as she is in our play, since the chorus consists of young Theban women who are divided in their sympathies. Accordingly, half of them go with Antigone to bury Polyneices, while the other half follow the official funeral cortège of Eteokles (presumably accompanied by Ismene).

There are difficulties, however, with viewing *Seven Against Thebes* as part of the literary and mythic background for *Antigone*. Many scholars believe that the end of *Seven* was composed later, *after* Sophocles' play, in order to cohere more neatly with it in later revivals. If this is the case, then we have virtually no evidence concerning Antigone or her story prior to Sophocles. But we do know that Antigone's own death was not an unalterable aspect of the myth, since Euripides composed a play (now lost) in which she survived, married Kreon's son Haimon, and bore him a son. We also know that Haimon played a different role in other versions: in the lost epic he was a victim of the Sphinx. Sophocles may also have enhanced the role of Ismene and invented that of Eurydike, Kreon's wife, whose sole dramatic purpose is to complete Kreon's punishment by adding her suicide to Haimon's (her name means "wide justice"). So even if Kreon's edict were an established part of the tradition, the audience of Sophocles' play would not have been certain of the outcome. The dramatist seems to have shaped the mythic materials in such a way as to emphasize personal conflict, blood-kinship and gender issues.

RELIGIOUS BACKGROUND

"Religion" in classical Athens was not a distinct sphere of human activity grounded in a sacred text, but a diverse set of practices and stories woven into all aspects of the fabric of human life. The Greek landscape, both psychological and physical, is pervaded by divinities. These range in stature and importance from mighty cosmic powers to minor local divinities, such as tree-nymphs and river-gods, all of whom must receive their due (cf. e.g. n. on *Ant.* 1131). The most conspicuous and familiar of these powers are the Olympian or "sky" gods (so called because they live in the sky up on Mount Olympus), who include Zeus, Apollo and his twin sister Artemis, Athena, Poseidon, Aphrodite, Ares, Hermes, and Dionysos. But there are also important divinities living under the earth, known as chthonian or "earth" gods, who are especially associated with birth, fertility, and death. Their king is Hades, lord of the underworld. Apart from him, most of the powerful Earth gods are female, including Gaia or Earth herself (cf. *Ant.* 339) and the two "great goddesses," namely the earth-goddess Demeter and her daughter Persephone, bride of Hades and queen of the underworld (cf. *Ant.* 894). The underworld is also home to many sinister female divinities, including the Erinyes or Furies and Hekate, a goddess associated with the junctions of roads, who is sometimes identified with Persephone.

Each divinity is associated with one or more aspects of human life. Thus Athena, patron goddess of Athens, is goddess of warfare and wisdom, weaving, horses and olives. Poseidon, another important divinity at Athens, is the god of the sea, of earthquakes and of horses. Both these divinities are celebrated, along with others, in the famous choral song in praise of Attica in *OC* (668-719). Hermes, who escorts Oidipous to his death in the same play, is the herald and messenger of the gods, and also the god of travel, lucky finds, herdsmen and thieves. Demeter is the principal goddess of fertility and food from the earth. Artemis is a goddess of hunting, animals, and children, especially girls. Hephaistos, the blacksmith god, is also the god of fire. His name may be used to signify "fire," just as Ares may mean "war," or Hades "death."

Zeus, often called "father of gods and men," is the chief god and patriarchal king of the ancient Greek pantheon. He rules over the Olympian gods and oversees many aspects of human life, including kingship, hospitality, justice, oaths, the family, friendship, and the weather. His characteristic weapons are thunder and lightning (cf. *Ant.* 127-33), which serve as signs of Oidipous' approaching death (*OC* 95, 1456-85). He is also the protector of strangers and suppliants. Supplication was a ritual whereby anyone in trouble, especially a fugitive, might seek refuge and protection by sitting at a more powerful person's feet or at a sacred spot, such as a shrine or altar. It involved various ritual gestures, especially touching the cheek or knees of the person supplicated, and sometimes props, such as branches wreathed with wool (cf. *OT* 19). This ritual imposes social, moral and religious pressure on the more powerful person to grant the suppliant's request, but also places the speaker in a socially subordinate or even humiliating position. Supplication was an established practice in real life, made use of, for example, by criminals and political fugitives. It is also a common theme in legend, and many tragic plots are built around it. It provides a natural source of tension between fugitive, pursuer and rescuer, which makes it a useful focus for dramatic action. In these plays, it helps to dramatize Oidipous' shifting fortunes: he starts *OT* as a powerful man supplicated by others (*OT* 40-42), arrives at Athens in *OC* as a suppliant himself, and ends up once again the object of another's supplication.

Another prominent god, who is particularly important for Oidipous, is Apollo. He is the patron of many areas of human life, including prophecy, archery, music and poetry, sickness and healing, light, purification and self-understanding. (On his temple at Delphi were inscribed the words "know yourself.") Like most important gods, he has numerous names and titles, many of which appear in these plays. As god of the bow, he is traditionally described as "far-shooting" (cf. *OT* 162). As a god of light, he is often called Phoibos ("Bright"), and sometimes identified with Helios, god of the sun. The latter is portrayed as traveling through the sky in a golden chariot, and hence seeing everything that happens on the earth (cf. *OC* 868). This makes him an important god of oaths, because in his journey across the sky he sees all things and is therefore aware of anyone who commits perjury. "Lykeian" is another frequent title for Apollo, of uncertain meaning and origin. Since it resembles a root meaning "light," it connotes primarily brightness. But it also evokes the epithet "Lycian" (see n. on *OT* 208), and sometimes alludes to Apollo's role as a protector—specifically, against wolves—since the root *lyk-* resembles the word for a wolf (*lykos*). The title "Pythian" echoes the name Pytho, sometimes given to his oracle at Delphi, as well as the title of the priestess who voiced his prophecies, who was called the Pythia. Yet another common name for him is Loxias. Though its etymology is disputed, the ancient Greeks associated it with a word meaning "oblique," and thus with Apollo's oracular evasiveness.[12]

We have already met Dionysos (sometimes called Bacchus) in his guise as god of the theater (above, p. 7). He is also a god of wine and irrational frenzy, vegetation, sex, fertility and growth. He was born in Oidipous' home city of Thebes, from Zeus and a Theban princess, Semele (see n. on *Ant.* 1117), and remained that city's most important divine patron. Thus in *Antigone* the chorus of Theban elders pray for him to come and heal or "purify" the city's "sickness" (1141-5; cf. 1015-16). But like all Greek gods, Dionysos is ambiguous in his gifts and powers. A god who brings healing may also bring destruction, sometimes simultaneously. Dionysos is a god of fire and night (cf. *Ant.* 1146-54), of madness and transgression, whose myths involve kin-murder and the rending and eating of raw flesh (sometimes human). His more sinister aspects are hinted at throughout *Antigone* (e.g. 135-6, 154, 955-65). The city will indeed be "healed," but only at the cost of disaster for its ruling family.

The other great gods of the irrational, along with Dionysos, are Aphrodite, goddess of sexual desire, and her son Eros, who, as his name suggests, embodies erotic passion. In tragedy, these gods are almost always destructive in their influence. Eros is the subject of a famous choral song in *Antigone*, in which the chorus laments his devastating effects on Haimon, Antigone's fiancé (781-800). The song evokes a wedding celebration, especially in its emphasis on the erotic attraction between bride and groom (795-7). Marriage is the culturally sanctioned institution for expressing and controlling the dangerous forces of Eros and Aphrodite. And at the song's conclusion Antigone is led out of the palace, like a bride leaving her father's house to be led to that of her new husband. But that "husband" will be not Haimon but Hades (cf. 575, 654, 805, 811-16, 891, 1205). The idea that a girl who dies before marriage is marrying death, a frequent theme in Greek culture, follows the mythic archetype

---

[12] Oracles are discussed further below, pp. 24-5.

of Persephone, who was stolen away from her mother by Hades and married to him in the underworld.

In such contexts, Hades is an unobtrusive but pervasive presence in tragedy. The most conspicuous "earth" gods in the Theban plays are, however, the Furies, or Eumenides. These sinister goddesses, whose shrine provides the dramatic setting for *OC*, are in Hesiod children of Earth (*Theogony* 414), in Aeschylus of Night (*Eumenides* 416, 844), and in Sophocles of Earth and Dark (*OC* 40, 106). Their shrine at Athens, like the one portrayed in the drama, was near a cavern believed to lead to the underworld. As the stranger tells Oidipous, they were worshiped under a variety of names in different places (*OC* 42-3). In Thebes they were called "Ladies" (Potniai) (as Oidipous addresses them at *OC* 84), while in Athens their cult name was "Solemn Ones" (Semnai) (note the word "solemn" at *OC* 41, 90, 101). The name Eumenides, or "Kindly Ones," is a euphemism, expressing a nervous desire for favor from goddesses who were in fact regarded with dread (similarly the Greek name for the hazardous Black Sea was the Euxine, which means "Hospitable").

The chorus' reaction at the beginning of the play gives us some idea of the feelings these divinities inspired (*OC* 125-32). This awe stems from their role as underworld goddesses of vengeance, in which aspect they are known as Erinyes or "Furies" (singular Erinys). In this capacity they are sometimes called "Curses" (Arai)—a title reflecting their role as the embodiment of vengeful curses, like those that pursue Oidipous for his dreadful deeds (see *OT* 417-19 with note). We have already met them as agents of Oidipous' own vengeful curse upon his sons in the earlier tradition (above, p. 19), a role they reiterate in *OC* (cf. *OC* 154, 864-5). The Erinyes often exert their will by driving their victims insane (most famously in the case of Orestes). They are especially associated with kin-murder, demanding blood for blood on behalf of the dead. This function is memorably depicted in Aeschylus' *Eumenides*, where they appear as the play's chorus, pursuing Orestes like bloodhounds for killing his mother. But Aeschylus' drama also presents them in a more positive light. At its conclusion they are installed in Athens, as embodiments of fertility and divine blessing, as well as of the "dread," or respect for authority, that is essential to social order.

Despite the more or less specialized roles of the various gods, Greek polytheism acknowledges the complexity of the human world and its many competing claims upon us by providing many different, often overlapping, functions for the gods. Kreon in *Antigone*, who is punished severely for offending the gods, is a pious man in his own way (cf. 162-3, 288-9). But his attention is focused too narrowly on the "sky" gods, especially Olympian Zeus, whom he views as a ruler in his own image (184, 304; cf. 282-9, 758). The divine realm cannot be neatly packaged, however. Zeus is not only the god of kingship, but a protector of the hearth and family, and in this capacity Kreon defies him in blasphemous terms (*Ant.* 486-90, 658-9, 1039-43). Kreon is also contemptuous of Antigone's reverence for Hades, ruler of the dead (777-80). But here again he is too narrow in his focus, since Zeus himself was sometimes equated with Hades (see nn. on *Ant.* 452, *OC* 1606). This failure to understand the multivalence of the gods, and of Zeus in particular, ironically leads Kreon to muddy a distinction that the gods themselves hold dear—the distinction between the proper areas of concern of the gods of earth and sky (1067-76).

Human beings attempt to placate the gods, and to divine their wishes, in various ways, of which the most important are sacrifice, oracles, and divination. Blood-sacrifice is a ritual means of reaffirming human beings in their proper relationships towards gods, animals, the natural world and each other. Teiresias' failed sacrifice, in *Antigone*, is a powerful expression of the disruption of such relationships. The prophet's lurid description of the failure of his rites conveys the sense of chaos, the perversion of divine and human distinctions and categories, that has resulted from Kreon's decree. Sacrificial victims should burn, not ooze with moisture (cf. 1005-11); the altar is not the proper place for human flesh (cf. 1016-18); animals should serve as victims and hence as human food, not as "tombs" for human bodies (1021-2, 1080-83). Verbal echoes reinforce the close tie between the failed sacrifice and the state of Polyneices' body (cf. esp. *Ant*. 410, 906, 1008). The dead belong under the earth, and the living on top of it. The rituals surrounding death and sacrifice have been confused and perverted, like those of death and marriage.

Prophecies and oracles were pervasive and extremely important in Greek life. Apollo's principle oracle, at Delphi, which plays a central role in Oidipous' story (above, p. 17), was one of the most important, and exerted considerable political as well as religious influence throughout the classical period. In drama and legend oracles always come true, just as exposed babies are always found, and scars—like those on Oidipous' feet (*OT* 1034-6)—are always significant. In real life, a pious Greek would expect them to come true in some way or other, if they derived from a legitimate source. But priests and prophets were not all equally prestigious or credible. There were many kinds of prophet, priest and miracle-monger, and some of them (such as the beggar-priests of the eastern mother-goddess Cybele, alluded to at *OT* 388) were viewed by many people—especially the more educated—as money-grubbing charlatans deserving of suspicion and contempt. There were many spurious oracles in circulation. And even oracles from the most respected sources, like Delphi, were typically confusing and open to varying interpretations, which meant that their priests and diviners were not immune from suspicions of trickery. Oracles could also be manipulated for political purposes. Of particular concern to fifth-century Athenians was the fact that the Delphic oracle favored their enemy, Sparta, in the Peloponnesian War (Thucydides 1.118.3, 2.54). Skepticism about oracles and the traditional gods had been in the air since at least the time of the poet-philosopher Xenophanes early in the fith century, and is reflected in other Athenian writers of the period. The reliability of prophecies and oracles was therefore a contemporary issue for Sophocles and his audience.

This lies behind Jokasta's skepticism about oracles in *OT*. She is a pious woman, who has no doubt about the gods' ability to make their wishes known (724-5; cf. also 646-7, 698, 911-13, 1060), and she does not reject prophecy as such; but she does question its reliability as filtered through human interme-diaries (707-25). Besides, even the most faithful believer in prophecies knew that they might be fulfilled in unexpected, non-literal or symbolic ways, in history as well as myth (see e.g. Thucydides 2.17.2). This is exemplified in Oidipous' reaction to the death of his adoptive father Polybos. If Polybos died out of grief for his absent son, then Oidipous will have "caused" his death in a fashion that, while sad, is morally innocuous (*OT* 964-72). Jokasta points out that the prophecy of incest might be fulfilled in an equally harmless fashion, for example through a dream (980-82). It is worth noting in this connection that such dreams are not given a Freudian "Oedipal" coloring in the play, or in antiquity generally. Though often connected with autocratic rule, they are not viewed as specially significant or worrying, but as insignificant or even optimistic. Indeed, some have thought that Sophocles is alluding to a specific story told by the historian Herodotus: the former Athenian tyrant Hippias dreamed that he had sex with his mother and took this to mean that he would regain power in his motherland; but the dream was fulfilled in an utterly trivial fashion, when he lost a tooth in Athenian soil (Herodotus 6.107).

When Apollo predicts that Oidipous will kill his father and marry his mother, he reacts by trying to prevent the prophecy from coming true. This illustrates the important fact that Greeks typically did not view these messages from the gods as deterministic predictions that impaired their own freedom of action. The fact that Apollo's oracle spoke the literal truth does not mean human beings are mere puppets of the gods. The concepts of "free will" and "determinism"—and the philosophical problems they raise—were not developed until well after Sophocles' time. In any case, an oracle predicting future events does not *cause* those events to happen. If they are truthful predictions, then they are logically unavoidable and will "necessarily" come true. It is in this sense that Oidipous "must" kill his father and marry his mother (*OT* 792, 826, 854, 995-6). But this is not a denial of human agency or responsibility. For example, when Jesus in the Gospel predicts that Peter will deny him three times, and the prophecy is fulfilled, this does not mean Peter had no choice in the matter; instead, Peter bewails his own weakness after the fact (*Matt.* 26.75). As such stories make clear, divine foreknowledge and human free will can in principle coexist.

Besides oracles and sacrifice, the most important way in which we communicate with the gods—or attempt to do so—is augury (interpretation of the flight-patterns and behavior of birds). Birds, living as they do between earth and heaven, serve as messengers between gods and mortals (cf. *Ant.* 1040-1). But the song and behavior of birds are, to most humans, irrational and incomprehensible. Hence the need for the specialized prophet, who is able, through divine dispensation, to decode their movements and twitterings. In the case of the prophet Teiresias, physical blindness is correlated with a more powerful inner vision that enables him to "see" and "read" these signs. The blind were thought especially capable of prophecy and divine inspiration, a power of mental "vision" compensating for their physical blindness. The breakdown of relationships between gods and mortals in *Antigone* is expressed in the prophet's inability to comprehend the bird-song that is a guide to the divine will (999-1004).

The gods take a lively interest in human affairs, and are often instrumental in causing various outcomes (in tragedy, usually for the worse) by influencing the actions of human beings. They will punish without hesitation anyone who offends them. In particular, they often disapprove of arrogant or boastful behavior (cf. e.g. *Ant*. 127-8). Punishment for such transgressions may be slow in coming (cf. *Ant*. 1074, *OC* 1536), but it usually arrives eventually, at least in myth. Thus Kreon suffers in *Antigone* for preventing the burial of dead kin—a powerful social and religious obligation that Antigone places among the immortal and unwritten "laws of the gods" (*Ant*. 450-60).[13] The gods not only punish this violation, but ensure that their law is eventually carried out. There are several hints that they are at work in the burial of Polyneices' corpse, for example by sending a quasi-miraculous dust-storm to conceal Antigone's movements (*Ant*. 421; cf. 257-8, 278-9). This is typical of the way in which gods usually accomplish their will in Greek mythology, not by direct action but by inspiring and assisting human agents.

The gods were traditionally thought to lead into trouble those whom they wished to destroy (cf. e.g *OC* 252-3). The resulting disaster may also be attributed to "fate" or "destiny," as it is, for example, by Kreon (*Ant*. 1273-5, 1296, 1346). Nevertheless, Kreon takes full responsibility for all his actions (1268-9, 1318-21; cf. 1112-3). The chorus likewise speak of inescapable fate (1337-8; cf. 235-6), but still hold Kreon responsible (1259-60). Both he and they are employing a mode of thought sometimes called "double determination," whereby human character is not clearly separable from divine causation. This means that an act may be viewed as caused on a divine and human level simultaneously, without removing human responsibility for purposeful action. Destiny or "fate," in Greek thinking, denotes not a coercive force but the shape of the life that one happens to live out, which is known in advance by the gods but leaves us responsible for our own choices.

Likewise, the fact that what happens to Oidipous in *OT* is his "destiny" (376, 1458; cf. 713, 863) does not remove his personal responsibility for the choices he makes in working out that destiny. In contrast to the unwitting deeds of the past, his actions within the play are freely chosen (cf. esp. 1230). When the chorus ask him what god incited his self-blinding (*OT* 1327-8), he replies that it was Apollo who "fulfilled" his sufferings, but his own hand that struck the blow (1330-33). This combination of divine and human factors echoes the messenger's account, with its hints that supernatural forces were at work (1258, 1261). But this does not mean Oidipous considers the blinding to be a divine punishment, or blames Apollo for it. He takes full personal responsibility for his deed. The chorus likewise treat him as a responsible agent who has made a choice, despite Apollo's instigation (1327-8). At the same time, the fact that the blinding was Oidipous' own choice does not prevent it from also fulfilling Apollo's divine agenda (cf. *OT* 376-7). As usual, the gods function

---

13   Denial of burial was a punishment sometimes meted out to traitors, and other extreme criminals, in Sophocles' Athens. But the family of a dead traitor was permitted to bury the body outside Athenian territory—a compromise juggling the competing demands of state and family, public needs and religion, policy and personal feelings.

through—not in opposition to—human feelings and behavior.

Sometimes divine punishment may extend over several generations, through the playing-out of an ancestral curse. Antigone inherits her malignant doom from her father, who in turn inherited it from his father Laios, who (at least according to some versions of the myth) offended the gods and was warned by Apollo not to have any children. This is mentioned, for example, by Aeschylus (*Seven Against Thebes* 742-52). Similarly in a poem by Pindar the Erinys causes the mutual fratricide of Eteokles and Polyneices as a direct consequence of Oidipous' parricide (*Olympian* 2.35-9). In *OT* this aspect of the story receives little emphasis. The family curse is only touched on, and no blame is ascribed to Laios, since the oracle he received was simply a prediction, not an injunction. But *OC* alludes several times to the doom or curse upon the family (e.g. 369, 596, 965), and it is clearly present in the background of *Antigone* (cf. 1-6, 49-60, 593-603, 856-71).

The gods are severe in their treatment of those who displease them. Yet these divinities are not, in any simple sense, moralistic. That is to say, they do not serve as arbiters of human morality, rewarding the virtuous and punishing the good—at least not in any reliable fashion—no matter how fervently humans may wish for this to be the case. In particular, they do not strike down only those who deserve it. Thus in *Antigone*, Kreon is crushed for defying the gods' laws, but Antigone, who does their will, dies a horrible death with no personal sign of divine approval (cf. 921-8). As for Oidipous, he is stricken for transgressions of which he was entirely ignorant. When he calls himself hateful to the gods (*OT* 816, 1346-7, 1519), this does not mean that he thinks they have punished him for a moral offense. Greek gods can mistreat mortals for a wide variety of reasons which may remain entirely mysterious to their victims.

Some modern readers have mistakenly assumed that Oidipous' quick temper, which leads to Laios' death, is a "fatal flaw" of character for which he is being punished by the gods. This familiar but misleading phrase derives ultimately from Aristotle, who declares in his *Poetics* that the central character in a tragedy falls because of a *megalē hamartia* or "great error" (1453a15-16). But *hamartia* does not mean "character flaw." In its original context, the phrase is more accurately translated as "huge mistake." In Oidipous' case, the mistake is quite obviously his ignorance of who his parents really are. And this is not, by any standard, a crime or flaw of character. This does not mean Oidipous' character is spotless. Like his father, he is impetuous and quick to anger. But his downfall is not a punishment for these minor defects of character. If all quick-tempered people were to suffer the fate of Oidipous, the world would indeed be a horrific place. Nor is there any sign within the play that the gods are angry with Oidipous for this reason.

Nor is Oidipous guilty of *hybris* against the gods. Contrary to modern popular usage, *hybris* (translated as "outrage") does not, in general, denote an arrogant attitude towards the gods. It is not a quality of character, nor is it intrinsically religious. Rather, it standardly refers to excessively violent or abusive behavior, in word or deed, which violates another person's proper status. In Athenian law, *hybris* refers to mental or physical abuse, including rape, unprovoked assault and certain kinds of verbal insult, directed at another human being as a way of asserting one's own superiority. Thus Kreon uses it in *Antigone* for defiance of his authority, whether real or imagined (*Ant*. 309, 480-82), and in *OC* for his own attempt to abduct Oidipous (883). The gods, of course, do not like such treatment any more than anyone else, and disrespect for their power and status, along with other impious behavior, may be severely punished (see esp. *OT* 873-96). But *hybris* is not a religious offense per se. And there is no evidence that Oidipous has behaved in any such fashion towards the gods.

Nor is it plausible to view Oidipous' fate as a divine punishment for any other failing. If parricide and incest are the "crimes" for which he is being punished, they cannot also be the punishment. He himself views these deeds as *evidence* of divine hatred, not as its cause. He is certainly not being punished for fleeing the oracle about his parents (*OT* 794-8). By trying to invalidate it, he is not showing disbelief in the gods and their power (rather the opposite). He is also, in practice, increasing the chance that the prophecies could be fulfilled in some unexpected or symbolic way that may leave him innocent (cf. above, p. 25). Nor is the outcome a punishment for killing an older man or marrying an older woman. Since Oidipous is convinced that he knows who his parents are, the worst he could be accused of is foolishness.

Despite Oidipous' innocence, however, his unwitting deeds have made him a polluted man. Religious pollution, or *miasma*, is an invisible religious taint that incurs divine displeasure. It is caused by various kinds of crimes and transgressions, especially murder, whether intentional or not. Pollution is not the same as guilt, since a legally and morally innocent person may still be polluted, for example for causing an accidental death. Since Oidipous acted in ignorance and (in the case of the parricide) in self-defense, he would be found innocent in a court of law, ancient as well as modern—as he himself argues so passionately in *OC*. But despite his innocence, he is a polluted man. His self-blinding, on discovering the truth, is not an admission of guilt, but an acknowledgment of horror, shame and pollution.

Pollution is normally infectious, affecting the polluted person's immediate relatives most directly, but also making it dangerous for others to approach and especially to touch him or her (cf. *OC* 1132-6). Thus Oidipous' terrible pollution has brought down a plague on the whole city of Thebes (*OT* 95-8). At the end of *OT*, he declares that his pollution can be transmitted to no one else (*OT* 1413-5). But this is a figure of speech, a rhetorical way of expressing the uniqueness of his case. Kreon, by contrast, says that Oidipous' very presence outside the house is polluting the sun and the whole of the natural world (*OT* 1424-31). In Athenian law, polluted persons could normally cleanse themselves by carrying out certain rituals of purification. But Oidipous' pollution is uniquely terrible and infectious, owing to the appallingly transgressive nature of his deeds, and cannot be cleansed by any simple ritual. The only way to free Thebes from the contamination of his presence is for him to leave the city. He begs for exile not simply because he killed a man—intentionally or otherwise—but because of the unparallelled pollution caused by his combined parricide and incest.

Oidipous' pollution follows him to Athens. When he reveals his identity to the chorus of *OC*, they are so afraid of the consequences of his presence that they break their promise to protect him (*OC* 234-6, 256-7). And Kreon argues that such a polluted man should not receive sanctuary (947-9). Oidipous himself does not deny his pollution (cf. 1130-36). But he does deny most vehemently that it justifies treating him as a guilty man. This view is confirmed by the behavior of Theseus, the city's authoritative mouthpiece, who displays a more enlightened and humane conception of piety, whereby the obligation to protect a suppliant take precedence over the potential risk of sheltering a polluted man. He shows so little fear of pollution that he is even willing to welcome Oidipous under his own roof (643). This is consistent with other tales in which Athens accepted polluted killers, not just morally innocent ones like Oidipous and Herakles, but deliberate murderers such as Orestes and even Medea.[14]

In *OC*, Oidipous' troubled relationship to the gods takes a different turn, as he assumes the identity of an Athenian cult hero. "Hero" in this sense does not mean simply the principal character in a play or legend (though these legendary characters are often also cult heroes), but a great figure from the past who was honored with special rites after his death. The dead in general were regarded with great reverence in Greek society. As *Antigone* makes all too clear, a proper burial was of huge importance. Athenians made regular visits to their family tombs, bringing offerings of food and drink and decorations such as wreaths, which were thought to bring honor and perhaps pleasure to the dead. The most common gifts were drink-offerings, of honey, milk, water, wine and olive oil, which would be poured onto the grave, or even into it through special feeding tubes. Such offerings were accompanied by prayers to the dead, that they show benevolence towards their surviving relatives. Cult heroes, however, were in a special class, with a public significance extending beyond their immediate family. Unlike the ordinary dead, they were regularly honored with animal sacrifice as well as drink-offerings and other gifts. They were believed to have—and to use freely—exceptional powers to help or harm their living friends and foes from beyond the grave. They thus embodied the essence of traditional Greek morality, which was based on reciprocal help between friends and harm between enemies.[15]

Since they lie buried in the earth, cult heroes are, like the Eumenides, chthonian or "earth" powers. They have a strongly local significance for the region where they are buried. If properly appeased they may bring the com-

---

[14] Aeschylus' *Eumenides* dramatizes the Athenian acceptance of Orestes, who killed his mother Klytemnestra at the command of Apollo. For Herakles, who killed his children in a fit of insanity, and Medea, who killed hers in cold blood, see Euripides' *Herakles* and *Medea* respectively. In *Herakles* Theseus plays a welcoming role comparable to his role in *OC* (cf. esp. 1398-1400).

[15] For a fuller discussion of this code and its significance in Sophocles' plays see Blundell 1989.

munity fertility, prosperity, and above all, help in battle. During the Persian Wars, Theseus allegedly appeared and helped the Athenians win the battle of Marathon, and Ajax assisted at the battle of Salamis (the island of his birth). Another Greek people, the Locrians, used to leave a gap in the battle line for their local hero to defend. In order to gain these benefits, the actual presence of the hero's body was of great importance. The Athenians repatriated the bones of Theseus, and the Spartans those of their hero Orestes, in the latter case specifically to ensure a military victory. This explains the importance attached in *OC* to the location of Oidipous' grave. Although he disappears physically at the end of the play, it is clear that he is to be thought of as remaining present somehow in Athenian soil (cf. esp. 621-2).

The tombs of cult heroes were treated as shrines, and located strategically, in keeping with the role that heroes played as military defenders. Unlike ordinary graves, which were placed outside the city walls, theirs might be within the city, or built into the city-wall, or placed inside a religious sanctuary. Such practices are reflected in *OC*, in Oidipous' disappearance at a sacred spot which is well-placed for defending Athens from invaders. The Thebans also hope to win such benefits by placing him just outside Theban territory (*OC* 399-405). This plan is a naive one, however, for it neglects the fact that in addition to a hero's body, his good will must be secured (cf. *OC* 402-3). Otherwise he may strike the land with plague, barrenness or war.

Heroic status was by no means confined to virtuous or benevolent figures. Some bizarre and even criminal characters received such honors after their death. At Astypalaea in the eastern Aegean, a boxer killed his opponent in a match, went berserk and destroyed a school full of sixty children, and yet was honored after death as a hero. The only thing all heroes have in common is that they are mighty figures of special local significance, for better or worse. "It is some extraordinary quality that makes the hero; something unpredictable and uncanny is left behind and is always present" (Burkert 1985: 208). Despite this quality, however, and despite their supernatural powers, cult heroes remain clearly distinct from the gods proper. They are dead mortals with special powers, rather than immortal gods. Unlike the gods, their sphere of influence is confined to the immediate vicinity of their tomb. And although many cult heroes are legendary characters, ordinary mortals continued to be promoted to their ranks. The tomb of the Athenian statesman Solon in Salamis was thought to protect the island, and Sophocles himself was made a cult hero after his death (above, p. 4).

In the course of *OC*, we see Oidipous transformed from a helpless, blind old beggar into an awe-inspiring figure, with unearthly powers for good and ill. The play thus dramatizes the process of "heroization," and this makes it a unique document. In particular, Oidipous' mysterious disappearance through the direct intervention of the gods is unparalleled. It is the climax of the special destiny the gods have promised him, which enables him, despite the taint of his terrible past, to call himself "sacred" and "reverent" (287). This gives him an extraordinary right to enter into the forbidden grove of the Eumenides, with whom his cult as a hero was historically associated. There was a shrine to him at Colonus, and a tomb of Oidipous in the shrine of the "Solemn Ones" (Semnai) at Athens (no doubt reflecting a rival tradition about his death).

So too in Sophocles' play, he enjoys a special kinship with these goddesses. The grove of the Eumenides is a place of dread for ordinary mortals like the stranger (39-40) and the chorus (125-32). But Oidipous enjoys a special affinity with this spot and its fearsome occupants. He claims a right to enter the grove as a suppliant of the goddesses, who to him are paradoxically "sweet" (106). This affinity is brought out by numerous details in the text. The chorus' reaction to Oidipous as "Dreadful to see and dreadful to hear!" (141) echoes their response to the goddesses, who are "dread-eyed" (84) and must be passed without a look or a word (128-32; cf. also 490). The shrine of a cult hero, was likewise passed by in silence (cf. 1762f.), and Oidipous' grave—a special instance of such a shrine—must not be looked upon (1641-2, 1652). Both Oidipous and the goddesses are in a mysterious sense "all-seeing" (43, 74), and both bring their friends the gift of supernatural "kindness" (486-7, 631). Oidipous even underlines his kinship with these goddesses, who do not accept offerings of wine, by saying that he comes "sober" to the "wineless" (100).

Oidipous also shares the double nature of these goddesses, their ability to bless and curse. Their benign aspect, as Eumenides or "Kindly Ones," is expressed not only in the benevolent welcome that he receives from them and from Theseus, but also in the blessing he himself bequeaths to Athens. With this blessing is bound up the destruction of his enemies through his curse. The curse, which Polyneices attributes to his father's Erinys or "Fury" (1299, 1434), reflects the goddesses' dark side, their role as avenging Furies, which complements their benevolent aspect. Their destructive potential, emphasized by the nervous chorus at the beginning of the play, is realized in the course of it through the person of Oidipous, their suppliant, who will soon join them as a chthonian or "earth" power, and a willing agent of their dual power for vengeance and blessing.

Oidipous' miraculous death is not a divinely-bestowed reward that he has earned by atoning for the deeds of the past. It is "amazing" (*OC* 1664; cf. 1586), but it is not the gateway to a blissful hereafter. Oidipous is mortal, and throughout the play the finality of death is emphasized (e.g. 1220-23). He himself longs for death not as a glorious future, but as a terminus and respite from his sufferings (see esp. 84-110). To look on his story as a drama of guilt, atonement and eternal reward is to view it through anachronistic Christian eyes. When the chorus say Oidipous has ended his life "blessedly" (1721), the "blessing" is that he has died, and done so without pain. In Theseus' words, he is one of those for whom death itself comes as a "favor" (1751-3).

Nevertheless, while Oidipous' fate may be no Christian heaven, the gods who caused his downfall have in some sense raised him up (cf. 394, 1453-5, 1565-7), not only by granting him a miraculous and painless death, but by enabling him to help his friends and harm his enemies from beyond the grave. Despite his mysterious disappearance, the audience would think of him as somehow still present under the earth at the spot where he died, and highly sensitive to the behavior of his friends and enemies. The gods have compensated him in their inexplicable way, by giving him a demonic power that in many ways resembles their own. His wrath, like theirs, is harsh, unforgiving and effective, and his protective power correspondingly great. It was in this capacity that Oidipous would have been most familiar to Sophocles' original audience: awe-inspiring not only as a paradigm of human misery during life, but as a heroic figure exerting supernatural power from beyond the grave.

ANTIGONE

CHARACTERS

ANTIGONE, daughter of Oidipous (former king of Thebes)
ISMENE, daughter of Oidipous
CHORUS, fifteen aged noblemen of Thebes
KREON, king of Thebes, uncle and guardian of Antigone and Ismene
GUARD, an aged and lowly soldier under Kreon's command
HAIMON, son of Kreon
TEIRESIAS, an aged prophet
MESSENGER, an attendant of Kreon
EURYDIKE, wife of Kreon
Guards and attendants of Kreon, Teiresias and Eurydike

Setting: Outside the royal palace of Thebes. The scene shows the façade of the palace, which has a large central door. The time is just before dawn, on the morning following the successful defeat of Polyneices and his allies in their assault on Thebes.

[Enter Antigone and Ismene from the palace. Antigone addresses her sister in iambic trimeters, the meter of dialogue (Introduction, p. 15).]

ANTIGONE

Ismene, my own sister, sharing the self-same blood,
of all the evils that descend from Oidipous
do you know one that Zeus does not fulfill for us,
the two still living?[1] There is nothing—no!—no grief,
no doom, dishonor or disgrace that I've not seen   5
counted among the evils that are yours and mine.[2]
Now this! What is this proclamation that they say

---

[1] Oidipous' children have inherited his misfortunes. (Introduction, p. 27). On Zeus see Introduction, p. 21.

[2] In *OC*, the sisters are portrayed as suffering many hardships. Cf. also *OT* 1486-1502. On the word "evil" (*kakos*) see n. on *OC* 87.

the general has just made to all the city's people?[3]
Have you heard anything? Or are you unaware
that evils due to enemies approach our friends?[4]   10

ISMENE

To me no word of friends has come, Antigone,
sweet or distressing, since the time when you and I
were both deprived, we two, of our two brothers, both
struck dead by two-fold hand within a single day;
and since the army of the Argives disappeared   15
during the night just past, I have learned nothing new—
whether my fortune has improved or I am doomed.

ANTIGONE

I knew it well. That's why I brought you here outside
the courtyard gates, for you to hear me by yourself.

ISMENE

What is it? You are clearly brooding on some news.   20

ANTIGONE

What? Has not Kreon honored only one of our
two brothers with a tomb, and dishonored the other?[5]
Eteokles he has seen fit to treat with justice, so
they say, and lawfully[6] concealed beneath
the ground, there to be honored by the dead below;   25
but as for Polyneices' miserable corpse,
they say the townsfolk have received a proclamation,
that none may shroud him in a tomb or wail for him;
he must be left unwept, unburied, treasure sweet
for watching birds to feed on at their pleasure.   30
They say that this is what good Kreon has proclaimed
for you and me—yes, *me* as well!—and that he's coming

---

3   The "general" is Kreon, who has been made commander-in-chief as well as king
    of Thebes by the death of Eteokles and Polyneices. He also displays a military
    outlook in his capacity as king and father (see especially 639-80 and cf. e.g. 241,
    1033-4). "City" translates the word *polis* (see n. 1 on *OC*, below p. 155).
4   This line could mean "the evils inflicted on our (recently-vanquished) enemies," or
    "the evils appropriate to enemies (generally)," or "evils coming from our enemies
    (i.e. Kreon)." But however it is interpreted, it accords with the Greek code of
    popular ethics that required one to help one's friends and harm one's enemies.
5   The rituals of burial were enormously important in the Greek world (see Introduc-
    tion, p. 29).
6   This is the first occurrence of a key word in the play, *nomos*. It has been translated
    throughout as "law," but unlike the English word, *nomos* covers not only the
    written laws of a society, but also custom and tradition, including the "unwritten
    laws" to which Antigone will later appeal (450-57).

here to make his proclamation clear to those
who do not know;[7] nor does he view the matter as
a trivial one: the penalty prescribed for such   35
a deed is death from stoning by the city's people.
That's how things stand; soon you'll reveal if you're
noble by birth, or evil from good origins.

ISMENE

If that is how things are, unhappy one, what good
can *I* do, loosening or tightening the knot?[8]   40

ANTIGONE

See if you'll join in laboring to do a deed.

ISMENE

What deed of danger? What can you be thinking of?

ANTIGONE

See if you'll join these hands of mine to lift the corpse.

ISMENE

What, bury him? When it's forbidden to the city?[9]

ANTIGONE

Yes, bury my own brother—and yours too—if you're   45
not willing. *I* will not be caught in treachery.[10]

ISMENE

Audacious one! Against Kreon's express command?

ANTIGONE

He has no business keeping me from what is mine.

ISMENE

Alas! Just think, my sister, of our father—how
he perished, hated and in ill-repute, for failings   50
he himself detected, after he himself
gouged out his two-fold eyes with self-inflicting hand;[11]

---

7   The first proclamation was presumably made on the battlefield. Kreon's entrance
    speech will be an official proclamation to the city as a whole, as represented by
    the elders of the chorus.
8   A proverbial expression of helplessness in face of an insoluble problem.
9   This could also mean "by the city," in which case Ismene is equating Kreon with
    the city as a whole (cf. 79, 905).
10 Antigone means that she will never betray Polyneices, but from Kreon's point of
    view she will indeed be "caught in treachery."
11 Sophocles here appears to use a version of the story in which Oidipous stayed at
    Thebes (rather than being exiled) after blinding himself, and died there (though
    "perished" might simply mean "was ruined"). In *OC*, he dies at Athens with
    divine favor.

next how his mother-wife—a two-fold name in one—
blighted her life with woven strands of twisted rope;[12]
third, our two brothers in a single day both killed   55
themselves in one another—wretched pair!—inflicting
one shared doom with two reciprocating hands;
look now in turn at us two, left here all alone—
our death will be the worst by far, if we defy
the law, and go beyond the power and vote of kings.[13]   60
We must remember, first, that we two are by nature
women and not fit to fight with men; second,
that we are ruled by others stronger than ourselves,
and so must bow to this and even greater griefs.[14]
So I for one shall beg those underneath the earth   65
to pardon me, since I am overpowered by force;[15]
I shall obey those who are in authority,
for deeds that are excessive make no sense at all.

ANTIGONE

I would not urge you otherwise, nor would it bring
me pleasure if you did now wish to act with me.   70
You be as you think best, but I shall bury him.
To me it's fine to die performing such a deed.[16]
I'll lie there, dear to him, with my dear friend,[17] when I've
performed this crime of piety; for I must please
those down below a longer time than those up here,   75
since I shall lie there always. You, though, if you think
it best, dishonor what is honored by the gods.

---

[12] I.e. she hanged herself (cf. *OT* 1263-4).

[13] On the word "king" (*tyrannos*) see n. on *OC* 373. The word "vote" has democratic
associations which produce a jarring effect when juxtaposed with the word "king,"
especially in this autocratic context (cf. also 633).

[14] The idea that whoever is stronger either has the right to rule, or must in fact rule,
is common in fifth-century Greek texts, and is associated with the influence of the
sophists (Introduction, p. 4). But it would seem appropriately "feminine" in this
context.

[15] The plural ("those underneath the earth") may include the gods of the underworld
as well as Polyneices and Antigone's other dead family members.

[16] "Fine" translates *kalos*, a powerful evaluative term with moral, aesthetic, heroic
and aristocratic overtones (also used at 372, 723, 925).

[17] "Dear" translates *philos*, which means both "friend" and "dear," and often also
"kin" (since family members are presumed to be "friends"). Here and elsewhere
Antigone uses the language of friendship to express her deep commitment to
family loyalty. But the passage also has an incestuous coloring that hints at the
perverted relationships in this particular family, and at Antigone's later preference
for her brother over a husband (905-14).

ISMENE
I don't dishonor him; but it's impossible
for me by nature to defy the citizens.[18]

ANTIGONE
Make your excuses! *I* shall go and heap up earth   80
into a tomb to bury him, my dearest brother.

ISMENE
Alas! How full I am of dread for you, poor wretch!

ANTIGONE
Don't fear for *me*; guide your own destiny aright.[19]

ISMENE
At least be sure that you reveal this deed to no
one else; conceal it secretly. I'll join in that.   85

ANTIGONE
Alas! Speak out! You'll be more hateful still if you
stay silent. No, proclaim my plan out loud to all!

ISMENE
You have a heart within you hot for chilling deeds.

ANTIGONE
I know that I am pleasing those I should please most.

ISMENE
Perhaps; but you're in love with the impossible.   90

ANTIGONE
Then when I've used up all my strength, I shall have done.

ISMENE
One should not hunt for the impossible at all.

ANTIGONE
If you speak so, you'll be a hateful enemy
to me, and justly hated by the dead man too.
Let me and the ill counsel that derives from me   95
suffer this awful fate; what I shall suffer will
be far less dire than dying an ignoble death!

---

[18]   The word translated here and elsewhere (90, 92, 175, 363) as "impossible" (*amēcha-nos*), is a significant one. It can be used actively, as here, to mean "lacking resources or devices," or passively, to mean "intractable, unmanageable, inaccessible to any resource or device."

[19]   On "destiny" see Introduction, p. 26. The word translated "aright" (*orthos*, meaning "straight," "upright," or "correct"), is a key word in the play, especially for Kreon (163, 167, 190, 403, 494, 675; cf. also 99, 636, 686, 706, 994, 1158, 1178, 1195. Besides "aright," I have translated it as "right," "rightly," or "upright."

ISMENE

Go, if you think it best; know that you're senseless to
be going, and yet rightly to your dear friends dear.[20]

*[Exit Antigone along the side-entrance representing the path to the upland plain
where the battle took place and Polyneices' body lies. Exit Ismene into the palace.
Enter the chorus of fifteen old, white-haired noblemen of Thebes, singing and dancing.
They enter along the other side-entrance, which represents the road from the city of
Thebes proper.[21]]*

CHORUS

Oh bright beam of the sun,[22]	*Strophe A*
loveliest light that ever shone	101
on seven-gated Thebes,[23]	
at last you have appeared,	
oh eye of golden day,	
rising on Dirce's streams,[24]	105
stirring to headlong flight	
with sharply piercing bit	
the Argive, shielded in white,	
in all his panoply, gone.[25]	

Polyneices, roused by a two-edged quarrel,[26]   110
led him here to attack our land;
over our land he flew with a piercing
scream like an eagle, covering us with a

---

20   The Greek word (*philos*) is both active and passive, covering "dear" as well as
"friend," so Ismene's words are ambiguous between "rightly showing friendship
to your friends/dear ones" and "rightly dear to your friends/dear ones."

21   The chorus' entry song or *parodos* consists of just two strophic pairs, and each
strophe and antistrophe is followed by seven lines of anapests (see Introduction,
p. 15).

22   The chorus invoke the newly risen sun in thanksgiving for the previous day's victory over the army of Polyneices and the Argives. Light is a common metaphor
for escape from threatened disaster.

23   Thebes was famous for its seven gates. In his assault on the city, Polyneices brought
six leaders, each of whom attacked one of the gates while Eteokles and his six
allies defended them (cf. *OC* 1301-25).

24   Dirce was a river to the west of Thebes, often used to symbolize the city.

25   This "warrior" represents the Argive army as a whole, not Polyneices or any individual fighter. The Argive shields are either painted white, or brightly shining.
(The text is corrupt here, but this is the general sense.)

26   "Two-edged" means "disputatious," but also indicates that the brothers' quarrel
was mutual, and suggests that there may have been fault on both sides. The word
for quarrel (*neikos*) puns on the name of Polyneices, which means "much quarrel-
ing."

snow white wing,[27]
he with his numerous weapons and helmets   115
crested with horse-hair.

Over our halls he hovered,   *Antistrophe A*
maw gaping wide,[28]
murderous spears encircling
our city's seven-mouthed gates,   120
but was gone before he could glut
his jaws with our streaming blood,
or pine-fed Hephaistos could consume
our crowning wreath of ramparts[29]—
such a crashing of Ares surged at their backs,[30]   125
tough task for the dragon who wrestled him.[31]

For Zeus exceedingly hates the boasts
of a mighty tongue.[32] *When he saw those men*
coming on in a copious flood,
with the supercilious clanging of gold,   130
he struck one down with brandished fire,
a man at his topmost goal, who rushed
to raise up the victory cry.[33]

He teetered and fell to the resistant earth,   *Strophe B*
bearing fire he rushed madly on,   135
breathing on us, in frenzied Bacchanal,
blasts of most hateful winds of enmity.[34]
But he failed in his attempt; mighty Ares,

---

[27] This refers to the white or (bright) Argive shield (cf. 107).
[28] The antistrophe continues the strophe's striking blending of monstrous eagle and battle imagery.
[29] Hephaistos, the blacksmith god, is also god of fire, and here stands for fire itself. He is "pine-fed" because torches were made of pine wood.
[30] Here, as often, the name of Ares the war god is used to stand for war itself (cf. 952).
[31] The "dragon" stands for the Thebans, who originated from dragon's teeth sown in the ground by their founder Kadmos. The dragon's "wrestling foe" is the Argive eagle.
[32] This is a variation on the theme of "mighty words" or "mighty thoughts," common Greek expressions for arrogance (cf. 478-9, 768-9, 1351).
[33] This is Kapaneus, one of Polyneices' allies. When he reached the top of the ramparts Zeus struck him down with lightning for his arrogance.
[34] Kapaneus is likened both to a storm and to a Bacchant, one of the frenzied torch-bearing worshipers of Dionysos, patron of Thebes (who is also called Bacchus, as at 154). On Dionysos see Introduction, pp. 7 and 22.

our right-hand trace-horse,[35] struck down hard,
dispensing other deaths to other men.   140

Seven captains at seven gates,
seven matched with an equal number,
left bronze tribute for Zeus, battle-turner.[36]
But that abhorrent pair of brothers,[37]
born from a single father and mother,   145
fixed two powerful spears in each other,
and both have their share in a double death.

But Victory of mighty name has come,   *Antistrophe B*
with joy responding to the joy
of many-charioted Thebes.[38]   150
Now war is past, bring on forgetfulness!
Let us visit all the gods' temples
with night-long dance and song!
May Bacchus, shaker of Thebes, lead on![39]

But here comes Kreon, the son of Menoikeus,   155
king of the land, and our new ruler since
this new fortune has come from the gods.[40]
What plan is he plying?[41]
Why has he called for a special assembly

---

35   In a four-horse chariot race, the trace-horse (i.e. the horse on the outside right) did
the most work, because it had to run furthest at the turns. The metaphor indicates
that Ares, god of war, took an exceptional part in the battle and caused it to turn
in favor of the Thebans.

36   It was customary after a victory to pile up the defeated enemy's armor and weapons
as a thank-offering to a god, in this case Zeus in his capacity as "turner of battles"
(*tropaios*, the word that gives us "trophy").

37   Eteokles and Polyneices.

38   Victory was worshiped as a goddess, often winged, and sometimes identified with
Athena, patron goddess of Athens. She had a small but prominent temple on the
Athenian Acropolis. Her joy "responds" to that of Thebes because it forms part
of the reciprocal exchange of pleasures and favors between mortals and gods that
underlies Greek religion.

39   Bacchus (Dionysos) was often worshiped at night. Through the gift of wine he
provides happy "forgetfulness" of human cares. Here, as often, he is envisaged
as leading the dance in his own honor. He "shakes" Thebes with the thunder of
dancing feet, but the image also foreshadows his role as the destructive purifier
of the city (cf. 1115-54).

40   Kreon has become king now that both of Oidipous' sons are dead. The emphasis
on his newness warns us that he may be inexperienced and rash.

41   The verb literally means to row or "ply an oar," but is often used metaphorically
for vigorous activity.

    of elders to meet here,[42]   160
    sending a shared proclamation to all?

[Enter Kreon, along the side-entrance leading from the battlefield. He may still be wearing armor, and is accompanied by armed men. The parodos ends, and the meter returns to the iambic trimeters used for spoken dialogue.]

KREON

    Oh men, the gods who tossed our city's ship on mighty
    waves have safely righted it once more.[43] And so
    I sent my messengers to summon you to come
    away from all the rest, because I know you always   165
    did revere the power of Laios' throne;[44] so too
    when it was Oidipous who steered the city right;
    and when he perished, you remained still loyal to
    their children, steadfast in your purpose and your thoughts.
    So, since his sons have perished in one day, two brothers   170
    by a two-fold destiny, both striking and
    struck down, hands foully stained with mutual fratricide,[45]
    it's I who now possess the throne and all the power,
    through my close bond of kinship with the perished dead.
        It is impossible to learn in full the spirit   175
    of a man, his purpose or his judgment, till
    he's shown up by experience of rule and law.[46]
    For anyone who rules the city as a whole
    and does not hold on to the counsels that are best,
    but keeps a lock fixed on his tongue because of fear,[47]   180
    I think that man most evil, and I always have;
    and he who thinks a friend is more important than
    his fatherland, he's nowhere in my reckoning.

---

[42] Some of the language here echoes Athenian democratic terminology.

[43] The metaphor of the ship of state, which already occurs in earlier texts, reappears at 189-90, and indirectly at 715-17 (cf. also n. on 158).

[44] "Reverence" (*eusebeia*) covers a wide range of obligations, including religious piety (e.g. 304, 778, 922-4, 1349-50) and various forms of respect for human beings, such as family members (e.g. 511), authority figures (cf. e.g. 744), and others (e.g. 730). These forms of "reverence" may sometimes conflict (cf. n. 872).

[45] Killing one's own kin brought an exceptionally terrible stain of religious pollution (see Introduction, p. 28).

[46] Kreon is aware that as a new king he must win his people's loyalty not only by the claim of birth but by his performance as a ruler.

[47] A leader might fear, for example, the consequences of unpopular policies (like Kreon's own). But it is usually subjects rather than rulers who keep their tongues "locked out of fear" (cf. 505). The statement thus strikingly exemplifies Kreon's inappropriate application of truisms.

For I—bear witness Zeus, who sees all things always!—
I'd not keep silent if I saw some doom instead   185
of safety moving on the people of this town;
nor would I ever count as my own friend a man
who felt ill will towards this land; I recognize
that this ship keeps us safe, and only when we sail
upon it upright can we make friends for ourselves.   190
    Such are the laws with which I make this city great.
And brother to them is my proclamation to
the townsfolk in regard to Oidipous's sons.[48]
Eteokles, who perished fighting for this city,
performing all the best feats with his spear, will be   195
concealed within a tomb with all the offerings
that go down to the best among the dead below.[49]
But as for his blood-brother—I mean Polyneices
who returned from exile willing to burn down
with fire from top to bottom his own fatherland   200
and his own family gods,[50] willing to gorge himself
on blood he shared,[51] and make his countrymen his slaves—
this city has received a proclamation not
to honor him with funeral rites or wail for him,
but all must leave his body unentombed, to be   205
the food of birds and dogs, an outrage to behold.
Such is my purpose; never shall evil men be held
in higher honor than the just, at least by me;
but he who bears good will towards this city will
be honored by me equally in life and death.   210

CHORUS

It pleases you, Menoikeus' son, to treat like this
the man who shows ill-will towards this city and
the kindly one. You have the power to use what law
you like regarding both the dead and us who live.

---

48   The use of "brother" to mean "closely allied" is not exceptional in Greek, but it
     has special resonance here because of the subject of the play.
49   An honorable burial included ritual lamentation and offerings to the dead, espe-
     cially libations, i.e. poured liquids, which literally "go down to the dead below."
     Libations might be of honey, milk, water, wine or olive oil. Other offerings included
     flowers, wreaths of wool, and locks of hair from the next of kin.
50   I.e. the temples of the gods of Thebes, worshiped by his family (cf. 284-7).
51   Primarily the blood of his brother Eteokles, but also that of the Thebans generally
     (his broader kin).

KREON
> See to it, then, that you watch over what I've said.   215

CHORUS
> Assign this burden to some younger man to bear.

KREON
> There are already watchers set to guard the corpse.

CHORUS
> What else besides that would you order us to do?

KREON
> Not to collaborate with those who disobey.

CHORUS
> No one's so foolish as to be in love with death.   220

KREON
> That is indeed the payment: death. But all the same,
> profit destroys men often, through the hope of gain.

[Enter the Guard, an old man dressed as a lowly soldier. He enters slowly and hesitantly along the side-entrance leading from the battlefield.]

GUARD
> My lord, I really cannot say that I've arrived
> here out of breath with speed or light and fleet of foot.
> No, many times my anxious thoughts brought me up short,   225
> making me wheel round in the road to travel back.
> My spirit spoke to me loquaciously, like this:[52]
> "Poor fool, why go where you will pay the penalty?"
> "Stopping again, you wretch? If Kreon hears about
> this from some other man, you're bound to suffer grief!"   230
> These ruminations made my progress leisurely
> and slow, until a short road turned into a long.
> But in the end, the plan of coming to you won,
> and if my words mean nothing,[53] I'll speak anyway:
> I've come here clinging to the expectation that   235
> I cannot suffer anything except my fate.[54]

---

[52] Personal uncertainty is often represented in Greek as a dialogue between a speaker and his or her mind or spirit (cf. 376 and the English idioms "a divided mind" and "in two minds"). The guard's "spirit" argues both sides of the case with him.

[53] This phrase apparently means that since the doer of the deed is unknown, the guard's narrative will be useless. But it could also conceivably mean "if I speak my own death-warrant."

[54] This is not a denial of free will, but a cliché equivalent to "que sera sera." On "expectation" see n. on *OT* 487.

KREON

What is the reason for this apprehensiveness?

GUARD

I want to tell you my own situation first.
I did not do the deed, or see the one who did,
and it would be unjust for me to come to harm.   240

KREON

You're aiming well and building fences round the deed.[55]
It's clear you've something unexpected to report.

GUARD

Great hesitation is induced by awful things.

KREON

Won't you speak up at last, and then get out of here?

GUARD

All right, I'm telling you. The corpse—someone just now   245
has buried it and gone; they sprinkled thirsty dust
upon its skin and carried out the proper rites.

KREON

What are you saying? What man dared to do this deed?[56]

GUARD

I do not know. There was no mark from pick-axe blows,
no earth thrown out by mattocks;[57] no, the ground was hard   250
and dry, not broken up or furrowed by the weight
of wagon wheels. The doer was one who left no sign.[58]
When our first watcher for the day pointed this out,
uncomfortable amazement came upon us all.[59]
The corpse had disappeared—not buried in a grave,   255
but covered with light dust as if to deflect a curse.[60]
No sign was visible that any dog or any

---

55 The guard's preamble is a "fence" of words to protect himself from blame. "You're aiming well" may mean that he is on target in his fears for the future, or that he is protecting himself from behind his "fence."

56 Note Kreon's assumption that the doer was male (cf. 61-2, 221-2, 307).

57 A mattock is a large heavy hoe, used to break the ground for farming.

58 This slightly mysterious phrase and the miraculous air of the whole description will prompt the chorus to suggest that the gods played a part in the burial (278-9).

59 Their astonishment is "uncomfortable" both because they are baffled and because they fear the consequences of their discovery.

60 Anyone who passed an unburied corpse without covering it with dirt was considered cursed or "polluted" (cf. Introduction, p. 28).

savage beast had been there tearing at the corpse.[61]
Abusive words began to rumble back and forth,
with guard accusing guard, and in the end we would   260
have come to blows—no one was there to hinder it.
For each and every one of us had done the deed,
but no one clearly so,[62] and all pled ignorance.
We were prepared to take up red-hot iron in
our hands,[63] to walk through fire, to swear oaths by the gods   265
that we had not done this ourselves, and had no knowledge
of who else had planned or carried out the deed.
    When our inquiries got us nowhere, then at last
one man spoke up who made us all bow down our heads
towards the ground in fear; there was no way for us   270
either to contradict him or to do as he
advised and fare well from it. He said that this deed
should be reported to you rather than concealed.
This view won out, and I, ill-fated one, became
the one condemned by lot to win this fine reward.   275
I'm here against my will; against yours too, I know;
for no one likes a messenger who brings bad news.

CHORUS

My lord, my mind has been suggesting for some time
that possibly this deed was prompted by the gods.

KREON

Stop speaking now, before you stuff me full of anger,   280
or you'll be found to have no sense in your old age.[64]
The words you speak are unendurable—to think
divinities might be concerned about this corpse!
Did they conceal his body to bestow a special
honor on a benefactor—he who came   285
to burn their pillared temples and their offerings,

---

61 A light sprinkling sufficed for ritual purposes, but one would not expect this to
    deter scavenging animals (257-8). Despite this hint of divine preservation, which
    suits the dramatic moment (cf. 278-9), the text elsewhere suggests that Polyneices'
    body is in fact rotting and torn by wild animals (409-12, 1016-22, 1198, 1202; cf.
    29-30, 205-6, 1080-83).
62 I.e. they all accused each other, but none of them had proof.
63 This recalls the medieval European "trial by fire," in which an innocent person
    could supposedly hold red-hot iron in the hand without injury. But there is no
    other evidence for such a custom among the ancient Greeks. "Walking through
    fire" is presumably a similar "test" of guilt or innocence.
64 The old were expected to have the wisdom of their years (cf. n. on 735). To be
    simultaneously old and foolish was therefore doubly reprehensible.

to scatter into pieces their own land and laws?
Do you see gods bestowing honor on the evil?
It cannot be! No, there are men who chafe at me
within the city, rumbling at me secretly   290
for some time now,[65] heads tossing, necks not justly held
beneath the yoke in due contentment with my rule.
I understand the situation well: the guards
were bribed by them with payment to perform this deed.
Money! No institution that's so evil ever   295
sprang into existence for the human race.[66]
This wipes out cities, forces men to leave their homes,[67]
re-educates and warps the minds of mortals that
were good, inducing them to turn to shameful things,
shows human beings how to undertake all crimes,   300
and come to know impiety in every deed.
     Yet those who hired themselves for cash and did this deed
ensured that they would pay the penalty in time.
But by the reverence that Zeus receives from me,
know this full well—and I am speaking under oath: 305
if you guards do not find the one whose hand performed
this burial, and show him clearly to my eyes,
Hades won't be enough for you; before you die
you'll hang alive until you make this outrage plain,[68]
so that in future you may seize your plunder knowing   310
where to get your profits from, and learn that you
should not be fond of profiting from every source.
For you will see that after shameful takings the
majority of people end up doomed, not saved.

GUARD
Will you grant me a word, or shall I just turn and go?   315
KREON
Do you not know that even these words trouble me?

---

[65] I.e. the burial reflects the kind of dissatisfaction with Kreon that some of the citizens had voiced privately even before the decree.
[66] The word translated "institution" (*nomisma*) is closely related to the word *nomos* (see n. on 24). In prose, it normally means "current coin" or "money."
[67] Greed for money causes warfare (including civil strife), which in turn causes displacement and exile.
[68] Hades, divine ruler of the underworld, here (as often) stands for death. Kreon means that mere death will not be good enough for the guards, but they will die only after hanging up until they confess their guilt. The reference is not to death by hanging, but to a form of torture that might result in death.

GUARD

But is their bite felt in your spirit or your ears?

KREON

Why try to pin down the location of my pain?

GUARD

The perpetrator pains your mind, but I your ears.

KREON

Oh what a natural chatterbox you are, that's clear!   320

GUARD

Perhaps; but I am not the one who did this deed.

KREON

You did it, and you sold your life for money too.

GUARD

Ah!

How awful to believe when your beliefs are false!

KREON

Play with the word "belief."[69] But if you don't reveal
the perpetrators of this deed to me, then you'll   325
admit disaster comes from profits basely won.

[Exit Kreon, into the palace.]

GUARD

Above all else may he be found. But whether he
is caught or not—that is for fortune to decide—
there's no way you shall see me coming here again.
This time I'm safe, despite my expectation and   330
my judgment, so I owe the gods great gratitude.

[Exit Guard, along the same side-entrance by which he arrived.]

CHORUS[70]

Awesome wonders are many,[71]   *Strophe A*

---

69   Kreon is scoffing at the clever rhetorical wording of the guard's previous line. Such
concepts as belief, opinion and knowledge were much discussed by philosophers
interested in exploring the difference between appearance and reality, or belief
and knowledge, and by rhetoricians whose art was designed to induce belief in
the hearer.

70   The chorus now dance and sing the first *stasimon* ("song in position"), which is
followed by eight lines of anapests, introducing the scene that follows (376-83).
The starting point for their meditation on the nature of humanity is the extraordinary, almost miraculous feat of burial that the guard has just described. But the
famous song has far-reaching implications for many of the broader themes of the
drama.

71   The word translated "awesome" or "awful" in this play (*deinos*) is ambiguous
between "clever," "wonderful" and "dreadful."

but none of them more awesome
than the human race.[72]
This creature travels the grey sea   335
before the stormy winter wind,
pressing through surging waves that crest about him;
the highest of gods he wears away,
the tireless immortal Earth,[73]
turning her with the offspring of horses,[74]   340
as the plow runs to and fro from year to year.

The tribe of light-headed birds,   *Antistrophe A*
all kinds of savage beasts,
and creatures born in the salty sea,
he traps with his intricate coiling nets   345
and leads away—ingenious man!
With devices he overpowers
the mountain-roaming beast
that dwells in the wilderness,
he breaks the shaggy-necked horse with a yoke   350
on its neck, and the tireless mountain bull.

Speech and wind-swift purpose,   *Strophe B*
these has he taught himself,
and the passion for civic law,
and how to escape the shafts   355
of the inhospitable frosty sky
and the harsh shafts of the rain—
all-resourceful! Resourceless
he meets nothing the future holds.
Only from Hades will he fail   360
to find escape; and yet escape
from impossible sicknesses,
this he has devised.

---

72 The Greek word here is *anthrōpos*, which means "human being" as opposed to
"man." But later the word "man" (*anēr*) is used (346), reflecting the Greek tendency
to regard the male as the norm and standard of humanity. The activities described
are also those primarily associated with the male. It is therefore not inappropriate
to use "he" as the subject of the verbs.

73 Earth does not rule the other gods, but she is "highest" because she is both oldest
(age implies dignity) and the mother of all.

74 This probably refers to mules (offspring of horses and donkeys), which were normally used for plowing. The taming of horses is mentioned in the antistrophe.

By means of skillful contrivance,   *Antistrophe B*
clever beyond expectation,   365
he comes to evil sometimes,
sometimes to good.
When he weaves in the laws of the earth,
and the gods' sworn justice,[75] he is
high in his city;[76] citiless   370
is he whose daring makes him
keep company with what is not fine.
May he never share my hearth,
may I never share his thinking,
he who would do such things.   375

[Enter Guard leading Antigone, along the side-entrance by which he exited. Antigone's eyes are cast down.]

My mind is divided! Is this a divine
portent?[77] I know her! How can I argue that
this girl here is not Antigone?
Unhappy one, and child of an unhappy
father, of Oidipous! What does this mean?   380
Surely they are not leading you here,
found disobeying the laws of the king,
caught in an act of foolishness?

GUARD

This is the woman who performed the deed. We caught
her in the act of burial. But where is Kreon?   385

[Enter Kreon from the palace, with attendants.]

CHORUS

He's here, returning when we need him from the house.

KREON

What chance event makes my arrival opportune?

---

75 The "laws of the earth" suggest both human laws like Kreon's, and the laws of the underworld. "Weaves in" means that he maintains these laws as part of his life (but the text here is thought by many to be corrupt). "The gods' sworn justice" means justice that he has sworn by the gods to uphold.

76 The wording also suggests "his city stands high." Both meanings are particularly relevant to Kreon. "Citiless" in the next clause suggests not only that a wrongdoer may be exiled, but that a city composed of such people cannot stand firm. Note the close structural and verbal echo of 358, which falls in the same place in its strophe.

77 The arrival of the royal princess under guard is so shocking to the chorus that they cannot believe their eyes, and suggest there must be a supernatural explanation (cf. Introduction, p. 26).

GUARD

My lord, there's nothing mortals should forswear, since sworn
resolve is falsified by second thoughts. Take me:
I was insisting I would not be back here in   390
a hurry, after being stormed at with your threats.
But unexpected joy that we have prayed for is
beyond all other pleasures in extent; and so
I've come—despite the oaths I swore that I would not—
leading this girl here, who was caught performing rites   395
of burial. This time there was no drawing lots;
this lucky find belongs to me, and no one else.
Now take her, as you wish, my lord, yourself; you can
interrogate her and convict her; but it's just
that I should leave here fully free from all these evils.   400

KREON

Where did you catch this girl you're leading here, and how?

GUARD

We caught her burying that man; now you know all.

KREON

Do you know what you're saying? Do you speak aright?

GUARD

I saw her burying the corpse to which you had
forbidden burial. Are these words clear enough?   405

KREON

And how was she observed and taken in the act?

GUARD

What happened was like this. When we got back to our
position, subject to those awful threats of yours,
we brushed off all the dust that had been covering
the body, stripping bare the putrifying corpse,   410
and sat down on the hilltop with the wind behind
us, to escape from being stricken by the stench,
each man alert, and rousing one another with
loud taunts at any who might slacken from the task.
    This lasted for the time it took the shining circle   415
of the sun to reach the center of the sky.
The heat was burning. Suddenly a whirlwind raised
a dusty column from the earth, a trouble high
as heaven, which filled up the plain, defacing all
the foliage of the trees, and choked the mighty sky.   420
We shut our eyes and bore the sickness sent by god.

It took a long time for the storm to pass. And then
we saw this girl here wailing bitterly aloud,
in the piercing voice of a mother bird who sees her nest
is empty and her bed bereft of baby chicks.   425
Just so did she, on seeing that the corpse was bare,
cry out in lamentation, and call evil curses
down upon the ones who had performed this deed.[78]
At once she gathered thirsty dust with her bare hands,
and lifting high a brazen pitcher, finely-wrought,   430
she crowned the corpse by pouring three libation-streams.[79]
    The instant that we saw her, we rushed forward and
hunted her down; she was completely unperturbed.
We charged her with the deeds of burial, both this
one and the first, and she did not deny a thing—   435
a fact that brought me grief and pleasure both at once:
it is most sweet to have escaped from evils for
oneself; and yet to bring a friend to evil is
distressing.[80] But it's only natural that all
of this means less to me than my own safety.   440

KREON [to Antigone]

You there! You, bowing down your head towards the ground!
Do you admit it or deny you did the deed?

ANTIGONE

I don't deny it; I admit the deed was mine.

KREON [to the guard]

You may now take yourself away, wherever you
may wish, free and unburdened of this heavy charge.   445

[He turns back to Antigone.]

But as for you, tell me succinctly, not at length:
you knew a proclamation had forbidden this?

ANTIGONE

I knew. How could I not? It was made plain to all.

KREON

And yet you had the daring to transgress these laws?

---

[78] Note the echo of 384. The similarity in the descriptions of the two deeds under-
       lines the similarity of Antigone's and Kreon's outlooks, and at the same time the
       diametrical opposition between their views.

[79] Libations are liquids poured out in honor of the gods, or in this case, the dead (see
       n. on 197). Three was the usual number.

[80] The guard would not be a "friend" of Antigone's in a personal sense, but as a
       servant of the family he wishes her well and feels an obligation of loyalty.

ANTIGONE

It was not Zeus who made this proclamation;   450
nor was it Justice dwelling with the gods below
who set in place such laws as these for humankind;[81]
nor did I think your proclamations had such strength
that, mortal as you are, you could outrun those laws
that are the gods', unwritten and unshakable.[82]   455
Their laws are not for now or yesterday, but live
forever; no one knows when first they came to light.
I was not going to pay the gods just penalty
for breaking these, dreading the purposes of a
mere man. I knew that I must die—how could I not?—   460
regardless of the proclamation that you made.
But if I die before my time, I count that as
a profit. How can death not profit one who lives
surrounded by as many evils as myself?
For me, therefore, to meet this doom is equal to   465
no grief at all. But if I had endured the son
of my own mother to lie dead without a grave,
that would have brought me grief; but I'm not grieved by *this*.
And if you think my present deeds are foolishness,
perhaps the one who calls me foolish is the fool.   470

CHORUS

The fierce child clearly shows her father's fierceness; how
to yield to evils, this she does not understand.

KREON

Know well that over-rigid purposes most often
fall; the iron that is most powerful, that's baked
in fire until it is exceptionally hard,   475
you'll see most often shattered into little bits;
a slender curb, I know, will school the spirit of
a raging-tempered horse; it is impossible
to harbor mighty thoughts when you are someone's slave.
This girl knew well how to commit an act of outrage   480

---

[81] Justice is often personified as sitting beside the throne of Olympian Zeus (e.g. *OC* 1382). But Antigone is also appealing to Zeus as ruler of the underworld (equivalent to Hades). According to her, there is a corresponding Justice who lives down below, representing the rights of the underworld divinities. On "earth" and "sky" gods see Introduction, pp. 20–21.

[82] "Unwritten laws" are customs and traditions, as opposed to codified law (see Introduction, p. 26). Kreon's proclamation is not a "written law," but is equated here with the laws of the state, which would generally be written down.

when she first transgressed against the published laws;
and here's a second outrage: after doing it
to boast of it and laugh, exulting in her deed.
It's clear enough that I'm no man, but she's the man,
if she can get away with holding power like this.[83]   485
No, whether she's my sister's child, or tied to me
closer by blood than all my household under Zeus,[84]
she won't escape from a most evil doom, nor will
her sister, her blood-kin, the other whom I hold
equally guilty in the planning of this tomb.   490
Call her. Just now I saw her in a frenzy in
the house, no longer in possession of her mind.

[Two of Kreon's attendants exit into the palace.]

The heart of those contriving in the dark what is
not right is often caught out in deceit before
they act. But this I also loathe—when someone caught   495
performing evil wants to glorify the deed.[85]

ANTIGONE

Take me away and kill me. What more do you want?

KREON

No more. If I have that, then I have everything.

ANTIGONE

Then why are you delaying? There is nothing in
your words that's pleasing to me—may there never be!   500
And naturally you disapprove of mine as well.
Yet how could I have won more glorious renown
than by the act of placing my own brother in
a tomb? These people here would say my action pleases
all of them,[86] if fear did not lock up their tongues.   505
But this is one of kingship's many blessings—that
it can both act and speak just as it wishes to.

---

[83] Kreon reveals his own preoccupations by oddly describing Antigone's success
      with a word (*kratos*) normally used for political power (cf. e.g. 173, 873).
[84] Literally, "than Zeus of the courtyard." An altar to Zeus of the Hearth was placed
      in the central courtyard of the Greek house, where the whole household might
      gather for sacrifice.
[85] I.e. Ismene tried to conceal the deed, but has been betrayed by the unusual behavior
      resulting from her guilty conscience, whereas Antigone has been caught in the act
      and is not ashamed of it.
[86] Antigone gestures towards the chorus. But the audience might also feel themselves
      to be included among "these people here."

KREON

This view is yours alone of all these Kadmeans.[87]

ANTIGONE

It's their view too; because of you they curb their lips.

KREON

Aren't you ashamed of thinking differently from them?   510

ANTIGONE

There's no shame in revering one's own flesh and blood.

KREON

Did he who died opposing him not share that blood?

ANTIGONE

He shared it, from one mother and one father too.

KREON

Then why give honor that's irreverent in his eyes?[88]

ANTIGONE

The dead man's corpse will not bear witness to your words.[89]   515

KREON

Yes, if you honor the irreverent equally.

ANTIGONE

No, for it was his brother, not some slave, who died.

KREON

Died trying to sack this land, the other in defense.

ANTIGONE

Despite that, Hades longs to see these laws fulfilled.[90]

KREON

But good and bad should not share in them equally.   520

ANTIGONE

Who knows if this is not untainted down below?[91]

KREON

An enemy is not a friend, even in death.

---

[87] "Kadmean" means "Theban," after Kadmos, the founder of Thebes.

[88] Since the two brothers were enemies, Kreon expects the dead Eteokles to be angered by Antigone's respectful treatment of Polyneices.

[89] Antigone may mean that since Eteokles is dead he is not available as a witness, or that he will not take the view Kreon imputes to him.

[90] These "laws" are the traditional rites of burial.

[91] I.e. perhaps in death Eteokles will respect his brother's right to burial. Kreon's response, that enmity extends even beyond the grave, is more plausible in terms of traditional Greek attitudes.

ANTIGONE

My nature joins in friendship, not in enmity.[92]

KREON

If you must show them friendship, go and do so down
below! But while I live a woman shall not rule.[93]   525

[The two attendants return from the palace leading Ismene. She is distraught.]

CHORUS

But here is Ismene in front of the gates,
pouring the tears of a loving sister;
a storm-cloud is hanging over her brow,
blighting her visage flushed with blood,
wetting her lovely cheek with rain.   530

KREON

You there, who lurked inside the house, a viper sucking
out my blood without my knowledge—I was not
aware of nurturing two dooms to overthrow
my throne—come, tell me, will you too admit you helped
perform this burial, or swear your ignorance?   535

ISMENE

I did the deed—if she will join in saying so.
I share in bearing the responsibility.

ANTIGONE:

Justice will not allow this, since you did not want
to do it, nor did I give you a share in it.

ISMENE

But in these evils I am not ashamed to make   540
myself a fellow-sailor of your suffering.

ANTIGONE

Hades and those below know who can claim this deed;
I do not like a friend who loves in word alone.

ISMENE

Don't, sister! Don't dishonor me by keeping me
from joining in your death and rites for him who died.[94]   545

---

92 In this line Antigone uses two unique words, which must have been carefully
    chosen (or coined) to express her essential nature. But her words should not be
    sentimentalized. For the Greeks, "friendship" with kin was a natural fact of birth,
    which should evoke loyalty regardless of personal sentiment.
93 This line is ambiguous. It could also mean "a woman shall not rule *me.*"
94 Ismene seems to think that by accepting blame for the burial she can also share
    the credit for it.

ANTIGONE

Don't try to share this death with me. Don't claim as yours
a deed you did not touch. My own death will suffice.

ISMENE

How can I long for life if you leave me behind?

ANTIGONE

Ask Kreon that; he is the one you care about.

ISMENE

Why cause me pain like this, when it's no help to you?   550

ANTIGONE

If I do laugh at you then it's because of grief.[95]

ISMENE

How then may I attempt to help you, even now?

ANTIGONE

Just save yourself; I don't begrudge you your escape.

ISMENE

Wretch that I am! Must I miss sharing in your doom?

ANTIGONE

You must; you made the choice to live, and I to die.   555

ISMENE

But not without me trying to talk you out of it.

ANTIGONE

One side approved your thinking and the other mine.[96]

ISMENE

And yet the two of us are equally at fault.[97]

ANTIGONE

Have confidence! You are alive, but my own soul
has long since died, that I may bring help to the dead.   560

KREON

One of these two, I say, has just been shown to be
senseless, the other's been that way since she was born.

---

[95] Mocking or gloating laughter was a standard way of expressing contempt for an
enemy or avenging oneself for an injury (cf. 483, 647, 839-42, 1084-5). Antigone is
retaliating against Ismene for the pain caused by her sister's failure to help her.
Ismene's response shows an attempt to repair their relationship even now.

[96] On one "side" of this imaginary debate is Kreon, on the other the gods and the
sisters' dead family members.

[97] Presumably Ismene means that she is equally guilty because she sympathizes with
Antigone's act. Or she may be referring to the fact that Kreon holds them equally
responsible.

ISMENE

Yes, lord; in evil fortune even people's inborn
sense does not remain within them, but departs.

KREON

Like yours, when you chose evil deeds with evildoers.[98]   565

ISMENE

How can I live my life without her, all alone?

KREON

She—do not speak of her as someone still alive.

ISMENE

But will you really kill your own child's bride-to-be?[99]

KREON

Yes; there are other plots of land for him to plow.[100]

ISMENE

Not like the harmony that fitted him to her.[101]   570

KREON

I loathe for sons of mine to marry evil wives.

ISMENE

Oh dearest Haimon, what dishonor from your father![102]

KREON

You pain me to excess, you and your marriage-bed.

ISMENE

Will you deprive him, your own offspring, of this girl?

KREON

It's Hades who will stop this marriage taking place.   575

---

98 Kreon wilfully misinterprets Ismene's reference to the sisters' "evil fortune," as if she meant bad behavior.

99 This is the first mention in the play of Haimon, Kreon's son. His betrothal to Antigone may have been invented by Sophocles (cf. Introduction, p. 20). If so, Ismene's words will have been quite a dramatic surprise for the original audience.

100 I.e. other marriage partners are available to Haimon. Kreon here echoes the Athenian marriage ceremony, in which the wife was given to the husband "for the plowing of legitimate children."

101 These words may suggest a special personal bond between the couple. But they may simply mean that they are well-matched dynastically.

102 Some commentators assign this line to Antigone rather than Ismene (to whom the manuscripts give it). Manuscripts do make such mistakes, but the arguments in favor of Antigone depend on a sentimental view of her relationship with Haimon, of which there is no other sign in the text. It would not be inappropriate for the affectionate Ismene to call Haimon "dearest." "Your marriage-bed" in the next line is normal Greek idiom for "this marriage that you keep going on about."

ISMENE

It has been settled, so it seems, that she must die.

KREON

Settled—for you as well as me. No more delays!
Take them inside the house, attendants. From now on
they must be women and not wander unrestrained.[103]
For even people who are bold will try to find   580
escape when they see Hades closing on their life.

[Attendants take Antigone and Ismene back into the palace. Kreon remains on stage.[104]]

CHORUS[105]

Blessed are they whose life has tasted no evil.   *Strophe A*
When a house is tossed by the gods,
no aspect of doom is lacking;
it spreads out over that family   585
like a surging wave of the salt sea
running over the surface
of murky darkness below;
blown by tempestuous Thracian blasts
it rolls black sand from the sea-bed,   590
and the wind-vexed headlands face
its blows with a groaning roar.

Ancient are the troubles I see   *Antistrophe A*
for the house of the Labdakids,[106]
heaped on the troubles of the dead;   595
no new generation frees the family,
but some god strikes them down

---

103   Respectable women were supposed to leave the house as little as possible. But on the stage, where the scene is always outside, it was necessary for them to appear outside if they were to participate in the drama. The dramatists often play on this tension between social propriety and dramatic necessity (cf. 18-19, 1183-5). Here Sophocles makes Antigone's freedom, necessary for dramatic purposes, into a further sign of her unruliness in Kreon's eyes.

104   It is usual in Greek tragedy for the actors to absent themselves during the choral songs. But Kreon seems to remain present, perhaps for all the play's remaining songs (cf. n. on 780).

105   The chorus now dance and sing the second stasimon (third choral song), which is followed by five lines of anapests introducing Haimon's entrance (626-30). In it they place the preceding events into the larger context of the inherited curse on the house of Oidipous. Like the previous song, it is most obviously relevant to Antigone but has broader implications extending to Kreon as well.

106   The Labdakids are the descendants of Labdakos, Oidipous' grandfather.

and they find no release.
Just now a light of hope shone forth
from the last root of Oidipous' house;   600
but in its turn it is cut down
by the bloody dust of the gods below,
by senseless words and a Fury in the mind.[107]

What transgression of men, oh Zeus,   *Strophe B*
can constrain your royal power?   605
Sleep that conquers all
cannot defeat it; nor can
the tireless months of the years.
A potentate unaged by time,
you occupy the dazzling   610
splendor of Olympus.
Both now and through the future,
as through the past, this law will stand:
no vast thing moves into mortal lives without doom.[108]

For widely-wandering hope   *Antistrophe B*
benefits many men; but many   616
it cheats with light-headed passions.[109]
it comes upon one who knows nothing
till he burns his foot in the hot fire.[110]
It was some clever person   620
who declared this famous saying:
evil seems good, sooner or later,
to someone whose mind

---

107 The text is difficult here, and the imagery, as we have it, is very bold. Antigone and
    Ismene are the "last root" of their family, because they are the last means of propa-
    gating it. Light is a common metaphor for hope and safety in Greek (cf. 100-109),
    but here it does double duty by signifying the nurturing sunshine that might have
    helped the "root" to grow. The "bloody dust" alludes to the dust that Antigone
    sprinkled on her brother's corpse. This, along with her rash ("senseless") words
    to Kreon and her own frenzied behavior, is responsible for her demise. Furies are
    goddesses of vengeance, who may exert their will by driving their victims insane
    (Introduction p. 23). This Fury represents divine vengeance manifested over the
    generations of the house of Oidipous. But Antigone is not the only one in this play
    who may be accused of "senseless words and a Fury in the mind" (cf. 1074-5).
108 This is an expression of the traditional Greek pessimistic view that great wealth
    and status lead human beings into disaster.
109 "Passions" here are literally *erōtes*, the plural of *erōs*, passionate desire (cf. 781-
    800).
110 The image is probably of someone walking confidently over what appear to be
    cold ashes and accidentally stepping on a burning coal.

a god leads towards doom;
he fares but the briefest of time without doom.   625

[Enter Haimon, along the side-entrance leading from the city proper.]

Here is Haimon, the last and youngest-
born of your children. Has he arrived in
grief at the doom of his bride Antigone,
is he distraught to be cheated out of his
marriage-bed with his promised bride?[111]   630

KREON

We'll soon know better than a prophet could. My child,
have you come here in frenzy at your father, hearing
of my settled vote against your bride-to-be?
Or am I still your friend, whatever I may do?

HAIMON

Father, I'm yours. Your judgments, being good ones, guide   635
my path aright, and I shall follow where they lead;[112]
no marriage shall be reckoned by me as a prize
more valuable than having you as my good guide.

KREON

Just so, my child; that's how your heart should be disposed:
to stand behind your father's judgment in all things.[113]   640
This is the reason men pray to beget and keep
obedient offspring in their house—that they may pay
back evil to their father's enemies, and give
due honor to his friends, just as their father does.
But he who fathers children that provide no help,   645
what can you say he propagates but labors for
himself, and peals of laughter for his enemies?
So do not ever lose your senses, child, just out
of pleasure in a woman, knowing that an evil
woman as a bed-mate in your house will make   650

---

111 Note the formal symmetry of the encounter between Haimon and Kreon: four lines
     each, a pair of long speeches, each followed by two lines from the chorus, two
     lines each followed by stichomythia, and finally four lines each before Haimon
     exits.

112 In Greek there is a subtle ambiguity in Haimon's words, which could mean *"when*
     your judgment is good, I follow it." There is a similar ambiguity in the latter part of
     638, which could mean *"when* you guide me well." Cf. also the ambiguity of "I'm
     yours" (635), which could mean either "I am your son" or "I am loyal to you."

113 There is military metaphor here: Haimon is to be a dutiful soldier obeying his
     father's judgment.

a chilly armful to embrace;[114] for what could be
a wound more serious than this, an evil friend?
So spit that girl away just like an enemy,
and let her marry someone else, in Hades' house.
For I have caught her disobeying openly,   655
this girl alone of all the city; and I shall
not falsify myself before the city, but
I'll kill her. Let her chant to Zeus as god of blood-
kinship; if I raise my own family to be
disorderly, outsiders will be even worse.   660
For he who is a good man in his household will
be shown to be a just man in the city too.
I am quite confident that such a man would both
rule well, and serve well as a subject under rule,
and in a storm of spears stand firmly in his place,   665
a just man and a good one at his comrades' side.
But that transgressor who does violence to the law,
or thinks to give commands to those who are in power,
whoever does this can receive no praise from me.
The one appointed by the city should be listened to,   670
in small things and in just things and the opposite.[115]
There is no greater evil than unruliness.[116]
It ruins cities and makes households desolate,
it breaks and turns to flight the ranks of allied spears.
But when the lives of mortals go aright, it is   675
obedience to rule that keeps most bodies safe.
Therefore we must defend the cause of order, and
by no means let a woman get the upper hand.
Better to fall, if we must do so, to a man;
then nobody could say a woman conquered us.   680

CHORUS

To us, unless time's robbed us of our wits, you seem
to speak with sense about the things you're speaking of.

HAIMON

Father, the gods implant good sense in human beings,

---

[114] Kreon's words ironically foreshadow Haimon's final embrace of Antigone (1236-7); compare also 653 with 1232.

[115] The idea that in order to preserve civic order one must obey even unjust commands by a ruler accords with Kreon's generally military outlook. The thought is not uncommon in Greek texts, but it is often associated with slavery.

[116] This is the first certain occurrence in Greek of the word *anarchia*, which gives us "anarchy." It means the collapse of rule and prevalence of disobedience.

the very best of all the things that we possess.
I could not say—and may I never understand   685
how to declare—that you're not right in what you say.
But things might also turn out well some other way.
It is my natural place to watch on your behalf,
at all that people say or do or criticize;
for awe before your face prevents the common man   690
from saying things that might displease you if you heard.
But I can hear, in dark obscurity, the things
the city says in lamention for this girl:
that she among all women least deserves to die
the evillest of deaths for deeds most glorious,   695
since she did not let her own brother, fallen in
the bloody slaughter, lie unburied or be torn
apart by fierce flesh-eating dogs or birds of prey.
Is golden honor not the lot that she deserves?
Such murky rumors are advancing secretly.   700
My father, no possession is more valuable
to me than your good fortune; for what greater treasure
can a child have than a father thriving in
renown, or can a father have than such a son?
Do not, then, clothe yourself in just one attitude—   705
that what you say, and only what you say, is right.
For those who think that they alone possess good sense,
or that no other has a tongue or spirit such
as theirs, when opened up expose their emptiness.[117]
No, even if a man is clever, there's no shame   710
in learning many things and not straining too tight.
When trees beside a swollen winter torrent bend
and yield, you see how every little twig stays safe;
but those that strain against it perish root and branch.
And on a ship, if he who holds the power strains   715
the rigging tight and does not yield, he overturns
his benches and completes the voyage upside down.[118]
So come, yield from your rage; allow yourself to change.
If there is judgment even in a younger person
like myself, I say it's best by far for men   720
to be by nature full of knowledge in all things.

---

[117] The image here may be that of a folded pair of writing tablets, which is opened
up to find nothing written on the waxed surface inside.

[118] Haimon describes the ship's captain in a way that is applicable to a political ruler
(cf. 738), and thus underlines the implications of the "ship of state" analogy.

If not—since things are not inclined to be that way—
it's also fine to learn from others who speak well.

CHORUS

It's fitting, lord, if he says something timely, that
you learn, and you from him, since both have spoken well.   725

KREON

Are men of my age to be taught to have good sense
by someone who has only grown to this man's age?

HAIMON

Only in what is just. And even if I'm young,
you should not look at someone's age, but at his deeds.

KREON

Revering the disorderly—at deeds like that?   730

HAIMON

I'd never urge you to revere an evildoer.

KREON

And is this not the sickness *she's* afflicted with?

HAIMON

That's not what all the citizens of Thebes are saying.

KREON

And shall the city tell me what I should command?

HAIMON

You see how like a very young man that was said?[119]   735

KREON

Am I to rule this land at someone else's whim?

HAIMON

There's no true city that belongs to just one man.[120]

KREON

By law is not a city his who holds the power?

HAIMON

You'd do well ruling in a desert by yourself.

KREON

He's fighting as the woman's ally, so it seems.   740

HAIMON

If you're a woman; you're the one I care about.

---

[119] Young men were expected to be rash and hot-headed, in contrast to the dignity
and restraint of maturity and the wisdom of old age (cf. 281, 726-7, 767).

[120] A city governed by a monarch might "belong to one man," but would not live up
to the ideals of the Athenian democratic *polis*.

KREON

Saying your father is unjust, most evil one?

HAIMON

Yes, since in justice I can see that you're at fault.

KREON

So I'm at fault to show due reverence for my rule?

HAIMON

Irreverence, trampling on the honors of the gods.   745

KREON

Vile character, to give a woman precedence!

HAIMON

At least you will not catch me conquered by disgrace.

KREON

Yet all you say is spoken on behalf of *her*.

HAIMON

Of you and me as well, and of the lower gods.

KREON

There is no way that you shall marry her alive!   750

HAIMON

Then she will die, in death destroying someone else!

KREON

Have you become so bold that you are threatening me?

HAIMON

What threat is it to speak against your empty judgments?

KREON

You'll weep for trying to teach me sense, when you have none.

HAIMON

If you were not my father, I'd say *you* lack sense.   755

KREON

Don't try to coax me with such words, you woman's slave!

HAIMON

You want to speak, yet hear no answer to your words?

KREON

Oh really? By Olympus here,[121] know well that you
will soon regret abusing me with your complaints.

[He addresses his attendants.]

---

[121] Olympus stands for the sky (home of the "heavenly" or "sky" gods), to which
Kreon gestures as he swears by it (cf. Introduction, p. 20).

Bring out that loathsome creature, so that she may die   760
at once, before her bridegroom's eyes, right at his side.

[Two attendants exit into the palace.]

HAIMON

No! No! She shall not perish at my side—do not
believe it! And you'll never see my face before
your eyes again; so you may rave on madly with
whatever friends still want to share your company!   765

[Haimon rushes from the stage along the side-entrance leading to the plain.]

CHORUS

My lord, the man has gone from us with angry speed,
and grief lies heavy on the mind of one so young.

KREON

Let him be gone to do, or think, things greater than
befits a man; he won't free those two girls from doom.

CHORUS

Have you indeed made up your mind to kill them both?   770

KREON

Not her who did not touch the deed; for you speak well.

CHORUS

By what doom do you plan to kill the other one?

KREON

I'll lead her to a place deserted by the steps
of mortals, and conceal her, living, in a cave
dug from the rock, with just a little food, enough   775
to let the city as a whole escape from taint.[122]
And there perhaps by praying to the only god
that she reveres—Hades—she may be spared from death;
or else she'll come to recognize at last that to

---

[122] The Greek suggests not a natural cave but a chamber hollowed out of the rock by
human hands, with a passage cut into the mountain leading to the mouth of the
chamber itself (1215-17). Tombs of this kind have been found in Greece. According
to Kreon's original decree, the punishment was to be death by stoning (cf. 35-6). But
since the perpetrator has turned out to be his kin, Kreon attempts to avoid the taint
of blood-pollution by letting Antigone die of "natural" causes rather than killing
her directly. Death by immurement was also felt to be appropriate to unmarried
women, since it leaves the body concealed and unpenetrated in death. Leaving
some food in the cave is a further symbolic attempt to evade responsibility and
pollution.

revere what Hades holds is labor in excess.[123]   780
CHORUS[124]

> Eros, unconquered in battle!   *Strophe*
> Eros, you plunder possessions,[125]
> you keep your night watch
> on a young girl's soft cheeks;
> you range over the sea   785
> and through wild rural shelters;
> not one of the immortals can escape you,
> not one of us human beings
> whose lives are but a day;[126]
> and he who has you has madness.   790
>
> You wrench aside minds to injustice,   *Antistrophe*
> even of the just, to their ruin;
> you have stirred up this quarrel too,
> between men who are blood-kin;[127]
> radiant desire is the victor,   795
> shining in the eyes of the bride
> who graces the marriage bed;[128]

---

123   Commentators disagree over whether Kreon exits at this point. If he goes into the palace, this would be the only time a male character besides the Messenger enters or leaves the female realm, except for Kreon's own final exit (see final note). If he remains on stage throughout, that might help to explain the chorus' lack of explicit support for Antigone. On the other hand, it seems strange for him to wait throughout Antigone's long lament before sending her off to her death at 885. If he does exit here, he returns at 882.

124   The short third stasimon is a hymn to Eros, god of passionate desire, to whom the chorus attribute Haimon's behavior in the preceding scene. It is followed by five anapests introducing Antigone (801-5).

125   Eros destroys material goods, not only by making people spend recklessly, but by provoking such destruction as the sack of Troy (caused by Paris's seduction of Helen).

126   This is a common way of expressing the brevity of human life in contrast to the immortality of the gods (cf. 456-7).

127   The word translated as "blood-kin" (*xunaimos*, also at 198, 488, 659), echoes and puns on the name of Haimon. Related words for blood (*haima*) are used at 122, 202, 486, 512, 529, 976, 1022, 1175.

128   The eyes are often viewed as both a locus and a cause of erotic desire. The phrase is thus suggestive of erotic reciprocity, indicating the bride's own desire as well as her attractiveness to her bridegroom. But there has been no sign of such desire in Antigone.

this sits in rule by the mighty ordinances;[129]
for the game-playing goddess
Aphrodite is invincible in battle.   800

[Enter Antigone, led by guards from the palace.]

But now at this sight I myself am carried
away past the bounds of such ordinances,[130]
I can no longer hold back the streams
of my tears, when I see Antigone pass
to the bridal chamber where all must sleep.[131]   805

ANTIGONE[132]

Look on me, oh you citizens   *Strophe A*
of this my fatherland,
as I travel my last road,
gaze my last on the light of the sun,
and never again.   810
Hades who puts all to sleep
leads me still alive
to the shores of Acheron.[133]
No wedding hymn is my lot;
no marriage song sung for me;   815
no, I shall be Acheron's bride.

CHORUS

But are you not going with praise and renown
to the place where corpses lie concealed?
You were not struck by a wasting sickness

---

129   The "mighty ordinances" are the laws sanctioned by the gods, like those to which
       Antigone appealed (450-60). Here the chorus is referring to the bond of loyalty
       that Haimon owes Kreon, as son to father. Eros evidently "sits beside" such laws
       "in rule" because he represents an equally powerful or even more powerful force.
       But many commentators have thought the text is corrupt here, since Eros often
       causes the violation of moral laws (cf. 791-2).

130   I.e. like Haimon, the chorus is carried away by an emotion which outweighs their
       loyalty to Kreon. The metaphor is from chariot racing, where the horses might get
       out of control and carry the driver outside the limits of the course (for the image
       cf. 139, 791-2, 1273-5).

131   On the theme of "marriage to death" see Introduction, pp. 22-3.

132   Antigone sings a monody, or lyric solo, consisting of two strophic pairs and
       punctuated by groups of lines from the chorus. This may also be viewed as a
       continuation of the third *stasimon*, in which case the entire lyric contains a total
       of three strophic pairs, one choral and two monodic.

133   Acheron is one of the rivers of the underworld (the name means "lamentation").
       It is personified in 816 as an embodiment of death.

or given the wage that is paid by the sword;[134]   820
you alone among mortals will go down
to Hades still living, a law to yourself.[135]

ANTIGONE

I have heard that Tantalos' daughter,   *Antistrophe A*
our guest who came from Phrygia,
perished most lamentably   825
upon the peak of Sipylus;[136]
like tenacious ivy the growth of rock
tamed her; as she wastes away
the pouring rains never leave her—
so the voice of men reports—nor does the snow,   830
and under her tearful brow
her neck is wet with streams;[137]
most like her a divinity puts me to sleep.

CHORUS

But she was a goddess and born from a god,
while we are mortals and human-born.[138]   835
And yet it is great if people should say
when you perish that you have shared in the lot

---

[134]   A violent death is the "wage" for taking up the sword.

[135]   Unlike some mythological characters (such as Orpheus and Herakles), Antigone will not actually reach Hades while still living. The chorus simply mean that she is going alive to her tomb. They are trying to comfort her by pointing out that this is an extraordinary fate (if not, as they suggest, a unique one).

[136]   Antigone counters the chorus' claim that her death is unique by pointing to the parallel with Niobe, whose end resembled her own entombment in the rock. Niobe, daughter of Tantalos, married Amphion, a king of Thebes (thus making her "our guest" to the Theban Antigone). When Niobe boasted that she had many children, whereas Leto, the mother of Apollo and Artemis, had only two, Apollo and Artemis killed all her children. Niobe returned to her original home at Mt. Sipylus (in Ionia), where she was turned into stone, in a rock-formation that some think is still visible today.

[137]   The chorus describe the misery of Niobe among the storms of the mountain-top, but the language shades into a description of her own unceasing tears for her dead children, which run down her petrified form as mountain streams. In Greek as in English the words "brow" and "neck" can be applied to mountains as well as people.

[138]   The chorus counter Antigone's parallel by pointing out what they view as an important difference between the two cases: Niobe was of divine ancestry (she was not, as they claim, a goddess, but her father, Tantalos, was the son of Zeus). The parallel thus enhances Antigone's glory, rather than diminishing it.

of the godlike in life and again in death.[139]

ANTIGONE

  Alas, you laugh at me![140]   *Strophe B*
  By my fathers' gods, why don't you save   840
  this outrage until I have gone?
  Why mock me in my presence?
  Oh city! Oh city's wealthy men!
  Oh springs of Dirce, sacred ground
  of Thebes of the fine chariots,   845
  you at least I call to witness
  how I'm going, unwept by friends,
  by what laws I go to the heaped-up prison
  of my strange tomb.[141] Unhappy me!
  I have no home among mortals,   850
  no home as a corpse among corpses,
  with the living or with the dead.[142]

CHORUS

  Stepping forward to daring's very brink,
  you stumbled with your foot, my child,
  on the lofty pedestal of Justice.[143]   855
  You're paying for some ordeal of your father's.

---

[139] Antigone resembles Niobe in life as well as in death because she too is meeting death prematurely, and will be covered by a rocky mountain. Her final moment of life, a gruesome confusion of life and death, resembles the moment at which Niobe began to turn to stone.

[140] Antigone interprets the chorus's words as mockery, presumably because she was seeking pity from them, but they have instead attempted to console her (cf. n. on 551).

[141] Antigone's language suggests the piling-up of earth for a grave such as Polyneices' more than a tomb carved into the rock. But the cave-tomb might have an artificially built-up mound on top. It will also be sealed with a pile of stones heaped up at the entrance (cf. 1216).

[142] Antigone laments that, as a living person assigned to the tomb, she belongs properly with neither the living nor the dead. She uses the word *metoikos*, which in fifth-century Athens denotes a resident alien, i.e. a non-Athenian who lives in Athens without civic rights. It also appears at 868 and 890.

[143] There is controversy as to whether these lines express approval or disapproval for Antigone's actions. Depending on the exact text adopted, they could mean that Antigone has "tripped over" justice, i.e. violated the justice of Kreon's decree, or "fallen at the feet of justice" as a suppliant, i.e. relied upon the justice of the unwritten laws. The chorus' words at 856 suggest a third interpretation: she has "stumbled against" a larger kind of justice than Kreon's, which requires her to "pay for" the misdeeds of her father Oidipous.

ANTIGONE

You touch on the most distressing   *Antistrophe B*
of all my cares, the thrice-turned
lamentation for my father,[144]
and for that whole destiny   860
allotted to us, the renowned
descendants of Labdakos.
Oh doom of a mother's bed,
ill-fated mother who slept
with her own son, my father!   865
Such was my unhappy birth.
To them I go thus cursed, unmarried,
to dwell without a home.
Oh my brother, the marriage you found
was ill-destined;[145] dying   870
you slaughtered me, who still lived.

CHORUS

There's reverence in revering him;[146]
but power—to those whom power concerns—
cannot permit transgression;
you're destroyed by your self-willed temper.   875

ANTIGONE

Unwept, unfriended, unaccompanied   *Epode*
by wedding song, I'm led away unhappily
along this road prepared for me.
No longer is it lawful for me,
wretch that I am, to look upon   880
the bright eye of this sacred torch;[147]
no friend laments my unwept destiny.[148]

KREON

Do you not know that no one would cease pouring forth

---

144   "Thrice-turned" means often repeated. The metaphor is from plowing.
145   This refers to Polyneices' marriage to Argeia, daughter of Adrastos, king of Argos, which brought Polyneices the allies he needed to mount his assault on Thebes, and thus indirectly caused Antigone's own death.
146   The chorus acknowledge that Antigone's action was indeed one of reverence, but refuse to dismiss the importance of other conflicting kinds of reverence (such as reverence for a king).
147   I.e. the sun. The dying often lament that they must leave the sunlight, which stands for life (cf. 809-10).
148   Antigone is not aware of Haimon's distress, and ignores Ismene's existence (cf. 895). In any case, these two are not present. The chorus have been moved to tears (801-5), but Antigone evidently does not count them as "friends."

songs of lament before their death, if that could help?
Lead her away as quickly as you can, and let   885
a covered tomb embrace her, as I said; then leave
her there alone, deserted, whether she desires
to die or live entombed beneath that kind of roof;
for we are pure as far as this girl is concerned;[149]
but she shall be deprived of any home up here.   890

ANTIGONE
Oh grave! Oh marriage chamber! Oh you caverned dwelling-
place, eternal prison where I go to join
my own, who perished in such numbers to be taken
in by Persephassa with the dead below.[150]
Now I am going down, the last of them, my death   895
the worst by far, before my destined share of life.
Yet I still nurse the hope that when I get there I'll
arrive dear to my father, dearly loved by you
my mother, and to you, my own dear brother, dear.[151]
For when you died, with my own hands I washed you and   900
laid out your bodies in due order, gave libations
to your graves; and now it is for tending your
corpse, Polyneices, that I'm reaping this reward.
     And yet, to those with sense, by honoring you I
did well; for if the oozing corpse were my own child,   905
or my dead husband, I would never have performed
this labor in defiance of the citizens.
In satisfaction of what law do I say this?[152]
My husband dead, I could have had another, and
a child from someone else, if I had lost the first;   910
but with my mother and my father both concealed
in Hades, no more brothers ever could be born.
By such a law as this I honored you, my own
dear brother, higher than them all; but Kreon thought
I was at fault in this and daring awful deeds.   915
And now he has me in his hands; he leads me off

---

[149] The method of execution is designed to avoid the pollution incurred by killing a blood-relative (cf. 775-6, with note).

[150] Persephassa is another name for Persephone, queen of the dead.

[151] I.e. Eteokles, as the change of subject in 902 makes clear.

[152] The curious argument, principle, or "law" that follows has a close parallel in Herodotus III.119. (There are also parallels in other cultural traditions.) Many have found the argument distasteful or inconsistent with other aspects of Antigone's character. But it suits her dedication to the dead members of her natal family.

unbedded, unaccompanied by wedding song,
without a share in marriage or the nurturing
of children;[153] thus deserted by my friends I go
alive, ill-fated, to the caverns of the dead.   920
What justice of divinities have I transgressed?
Why should I still, unhappy one, look to the gods?
What ally should I call on, when my reverent deed
has gained me condemnation for irreverence?
If this is viewed among the gods as something fine,   925
I'll find out, after suffering, that I'm at fault;
if these men are at fault, may what they suffer be
as evil as the unjust things they do to me.

CHORUS
Still the self-same blasts of the self-same winds
of the spirit are gripping this girl.   930

KREON
Therefore these men who are leading her off
will weep on account of their slowness.

ANTIGONE
Alas! That word has approached very close
to death!

KREON
I do not encourage her to have confidence   935
that this sentence won't be fulfilled.

ANTIGONE
Oh, my paternal town in the land of Thebes!
Oh, my ancestral gods!
Now I'm led off, there is no more delay.
Look on me, oh rulers of Thebes,[154]   940
the last of your royal house who remains,[155]
see what I suffer, from what kind of men,
for revering reverence.

[Antigone is led away by the guards along the side-entrance leading to the plain.]

---

[153] The analogy between marriage and death is enhanced by the verb "lead" (916, 931, 939), also used for a husband "leading" a wife to his house at their wedding.

[154] She is addressing the chorus, with the implication that their noble status gives them some authority and/or responsibility for events.

[155] Having cut off Ismene for disloyalty, Antigone apparently excludes her from membership of the royal house.

CHORUS[156]

Danae too endured to exchange	*Strophe A*
heaven's light for a bronze-bound dwelling.[157]	945
Concealed in a tomb-like bridal chamber,	
she too was yoked.[158]	
Yet she was of honored family, child,	
oh my child, and stored up the seed	
of Zeus in a flow of gold.	950
Fate is awesome in its power.	
Wealth cannot escape it,	
nor Ares, nor ramparts,	
nor black ships beaten by the salt sea.[159]	

And the son of Dryas, quick to anger, was yoked,	*Antistrophe A*
king of the Edonians, imprisoned by Dionysos	956
in rocky bondage for his raging taunts.[160]	
Thus did the awful blossoming force	
of his madness dwindle, drop by drop.	
He did not recognize the god	960
until he attacked him in madness	
with taunting tongue. He tried to stop	
the women possessed by the god,	
their fires and their cries of *Euoi!*	
and provoked the flute-loving Muses.[161]	965

By the waters of the dark-blue rocks,	*Strophe B*
and of the double sea,	

---

[156] The chorus now sing the fourth *stasimon*. Like many choral songs in tragedy, it uses mythic parallels to explore the tragic situation. The text of the song is exceptionally corrupt and obscure, but the various stories all involve a person of noble birth being imprisoned, like Antigone.

[157] Danae's father, Acrisios, was warned by an oracle that he would be killed by his daughter's son. So he shut up Danae to keep her from becoming pregnant. But Zeus impregnated her in the form of a golden shower, and she gave birth to the hero Perseus.

[158] I.e. she had to submit to her fate (cf. 956). But "yoking" is also a common metaphor for the "taming" of a woman by marriage.

[159] I.e. fate cannot be bribed with wealth, fought off with warfare, kept out by fortifications, or escaped by sea-faring.

[160] Lykourgos, son of Dryas, resisted the arrival of the god Dionysos in Thrace (north of Greece), so Dionysos drove him mad. He did many violent deeds and was finally imprisoned in a cave.

[161] The "women possessed by the god" are the Bacchants or Maenads, the female worshipers of Dionysos (cf. n. 34). *Euoi!* is their ritual cry (cf. 1134-6). The Muses (goddesses of music, poetry, song and dance) are also sometimes found in the company of Dionysos.

are the shores of Bosporus,
and Thracian Salmydessus,[162]
where neighboring Ares looked upon   970
the accursed blinding wound
dealt to Phineus's two sons
by his savage wife, a wound
that darkened the orbs of their eyes,
calling for vengeance, gouged out   975
by bloody hands and a sharp shuttle.[163]

Wasting away, that wretched pair,   *Antistrophe B*
they wept for their wretched fate,
offspring born of a mother
whose marriage was no marriage.   980
Her own seed made her queen
of the ancient-born Erechthids;[164]
she was nurtured in far-off caves,
among her father's storm-winds,
a horse-swift Boread over the steep hills,   985
a child of gods.[165] Yet on her too
the long-lived Fates bore down, my child.

[*Enter Teiresias, a blind old prophet, by the side-entrance coming from Thebes proper;
he is guided by a young boy.*]

TEIRESIAS

Oh lords of Thebes, we've come here by a road we shared,
two seeing through the eyes of one; for this is how
a blind man makes his way, with someone else to lead.   990

KREON

What is it, aged Teiresias? Do you have news?

---

162 Salmydessus is in Thrace, on the west coast of the Black Sea, near the entrance to
the Bosporus. Thrace was the home of Ares, god of war.
163 Kleopatra was the daughter of the wind-god Boreas and wife of Phineus, King of
Salmydessus. She bore her husband two sons, but he imprisoned her and married
another wife, named Eidothea. Eidothea blinded Kleopatra's sons with a shuttle
(a long, pointed, needle-like implement used in weaving), and had them imprisoned too. (Note that this Kleopatra has nothing to do with the famous Egyptian
queen.)
164 Kleopatra's mother was Oreithyia, daughter of Erechtheus, a mythical king of
Athens. His descendants are called the Erechthids.
165 Boreas the wind-god carried Oreithyia off to a distant mountainous region of
Thrace, where she bore him four children, one of whom was Kleopatra. His
daughters are called Boreads.

TEIRESIAS

I'll tell you. You, believe the prophet and obey.

KREON

I've not departed from your thinking in the past.[166]

TEIRESIAS

And that is why you've steered this city's course aright.

KREON

I can attest the benefits that I've received.   995

TEIRESIAS

Think you now stand again on fortune's razor-edge.

KREON

What is it? How I shudder at the words you speak!

TEIRESIAS

You'll find out when you hear the signs from my skilled craft.
As I sat on the ancient seat where I perform
my augury, a haven for all kinds of birds,[167]   1000
I heard the birds give unintelligible voice,
screeching in evil frenzy with a babbling noise.
I sensed them tearing at each other with their bloody
claws—the whirring of their wings was a clear sign.
At once, in fear, I tried to make burnt-sacrifice   1005
upon an altar duly kindled; but Hephaistos
did not blaze forth from the offerings;[168] instead
a putrid liquid from the thighs oozed out upon
the coals, and smoked and spattered, and the gall-bladder
exploded up into the air; the thighs, streaming   1010
with moisture, lay bared of their covering of lard.
I learned about these things—the failure of my rites
of prophecy, which gave no signs—from this boy here.
For just as I lead others onward, he leads me.
    And it's from *your* bad thinking that the city is   1015
so sick. Our public altars and our hearths have all

---

166 This may allude to the fate of Kreon's son Megareus (sometimes called Menoikeus), who was sacrificed, on the advice of Teiresias, to save the city from attackers (cf. 1301-5).

167 Birds were lured with food to a "haven" so that they could be more easily observed by prophets (see further Introduction, p. 25).

168 When augury fails, Teiresias turns to sacrifice, where omens were seen in the way the offering burned. The offering itself consisted of an animal's thigh-bones, wrapped with a double layer of fat, with intestines and gall-bladder on top. The use of Hephaistos' name for "fire" here suggests divine disapproval (cf. n. on 124).

been tainted, every one, by dogs and birds with food
from the ill-fated fallen son of Oidipous.
And this is why the gods accept our sacrificial
prayers no more, nor flames from burning victims' thighs,   1020
nor do the birds scream cries that give me signs,
for they have eaten of a slain man's bloody fat.
     Think on this well, my child. To be at fault is common
to all humans. But when someone is at fault,
that man's no longer foolish or unfortunate   1025
if he attempts to heal the evil he has fallen
into, and does not remain immovable.
Self-will is what incurs the charge of foolishness.
Yield to the dead and don't keep stabbing at a perished
man. What prowess is it to re-kill the dead?   1030
I think and speak for your own good; it is most sweet
to learn from one who speaks well, if it profits you.

KREON
Old man, you all keep shooting arrows at me, just
like archers at a target.[169] Even your prophetic
skill is used against me. For a long time now   1035
I have been traded by your breed like merchandise.[170]
Go, make your profits! Keep on trading silver-gold
from Sardis,[171] if you wish, and gold from India;
but you shall not conceal him in a tomb, not even
if the eagles, birds of Zeus, should wish to rend   1040
his flesh and take it up to Zeus's throne as food.[172]
Not even then will I let him be buried out
of fear of this polluting taint; for I know well
no human being has the strength to taint the gods.[173.]
But mortals, even those with many awesome skills,   1045
fall in a shameful fashion, aged Teiresias,
when they speak finely shameful words for profit's sake.

---

[169] "You all" must refer to the other imagined conspirators, and perhaps Haimon.
[170] I.e. Teiresias has allegedly taken bribes to plot against Kreon, and thus "sold" him.
       Kreon may be referring to the death of Menoikeus (see n. on 993).
[171] This refers to electrum, a natural alloy of silver and gold, also called "white gold,"
       which came from mines near Sardis in Lydia.
[172] The eagle, king of birds, was sacred to Zeus, king of gods.
[173] A human being could not literally taint the gods with pollution, but of course this
       does not mean Zeus approves of Kreon's behavior.

TEIRESIAS

Ah![174]

Does any mortal know, or take into account...

KREON

What thing? What commonplace pronouncement do you speak?

TEIRESIAS

...how far good counsel is the best thing to possess?   1050

KREON

As far, I think, as thoughtlessness does greatest harm.

TEIRESIAS

Yet this is just the sickness that's infecting you.

KREON

I'd rather not abuse a prophet in reply.

TEIRESIAS

You do so, when you say my prophecies are false.

KREON

They are! All prophets are a money-loving breed.   1055

TEIRESIAS

And kings a breed that loves to profit shamefully.

KREON

Do you not know that you are talking to a king?

TEIRESIAS

I know; for through me you have kept this city safe.

KREON

You are a clever prophet, but you love injustice.

TEIRESIAS

You'll make me tell things undisturbed within my mind.   1060

KREON

Disturb them! Only do not speak for profit's sake.

TEIRESIAS

Is that what I'm already doing, in your view?

KREON

Know that you'll never use my thinking for your trade![175]

TEIRESIAS

And you, know well that you won't live through many more

---

[174] Such an exclamation interjected into stichomythia (single-line dialogue) often indicates a power-shift in favor of the speaker (so also at 323).

[175] I.e. Teiresias will not be able to make money out of the alleged Theban conspirators by getting Kreon to change his mind.

swift-racing courses of the sun before you give   1065
a child of your own flesh and blood in turn, a corpse
to pay for corpses, since you have cast down below
one who belongs above, sending a living soul
to dwell dishonorably in a tomb, and keep
up here a corpse belonging to the gods below,   1070
deprived of rites, of offerings, of piety.
These things are no concern of yours or of the upper
gods, but you are violating them by force.
Therefore the ruinous late-avenging Furies of
the gods and Hades lie in wait for you, that you   1075
may be caught up in these same evils in your turn.
See if I'm saying this because I'm silver-plated![176]
A little time will test my metal and reveal
the wailing cries of men and women in your house.[177]
Moreover all those cities have been shaken up   1080
with enmity whose mangled flesh got funeral rites
from dogs, or beasts, or flying birds that carried home
the impious stench to every city and its hearths.[178]
    In rage have I let fly these arrows, archer-like,
into your heart, for you have pained me; they are sure,   1085
and running will not help you to escape their fire.
    Come, child, lead me away to my own house, so that
this man can let his rage fly forth at younger men,
and learn to nurse a tongue that is less active and
a mind with better thoughts than those he's thinking now.   1090

[Exit Teiresias, led by his attendant, down the side-entrance into the city.]

CHORUS

My lord, the man has gone from us with awful words
of prophecy. And ever since the black hair on
my head turned white, I've never known him make the city
any utterance that turned out to be false.

---

[176] Teiresias refers sardonically to Kreon's repeated claims that he has been bribed, or
       "covered in silver." The test of time, like a touchstone, will reveal that the prophet
       is not "plated" with any superficial appearances, but is authentic through and
       through.
[177] The phrase is ambiguous between "wailing *by* men and women" and "wailing *for*
       men and women," and both will turn out to be true (cf. 1207, 1227, 1303, 1316).
[178] Kreon has refused burial not just to Polyneices, but to all the dead of the attacking
       army (a central feature of the story in many other treatments). Their only "entomb-
       ment" has been within the stomachs of wild animals. This causes both pollution
       (transmitted by birds of prey) and resentment in the dead men's home cities.

KREON

I know it too, and I am shaken in my mind.   1095
To yield is awful; but, by standing firm, to strike
with ruin my proud heart—why, that is awful too.

CHORUS

You need to take good counsel now, Menoikeus' son.

KREON

What should I do then? Tell me, and I shall obey.

CHORUS

Go, set the girl free from her rocky chamber, and   1100
construct a tomb for him who's lying there exposed.

KREON

Is this what you advise? You think that I should yield?

CHORUS

As quickly as you can, my lord. The gods' avenging
Harms, swift-footed, cut down those with evil thoughts.[179]

KREON

Alas! Reluctantly I leave my heart's resolve: 1105
I'll do it. There's no fighting with necessity.

CHORUS

Go, then, and do it. Give this task to no one else.

KREON

I'll go at once. Go! Go, all my attendants, both
those present and those absent![180] Take up axes in
your hands, and rush towards the place—it's over there.   1110
And now that my opinion has reversed itself,
I shall be there to set her free, just as I was
the one who bound her. It is best, I fear, to live
until life's end preserving the established laws.

*[Exit Kreon with attendants, along the side-entrance leading to the plain. The chorus
now sings their final song.]*

CHORUS

Oh you of many names,   *Strophe A*
treasure of the Kadmean bride,   1116
child of deep-thundering Zeus,[181]

---

179 The Harms of the gods are personified forces of vengeance like the Furies.
180 Apparently an idiomatic expression meaning "every one of you."
181 Dionysos was the son of Zeus and Semele, daughter of Kadmos (founder of
     Thebes). Semele asked Zeus to appear to her in the form in which he showed
     himself to his divine wife Hera. He came with his thunder and lightning, and she
     was incinerated (cf. 1140).

who care for famous Italy,[182]
and hold sway in Demeter's
folding hollows at Eleusis,   1120
a sanctuary shared by all,[183]
oh Bacchus, dwelling in Thebes,
the Bacchants' mother-city,
by Ismenos' flowing stream,
at the sowing of the savage dragon's seed![184]   1125

The smoky flash of the torch   *Antistrophe A*
has seen you above
the double-peaked rock,
where the Corycian Nymphs,
the Bacchants tread,   1130
and so has the stream of Castalia.[185]
The ivy-covered slopes
of Nysa's mountains have sent you,
and the green shore clustered with grapes.[186]
Immortal songs cry out *Euoi!* to you   1135
watching over the streets of Thebes.

You honor this city most highly,   *Strophe B*
high above all the rest,
you along with your mother,
she who was struck by lightning.   1140
Since all of the city's people

---

[182]   There were many Greek colonies in southern Italy, and Dionysos often appears
        in art of that region.
[183]   Demeter is goddess of earth and fertility. Her most prominent cult was at Eleu-
        sis, near Athens. "Hollows" alludes to the topography of Eleusis, but also to the
        receptive bosom or womb of the earth mother. Dionysos was also worshiped here
        under the name Iacchus (cf. 1154). The Eleusinian cult was open to all, and many
        flocked to the festivals; hence it is "shared by all."
[184]   Kadmos founded Thebes by sowing dragon's teeth, from which the first Thebans
        grew (cf. 126 with note). It is the "mother-city" of the Bacchants because the god
        was born there. Ismenos was a river to the east of the city.
[185]   The Bacchants celebrated Dionysos with torches and dancing at night in the
        mountains. At Delphi they danced on the high ground of Mt. Parnassus above
        two rocky peaks but below the mountain's summit. The Castalian stream flows
        down from here to Delphi. Here the Bacchants are not human women, but local
        nymphs, named for the Corycian cave, a large cave on Mt. Parnassus a few miles
        from Delphi.
[186]   These mountains and vineyards are at Nysa in Euboea, an island north of Attica
        which was famous for its wine (see Map 2). Dionysos had an important cult here.
        Ivy and grapes were both sacred to this god.

are gripped by a violent sickness,
come now too with purifying foot,
over the ridge of Parnassus,
or the groaning waters of the strait.[187]   1145

Oh you who lead the chorus   *Antistrophe B*
of stars that breath forth fire,[188]
you who watch over the voices
that cry out during the night,
offspring born of Zeus,   1150
appear to us, oh lord,
with your attendant Thyiads,[189]
who dance all night in madness
for bountiful Iacchus!

[Enter Messenger, along the side-entrance leading to the plain. He is an attendant of Kreon, probably a slave.[190]]

MESSENGER

Neighbors of Kadmos and the house of Amphion,[191]   1155
there is no human life in any state that I
would ever praise or criticize as something fixed.
For fortune sets upright and fortune dashes down
whoever has good luck or bad at any time,
and mortals have no prophet for what's set in place.   1160
Kreon was once a man to envy, in my view.
He saved this land of Kadmos from its enemies,
gained total power in the land and guided it,
sowed children's noble seed and throve in them.
Now all is gone. When even a man's pleasures let   1165
him down, then I no longer count him as alive—
I just consider him to be a living corpse.
Heap wealth within your house, if you so wish, and live
with royal splendor; yet if joy is missing from
these things, I wouldn't pay smoke's shadow to a man   1170

---

[187] I.e. the strait between Euboea and the mainland.
[188] The heavenly bodies were thought to participate in the night-time rituals of Iacchus (Dionysos) at Eleusis.
[189] This is another name for the nymphs who accompany Dionysos.
[190] The Messenger is a standard formal device in Greek tragedy. He is a barely characterized minor figure whose function is to report off-stage events, often of a violent or shocking nature.
[191] Amphion was a king of Thebes who built the city walls by charming the stones into place with the music of his lyre.

to purchase all the rest of it, compared with pleasure.

CHORUS

What further weight of grief do you bring for our kings?

MESSENGER

They're dead. The living are responsible for death.

CHORUS

Who is the bloody murderer? Who lies dead? Speak!

MESSENGER

Haimon has perished, bloodied by a kindred hand.[192]   1175

CHORUS

Was it his father's hand that did it, or his own?

MESSENGER

He killed himself, in wrath at blood his father shed.

CHORUS

How right, oh prophet, did you prove your words to be!

MESSENGER

That's how things stand; you may take counsel for the rest.

[*Enter Eurydike from the palace, attended by maids.*[193]]

CHORUS

But here is Kreon's wife, wretched Eurydike,   1180
close by; I see her coming from the house. She must
have heard about her son, or else she's here by chance.

EURYDIKE

Assembled townsfolk, I was starting to go out
and overheard you. I was going to supplicate
the goddess Pallas,[194] to address her with my prayers.   1185
As I was loosening the bolts across the door
to open it, a voice assailed my ears with words
of evil to our house. I sank back, full of dread,
upon my serving-maids, quite stricken from my wits.
But speak again, whatever news you brought, and I   1190
shall listen—I'm experienced in suffering.[195]

---

192 The Greek word could mean "by his own hand" or "by the hand of a kinsman."
     Hence the chorus' need for further clarification. The pun on Haimon's name and
     the Greek word for blood (*haima*) is particularly striking here (cf. n. on 794).

193 This character may have been invented by Sophocles (cf. Introduction, p. 20). She
     has nothing to do with Orpheus' wife of the same name.

194 Pallas is a frequent name for Athena.

195 This presumably alludes to the death of her son Megareus (see n. on 993).

MESSENGER
 Dear mistress, I was there in person and I'll speak
without omitting even one word of the truth.
Why should I try to soothe you with soft words that will
be shown as falsehoods later? Truth is always right.   1195
  I went, attending on your husband as his guide,
up to the high part of the plain where Polyneices'
corpse still lay unpitied, mangled by the dogs.
We prayed first to the goddess of the road and Pluto
to restrain their anger and be kind,[196] and washed   1200
him with the ritual washing, then with branches freshly
plucked we burned the body—what was left of it—
and built a lofty grave-mound from the earth that was
his home,[197] then made our way towards the prison of
the girl, her bridal-cave of Hades, strewn with rock.[198]   1205
Near that unhallowed inner chamber someone heard
a distant sound of high-pitched wailing cries, and came
to tell our master Kreon of these signs. As he
drew closer, incoherent cries of misery
surrounded him; he moaned aloud and sent forth words   1210
of bitter lamentation, "Ah, wretch that I am,
am I a prophet? Is the path I'm moving down
the most unfortunate of all the roads I've ever
walked? My son's voice greets me. Servants, come,
go closer quickly! Go up to the tomb and enter   1215
by that gap where stones have been torn out, up to
the grave's own mouth, and look to see if I detect
the voice of Haimon, or the gods deceive my ears."
Commanded by our apprehensive master we
looked in; within the furthest recess of the tomb   1220
we saw the maiden hanging by her neck, tied up
there by a noose of finely woven cloth;[199] the boy
had flung himself around her waist in close embrace,
while he bemoaned his bridal-bed now lost below,

---

[196] The "goddess of the road" is Hekate, an underworld goddess to whom offerings
were left at the junctions of roads. Pluto is another name for Hades.

[197] After a corpse was burned, the bones were collected and a mound of earth piled
over them. Polyneices is buried in his native ("home") soil, but the Greek also
suggests that under the earth is where he, as a dead person, belongs.

[198] This is another inverted reference to marriage, since a bridal chamber should be
strewn with soft bedding, perfumed and decorated with flowers.

[199] Antigone has hanged herself with a piece of her own clothing, probably her veil—a
symbolic item in marriage rituals.

his father's deeds and his unhappy marriage-bed.   1225
When Kreon saw them, he moaned horribly and went
inside to him, and called out with a wailing cry:
"What is this deed that you have done, bold wretch! What were
you thinking of? What circumstance destroyed your wits?
Come out, my child, I beg you as a suppliant!"[200]   1230
His son glared back at him with savage eyes, spat in
his face, said nothing in reply, and drew his two-
edged sword. His father rushed back to escape and Haimon
missed his aim. At once, ill-fated boy, in anger
at himself, he tensed himself upon his sword-   1235
point, and drove half its length into his side. Before
his wits departed he embraced the maiden with
a wilting arm; gasping, he spurted forth a sharp
swift stream of bloody drops upon the girl's white cheek.
He lies there, corpse embracing corpse. He has received   1240
his marriage rites at last—poor wretch—in Hades' house,
and demonstrated to the human race how far
ill-counsel is the greatest evil for a man.

[Exit Eurydike with her maids into the palace.]

CHORUS

What do you think this means? The woman's gone again
without one word for good or evil from her lips.   1245

MESSENGER

I am astonished too. But I'm sustained by hope
that hearing of this grief for her own child she won't
think fit to make lament before the city, but
will set her maids to weep this household woe inside.[201]
Her judgment's too experienced to be at fault.   1250

CHORUS

I don't know; but I think that silence in excess
is just as weighty as extraordinary cries.

MESSENGER

I'll go inside the house, then I shall know if she
is really keeping something secretly concealed,
pent up within her raging heart. Your words are good: 1255
excessive silence also carries heavy weight.

---

[200] Kreon invokes the ritual of supplication (Introduction, p. 21).
[201] I.e. Eurydike should mourn unostentatiously, in antiphonal lamentation with her
       maids inside the house.

[Exit Messenger into the palace. Enter Kreon along the side-entrance leading from the plain, carrying Haimon's corpse.[202]*]*

CHORUS

But here is our lord himself; he comes
with a clear-stamped monument held in his hands.
If it's lawful to say so,[203] his doom wasn't caused
by any outsider—the fault was his own.   1260

KREON

Oh!   *Strophe A*
The rigid faults, death-dealing,
of thoughtless wrongful thinking!
Oh you who here behold us,
kinsmen who killed and died!
Alas for my counsels' misfortune!   1265
Oh my son, too young
for your youthful doom!
Aiai! Aiai! You died, you departed,
through my ill counsel, not your own!

CHORUS

Alas! You seem now to see justice, but too late.   1270

KREON

Alas!
I have learned, wretch that I am! On my head
a god with a mighty weight struck down
at that moment, and tossed me in savage roads,
overthrew my joy—alas!—to be trampled.[204]   1275
Ah! Ah! Oh alas for the labors,
the anguished labors of mortals!

---

202 Alternatively, Haimon's body may be carried in by attendants, while he embraces
it with gestures of mourning. (This would provide a closer dramatic echo of Antigone's final scene.) In either case, there is a contrast between what Kreon holds
"in his hands" now and previously (cf. 916, 1258, 1280, 1297, 1344). No further
mention is made, here or elsewhere, of Antigone's body.
There follows a *kommos*, or lyric dialogue of lamentation, between the chorus and
Kreon (1261-1347). It is preceded and followed by choral anapests (1257-60, 1348-
53). Kreon's lyrics alternate with spoken lines (iambic trimeters) from Kreon, the
chorus leader, and the messenger, in a complex symmetrical structure.

203 The chorus is hesitant because of Kreon's royal status and the enormity of the
charge they are making. The word they use for "lawful" is *themis*, which refers not
to human laws but to a sense of what is divinely permitted in the order of things.
A related word is used for the "mighty ordinances" in the ode to Eros (798).

204 The wording here suggests the image of a charioteer who drives recklessly into
disaster after a blow on the head.

[Enter Messenger, from the palace.]

MESSENGER
You seem, my master, to have come with evils, yet
you have more still in store; the first you bear in your
own hands, but soon you will see others in the house.   1280

KREON
What greater evil follows evils such as these?

MESSENGER
Your wife is dead—in truth the mother of this corpse[205]—
unhappy woman, killed just now by fresh-struck blows.

KREON
    Oh!   *Antistrophe A*
    Oh harbor of Hades, unpurifiable,[206]
    why, oh why are you destroying me?   1285
    Oh herald of sorrow's evil tidings,
    what word is this you utter?
    Aiai! You've re-killed a man destroyed!
    What are you telling me, boy?[207]
    What new slaughter do you say
    embraces me—*Aiai! Aiai!* —   1290
    on top of destruction a woman's doom?[208]

[The palace doors open to reveal the corpse of Eurydike.[209]]

CHORUS
She can be seen. She is no longer shut indoors.

KREON
    Alas!
    Ah wretched me! I see this second evil!   1295
    What destiny, what still awaits me?
    I've just held my child in my hands,
    wretch that I am, and now I see her,

---

[205] She is Haimon's mother "in truth" because his death drives her to suicide, thus showing that she is a complete mother, one who cares exclusively about her children.

[206] The underworld is here viewed as a harbor choked with an endless supply of
putrid corpses, and hence of pollution.

[207] This is addressed to the messenger. Slaves were commonly addressed this way,
or it could be merely the address of an older man to a youth.

[208] This phrase hints at Kreon's own emasculated condition.

[209] The *ekkyklēma*—a low wheeled platform (Introduction, p. 11)—may have been used
here, showing Eurydike lying at the altar where she stabbed herself. Alternatively,
attendants may bring out her body and place it beside Kreon, who is thus framed
by the two corpses. The latter would make good dramatic sense of 1340-42.

another corpse before me.
Ah, ah, miserable mother! Ah my child!   1300

MESSENGER

There at the altar with a sharply-whetted knife[210]
she let her eyes close into darkness, after she
wailed first for dead Megareus' empty bed and then
for Haimon's.[211] Last of all she chanted evil fortunes
down upon your head for killing your own sons.[212]   1305

KREON

Aiai! Aiai!   *Strophe B*
My heart leaps with fear! Why does no one
strike my chest with a two-edged sword?
Wretched am I—*aiai!*—   1310
dissolved in wretched anguish!

MESSENGER

Before she died, your wife denounced you as the one
responsible for both the dooms of your two sons.

KREON

By just what form of bloody slaughter did she go?

MESSENGER

She struck with her own hand into her liver, when   1315
she heard of her son's death, so piercingly bewailed.[213]

KREON

Alas! Alas!
To me, to no other mortal,
this responsibility will cling forever.
It was I who killed you, I, wretch that I am!   1320
It was I! I speak truly.
Oh, servants!
Lead me as quick as you can,

---

[210] This line is conjectural, since the Greek is corrupt.
[211] On Megareus see n. on 993. The phrase "empty bed" is an emendation, and its meaning is uncertain. It may refer to the fact that neither of Eurydike's sons reached maturity as marked by marriage, which would fit in well with the play's theme of thwarted marriage. Alternatively, it could mean she lamented her own bed bereft first of Megareus and then Haimon. On this interpretation, she is lamenting the loss of her young (cf. 424-5). This also resonates strongly with the play's themes of incest and thwarted motherhood.
[212] The curse of a suicide was believed to be especially powerful.
[213] Greek texts often speak of the liver, as well as the heart, as a seat of life and an organ affected by passionate emotions. But in this context it refers more loosely to the vital organs.

lead me out of the way,
I who exist no more than nothing.   1325

CHORUS

If any profit lies in evils, your advice
holds profit. Evils underfoot are best when briefest.

KREON

Let it come, let it come!   *Antistrophe B*
Let that finest of fates for me appear,
bringing my final day,   1330
supremely best of fates!
Let it come, let it come,
that I may never see another day!

CHORUS

That's in the future. Now we must perform what lies
at hand. These things concern those whom they should concern.[214]   1335

KREON

My prayer encompassed all my passionate desires.

CHORUS

Pray now no further. There is no deliverance
for mortals from whatever is ordained for them.

KREON

Lead me away, a worthless man.
I killed you, my son, without intending to,   1340
you too, my wife—ah, wretch that I am!
I cannot look towards either one.
Nowhere can I lean for support.
All in my hands is warped,[215]
and from outside   1345
a crushing destiny
has leapt down on my head.

[Kreon's attendants lead him into the palace.[216]]

---

[214] This may mean that the gods, in whose hands the future lies, will take care of the
future, including Kreon's death, or that the chorus themselves, and Kreon, will
take care of the present situation.

[215] There is an ambiguity here between "the situation I am handling" and "what I
have in my arms."

[216] It is possible that Kreon departs down one of the side-entrances, in a funeral cortège
with the bodies of Haimon and Eurydike. But an exit into the house is suggested
by 1324, and would provide a fitting symbol of his emasculation since the house
is the realm of the female.

CHORUS

Sound thought is by far the foremost rule
of happiness; when we deal with the gods
we should never act with irreverence.   1350
Mighty words of boastful men
are paid for with mighty blows which teach
sound thinking at last in old age.

KING OIDIPOUS

CHARACTERS

OIDIPOUS, king of Thebes
PRIEST of Zeus
KREON, brother of Jokasta
CHORUS of aged Theban noblemen
TEIRESIAS, a prophet
JOKASTA, wife of Oidipous
FIRST MESSENGER (a poor old man from Corinth)
SHEPHERD (an aged slave of the royal house)
SECOND MESSENGER (a servant from within the house)
Antigone and Ismene, daughters of Oidipous and Jokasta
Guards and attendants

Setting: Outside the palace of Oidipous and Jokasta at Thebes. The scene shows the façade of the house, which has a central door. Near the door is an altar of the god Apollo. One of the two side-entrances represents the road to the countryside (and thence to Corinth and Delphi), the other the way to the city of Thebes proper.

[Oidipous enters from the palace, a man in the prime of life whose costume indicates royal status and authority. Before him is a crowd of citizens of all ages, carrying olive or laurel branches twined with wool and sitting on the steps of the altar. In front of them stands the priest of Zeus, king of the gods (Introduction, p. 21). Oidipous addresses the crowd in iambic trimeters, the meter of dialogue (Introduction, p. 15).]

OIDIPOUS

My children, youngest nurslings of your ancestor
Kadmos,[1] why do you sit here so beseechingly,
bearing these suppliant branches garlanded with wool?[2]
The city is filled up alike with incense-smoke,

---

[1] Kadmos was the founder of Thebes and Laios' great-grandfather. This makes him
 Oidipous' own ancestor as well, but he is not yet aware of that fact.
[2] On the ritual of supplication see Introduction, p. 21.

alike with prayers to Paian and with groaning cries.[3]   5
I thought it was not right for me to hear this by
report from others, children, so I've come myself:
I, famed to everyone, the man called Oidipous.

[He turns to the priest of Zeus.]

Come, tell me, aged one—since you're the natural
and fitting spokesman for these others—why you're sitting   10
here: in dread or in desire? You can be sure
I wish to aid you fully. I would be immune
to grief, did I not pity suppliants like these.

PRIEST

Oh Oidipous! Oh you who rule my land in power!
You see what age we are who sit here at your altar—   15
some who are still not strong enough to flutter far,
others already burdened with the weight of age;
I am the priest of Zeus, and these are chosen youths;
the other Thebans, branches wreathed with wool, are sitting
in the market-places and at both the shrines   20
of Pallas and Ismenos's prophetic ash.[4]
As you yourself can see, the city's now so badly
storm-tossed that it can no longer keep its head
from sinking down beneath the tossing waves of blood;
it is decaying in the fruitful husks of earth,   25
decaying in the herds of pastured cattle and
in women's barren labor-pains; and the fire-bearing
god, most hateful plague, has swooped to scourge
the city, emptying the house of Kadmos while
black Hades is enriched with groaning and laments.[5]   30
It's not because we judge you equal to the gods

---

3   Paian is a healing god closely associated with Apollo (Introduction, pp. 21-2), with
    whom he is sometimes identified (see 155 with note).
4   Thebes had at least two market-places. Pallas is a common name for Athena,
    who had two temples in Thebes. Ismenos was one of the main rivers of Thebes.
    "Prophetic ash" probably refers to a temple of Apollo, which stood near the river,
    and where divination was practiced by means of burned sacrificial victims (cf.
    Introduction, p. 24).
5   On Hades see Introduction, p. 21. There is a rich interweaving of imagery in this
    description of the blight on the land, which takes three forms: sterility of crops,
    sterility or still-birth of humans, and the plague itself, which is likened to a mili-
    tary enemy bearing fire. The image of the ship of state, which recurs repeatedly
    throughout this play and elsewhere (cf. *Ant.* 162-3 with note), is here linked with
    the image of the state as an individual drowning in a sea of blood.

that I and these, your children, sit here at your hearth,[6]
but as the first of men, both in life's circumstances
and in dealings with divinities.[7] For you
came to the town of Kadmos and released it from   35
the tribute that we paid to the harsh singer,[8] though
you had no special knowledge and had not been taught
by us; no, it was through the aid of god that you
set our lives upright—that's what people think and say.[9]

    Now, royal Oidipous, most powerful among all,   40
we do beseech you, all those here as suppliants,
to find us some protection, whether you have heard
a god's voice, or perhaps know something from a man;[10]
for it is those with past experience, I've seen,
whose plans most often stay alive through their success.   45
Come, stand our city upright, best of mortals! Come,
think of yourself as well, for now this land calls you
its savior for your heartfelt vigor in the past;
may this, your rule, not be remembered as the time
when after standing upright we fell down again.   50
No, set this city upright in security!
Back then you offered us good fortune blessed by a
well-omened bird:[11] be equal to that now as well.
If you're to rule this land in power, as you do now,
it's finer to hold power with living men than in   55
a desert; ships are nothing, ramparts too, if they
are empty of the men who dwelt in them with you.

---

6   A domestic altar and a hearth were to some degree interchangeable. The hearth,
    which normally lay in a house's courtyard, was the symbolic as well as the literal
    center of the household, and as such was sacred both to Hestia, goddess of the
    hearth, and to Zeus.

7   The word translated as "circumstances" (*symphora*) is ominous, since it is usually
    used for disasters (cf. 833, 1347, 1525).

8   The Sphinx demanded "tribute" in the form of the lives of those who failed to
    answer her riddle. She is called a "singer" because she chanted her riddles in
    hexameter verse, the same meter used by epic poetry and the Delphic oracle.
    At line 391 she is called a "song-weaver" (*rhapsōidos*)—the same word used for
    professional reciters of epic. See further Introduction, p. 17.

9   Language of setting right or upright recurs throughout the play (cf. 50, 88, 419,
    506, 528, 696, 853, 1222 and n. on *Ant.* 83).

10 The line ends with the words *oistha pou*, meaning "perhaps you know." This is
    the first of many untranslatable puns on the name of Oidipous, which echoes the
    Greek verb *oida*, "to know" and *pous*, which means "foot" (cf. n. on 131, 926). The
    root *oid-* also means "swell" (cf. 1036).

11 The "bird of good omen" is metaphorical, but alludes to the practice of divination
    by observing birds (Introduction, p. 25).

OIDIPOUS

    Pitiful children, known—and not unknown—to me
    are the desires that bring you here; for I know well
    that all of you are sick; and yet, sick as you are,   60
    there is not one of you whose sickness equals mine.
    Your grief afflicts each person individually,
    in isolation from the rest; *my* spirit, though,
    weeps for the city, and myself, and you as well.
    You are not waking someone who was fast asleep;   65
    know that I have already let fall many tears
    and travelled many wandering roads of anxious thought.
    And looking closely into it I only found
    one cure, and I've enacted it: I've sent Kreon,
    Menoikeus' son, my own wife's brother, to Apollo's   70
    Pythian home,[12] inquiring how I may succeed
    in rescuing this city through my deeds or words.
    And as I measure up the days, the passing time
    pains me. How is he faring? He has now been gone
    unreasonably long, beyond the fitting time.   75
    But when he does arrive, I would be evil if
    I did not act on everything the god reveals.[13]

PRIEST

    Your words are opportune; these people here just gave
    a sign to me that Kreon is approaching us.

[Enter Kreon along the side-entrance leading from Delphi, wearing a wreath of bay laurel—a plant sacred to Apollo—as a sign of success.]

OIDIPOUS

    Oh lord Apollo, may he come to us with bright   80
    and saving fortune, even as his eyes are bright!

PRIEST

    His news is sweet, so I surmise; or else he would
    not come towards us crowned with thickly berried bay.

OIDIPOUS

    We'll soon know, now he measures close enough to hear.
    My lord, Menoikeus' son and my own kin, what word   85
    has your arrival brought us from the voice of god?

KREON

    A good one! Even what is hard to bear, I say,

---

12 On Apollo see Introduction, pp. 21-2. His "Pythian home" is Delphi, his most
    important oracle, also called Pytho (e.g. below, 153).
13 On the word "evil" (*kakos*) see n. on *OC* 87.

may end up in good fortune, if it comes out right.

OIDIPOUS

What were his actual words? What you have said so far
fills me with neither confidence nor apprehension.   90

KREON

If you desire to hear me talk with these folk present
I'm prepared to do so—or to go inside.

OIDIPOUS

Speak out before us all! I bear a greater weight
of sorrow for these people than for my own life.

KREON

I'll say, then, what I heard the god divulge. My lord,   95
Phoibos commands us clearly to drive out a taint
upon this land that has been nurtured here, and not
to nurse this thing until it is incurable.[14]

OIDIPOUS

To cleanse ourselves? But how? And from what circumstance?

KREON

By driving someone out, or paying blood for blood,   100
since blood is what engulfs our city in this storm.

OIDIPOUS

Does he declare upon what man this fortune fell?

KREON

My lord, before you kept our city on its course,
a man called Laios was the ruler of this land.

OIDIPOUS

I know of him—though just from hearsay, not by sight.   105

KREON

He's dead; and now the god commands us clearly to
lay hands in vengeance on the men who murdered him.

OIDIPOUS

And where on earth are they? Where will the doubtful track
of evidence be found for such an ancient crime?

KREON

Here in this land, he said. If something is sought out   110
it can be captured, while what is ignored escapes.

---

14 Phoibos ("Bright") is a name for Apollo. On religious taint or pollution see Introduction, p. 28.

OIDIPOUS

Did this man Laios fall in with his bloody death
at home, or in the fields, or in some other land?

KREON

He left here to consult the oracle, he said,
but after setting out he never came back home.[15]   115

OIDIPOUS

And was there no report, no fellow-traveler
who saw something of use, from whom one might have learned?

KREON

All died but one, who fled in fear, and he could tell
with knowledge nothing that he saw—except one thing.

OIDIPOUS

And what was that? One fact might lead to learning much,   120
if we could grasp some small beginning-point of hope.

KREON

He said the robbers that they met killed Laios not
with one man's strength, but striking blows with many hands.

OIDIPOUS

How could the robber dare to go so far, unless
he was suborned with silver from some Theban source?   125

KREON

That was our thinking; but with Laios dead, no one
arose as our defender at an evil time.

OIDIPOUS

What evil underfoot, the kingdom having fallen
thus, kept you from learning fully what transpired?

KREON

The devious-singing Sphinx led us to set aside   130
the mystery and look at what lay at our feet.[16]

OIDIPOUS

I'll start again then, and reveal these things as well.
For fittingly has Phoibos, and you fittingly,
paid such attention on behalf of him who died.

---

[15] Sophocles does not say why Laios was consulting the Delphic oracle, but in other
versions of the story he was going to inquire whether the baby he and his wife
had exposed on the mountain to die had in fact perished.

[16] Lines 128-31 provide the first, apparently innocuous, appearances of the "foot"
motif, which links Oidipous' name both with the riddle of the Sphinx (Introduction, p. 17) and with the pervasive theme of physical and intellectual travel.

So you will see me also, as their ally, justly   135
taking vengeance for this land and for the god.
I shall disperse this taint, not on behalf of some
more distant friend or kinsman, but for my own self,
since he—whoever killed that man—may wish perhaps
to use the same avenging hand against me too.   140
By aiding Laios, then, I also help myself.[17]
  Come now, my children, stand up from the steps as fast
as possible; remove these suppliant branches, and
let someone gather Kadmos' people here; be sure
that I'll do everything I can. We shall, with god's
help, be revealed as fortunate or fallen down.   145

*[Exit Oidipous into the palace, and Kreon along the side-entrance leading to the
city.]*

PRIEST

My children, let us stand. He's just announced to us
the very favor for the sake of which we came.
May Phoibos, who has sent these oracles, come both
to save us and to bring our sickness to an end.   150

*[Exeunt priest and suppliants along the side-entrance leading to the city. Enter the
chorus of Theban noblemen, representing the mass of the people just summoned by
Oidipous. They proceed into the orchēstra, singing and dancing the parodos or entry-
song.]*

CHORUS

Oh sweet-spoken Voice of Zeus,   *Strophe A*
  with what meaning have you come
from gold-rich Pytho to gleaming Thebes?[18]
Mind racked with fear, I quiver with dread,

---

17 The preceding lines are heavily ironic, since Oidipous is himself his father's clos-
    est kinsman (137-8). The word "justly" (135) suggests the obligation he would
    have, in Athenian law, to investigate the murder of his father as next of kin. His
    fear that the killer will turn "the same hand" on him in vengeance (139-40) will
    be literally fulfilled, when he puts out his own eyes. And by aiding Laios he will
    not help, but destroy himself.
18 Pytho is another name for Delphi, to whose oracular Voice the chorus address
    their song (for the personification cf. 158 and 188). Zeus is viewed as the author
    of the oracle, both because he is the ultimate ruler of human events and because
    Apollo is his son and messenger. Delphi was famously "rich in gold," both because
    it served as a kind of bank for the storage of precious metals and because of the
    numerous lavish offerings dedicated there by worshipers.

Delian Paian to whom we cry aloud, in awe at you.[19]   155
What debt will you ordain—something new,
or one that returns as the seasons revolve?[20]
Tell me, child of golden Hope, immortal Voice!

I call first on you, daughter of Zeus,
    immortal Athena.   *Antistrophe A*
I beseech too your sister Artemis, our land's support,   160
who sits on her glorious circular throne
in the market-place, and far-shooting Apollo.
Appear to me as three-fold protectors from doom,
if you banished the flames of disaster
when doom rushed over our city   165
in the past, come now as well![21]

Oh, oh! Uncountable   *Strophe B*
are the troubles I endure!
My whole company is sick;[22]
there's no spear of thought to protect us;   170
the offspring of the glorious earth grows not,
nor do women emerge with births
from the labor-pains where they cry aloud.[23]
You may see one after another,
like a strong-winged bird,   175
speeding swifter than savage fire

---

19   On Paian see n. on 5. Here the god is addressed as Delian because he is identified with Apollo, who was born on the island of Delos. Apollo was a god who
brought both plague (as at the beginning of the *Iliad*) and healing (as he is asked
to do here). Here the chorus identify the plague itself not with Apollo but with
Ares (190). Apollo, as the god most deeply implicated in Oidipous' story, is also
obviously in some sense the cause of the plague, but there is no reason for the
chorus to suspect this.

20   The contrast is between the possible need to propitiate the gods for some new
occurrence, and the revival of Thebes' past troubles with the Sphinx and Laios,
which may turn out to be causally connected with the plague, and as such require
a reiterated "payment" to the gods.

21   The chorus invoke a triad of important gods: Athena, Apollo, and Artemis (see
Introduction, pp. 20-22). It is a common feature of prayers to invoke past benefits
bestowed by the divinity in question.

22   The language suggests a ship's company, evoking the ship of state.

23   The procreation of children and production of crops are very closely associated
in Greek culture, and frequently represented as parallel or identical processes
(cf. 25-7, 260; *Ant.* 569). Since these homologous processes are both vital to the
flourishing of human life, the anger of the gods is expressed through a parallel
blight on both kinds of reproduction, as well as in the plague as such.

to the shores of the evening god.[24]

Through these deaths beyond count	*Antistrophe B*
the city perishes;	
offspring lie on the plain unpitied,	180
unmourned, bringing yet more death.[25]	
Wives and white-haired women	
ring the altars in supplication	
lamenting their grievous pains.	
The Paian shines forth,[26]	185
and voices groan in accompaniment;	
for all these things, oh golden daughter of Zeus,[27]	
send us the fair face of Protection!	

Grant that raging Ares, who flames at me now,	*Strophe C*
attacking without the bronze of shields,	191
surrounded by screaming,	
turn his back on my fatherland	
and run rushing in retreat,	
wafted away to Amphitrite's great bed-chamber,	195
or the Thracian waves inhospitable to anchorage;[28]	
for if night leaves something undone,	
the day undertakes to complete it.[29]	
Oh you who wield the power	
of fire-bearing lightning,	200
oh father Zeus, destroy him	
with your thunderbolt!	

---

[24] The "evening god" is Hades, whose realm is sometimes located in the west, and who is fittingly associated with the darkness of sunset, since this symbolizes the loss of the light of life. In early Greek art, the souls of the dead are often represented as winged creatures. In Homer, they are likened to a fluttering cloud of bats. Here, they are envisaged as a flock of birds streaming westward into a fiery sunset. At the same time, the fire imagery recalls the burning pyres that consume the bodies of the dead.

[25] This presumably refers to the contagiousness of the rotting corpses.

[26] The Paian is a song of thanksgiving to Apollo or another god, or, as in this case, a prayer for protection or healing.

[27] The chorus is again addressing Athena, to whom they will add Zeus, Apollo and finally Dionysos (Bacchus).

[28] Amphitrite is wife of the sea-god Poseidon, and her "bed-chamber" is the Atlantic Ocean. The "Thracian waves" refer to the Black Sea. These two bodies of water represent the most remote locations to east and west, to which the chorus hopes Ares will be dispatched.

[29] The exact meaning of these two lines, and their relationship to the context, are both uncertain.

Lykeian lord,[30] I also wish   *Antistrophe C*
the invincible arrows
from your gold-spun bowstring   205
to spread out, stationed in our defense,
and the fire-bearing gleam of Artemis' torches,
with which she darts through the Lycian mountains;[31]
and I call on the god of the golden head-dress,
who shares his name with this land,   210
Bacchus, face flushed with wine,
companion of the Maenads,
whose worshipers cry aloud *Euoi*,
to approach us flaming with gleaming pine-torch
and attack the god dishonored among gods.[32]   215

[As the chorus conclude their song, Oidipous re-enters from the palace.]

OIDIPOUS

You pray: if you are willing, as regards your prayers,
to listen and take in my words, thus tending to
your sickness, you may gain protection and lift up
your heads above these evils. I shall speak as one
who's foreign to this story, foreign to the deed,   220
for I could not get far in tracking it without
some clue. Since I became a citizen after
it happened, I proclaim to all you Kadmeans:
if anyone among you knows the man who killed
Laios, the son of Labdakos, I now command   225
that person to provide me with a full report.
If he's afraid, let him eliminate the charge
                    * * * * * * * * * * *
by coming forward, and he'll suffer nothing worse
than exile from this land with no harm to himself;[33]
but if he knows the murderer is someone else,   230

---

30 "Lykeian" is a frequent epithet of Apollo (Introduction, p. 22).

31 Lycia is a region of Asia Minor, often associated with Apollo, and in this case with his sister Artemis as well.

32 Ares, god of war, is often said to be unpopular with the other gods. Dionysos (Bacchus) is associated with the east and sometimes represented as wearing an orientalized head-dress. He was born at Thebes and is often referred to as "Theban," while Thebes is called "Bacchic." The Maenads were female worshippers who followed him in his travels and participated in his festivities, shouting the ritual Bacchic cry, *Euoi!*

33 The sense is obscure here (a line may be missing). But it seems clear that Oidipous is promising anyone who is secretly guilty of the murder that if he comes forward he will be exiled rather than killed in punishment.

or from elsewhere, then let him not be silent; I'll
pay him due profit and he'll have my thanks besides.
But if you do keep silent, if somebody fearing
for a friend, or for himself, does thrust aside
my words, in that case, you must hear what I shall do: 235
I solemnly prohibit anyone within
this land whose power and throne are mine to take him in—
the man who did this—or address him, or allow
him to participate in prayers or sacrifices
to the gods, or let him share the lustral water;[34]   240
no, all must thrust him from their homes, since he's the source
of the polluting taint upon us, as the god's
Pythian oracle has just revealed to me.
This is the kind of ally I shall be, then, both
to the divinity and to the man who died.   245
[I pray too that the perpetrator, whether it's
one person we are unaware of, or a group,
may evilly wear out his doomed and evil life.
I also pray that if he shares my hearth and home,
with my own knowledge, I myself may suffer these   250
same curses I have just called down on other heads.[35]]
    I do enjoin you to fulfill all these commands
for me, and for the god, and for this land that has
been wasted so by god-forsaken fruitlessness.
For even if this matter were not sent by god,   255
it still would not befit you to leave it uncleansed—
when he who perished was the best of men, and more,
your king—but to investigate it; as it is,
since it is I who now enjoy his former rule,
who share the sowing of his marriage-bed and wife,   260
and would have shared in children from a common womb,
had his descendants not been so unfortunate—
but as it is, ill-fortune leaped upon his head.
I therefore shall take up this fight on his behalf
as if he were my father, and pursue all paths   265

---

[34] Family sacrifices began with the head of the household dipping a brand from the
      altar in water, and sprinkling the assembled company. The presence of a guilty
      person at a sacrifice might render it inauspicious. By excluding any such person
      from sacrifice, the proclamation excommunicates him or her from the life of the
      household and from the shared cultural ties of religion.
[35] Some editors delete these lines, which mar the rhetoric of the speech and are
      redundant after 236-43. Others reorganize the order of the lines to make the speech
      more coherent.

seeking to catch the murderer of Laios, son
of Labdakos the child of Polydoros, son
of ancient Kadmos and Agenor long ago.[36]
    For those who don't do what I say, I pray the gods
may raise no crops up from their land, no children from   270
their women; may they go on being wasted by
our present destiny or one more hateful still.
As for you other Kadmeans, to whom these words
are pleasing, may both Justice, fighting as your ally,
and all the gods be with you always for the best.   275

CHORUS
I'll speak, my lord, as someone subject to your curse:
It was not I who killed him; nor can I point out
the killer. It was Phoibos' task—who sent us to
seek out this thing—to tell us who performed the deed.

OIDIPOUS
Your words are just. But no man can impose upon   280
the gods necessity to do things they don't want.

CHORUS
Then I would tell you what I think is second-best.

OIDIPOUS
If there's a third as well, don't leave your thoughts untold.

CHORUS
I know the lord whose vision is the closest to
Lord Phoibos is Teiresias; look into this   285
with his help, lord, and you'll most clearly learn the truth.

OIDIPOUS
I've not been sluggish in this action either; for
at Kreon's prompting I have sent two messengers
to bring him. I'm surprised he's not already here.

CHORUS
Aside from him, what others say is faint and old.   290

OIDIPOUS
What's this they say? I'm looking into every word.

CHORUS
It's said that he was killed by certain travelers.

OIDIPOUS
I heard that too. But no one saw who did the deed.

---

[36] Oidipous unwittingly recites his own line of descent—a line that has not, as he
thinks, been wiped out by the "ill-fortune" of extinction, but cursed with misfortune of a very different kind.

CHORUS

    If he's susceptible to dread at all, and hears
    the kind of curses you pronounced, he won't stand firm.   295

OIDIPOUS

    The deed did not appall him: he won't fear mere words.

[Enter Teiresias, a blind old prophet, led by a boy and guided by Oidipous' attendants, along the side-entrance leading from the city.]

CHORUS

    The one who'll show him up is present; for these folk
    are leading here the godlike prophet; he's the only
    human in whom truth is naturally inborn.

OIDIPOUS

    Teiresias, surveyor of all things—those taught   300
    and those unspoken, heavenly and walking on
    the earth—although you cannot see, you understand
    the sickness present in our city; we can find
    no champion and no savior from it, but for you.
    Phoibos—in case you haven't heard report of this—   305
    sent us this answer, when we sent to ask him: that
    we'll be released from this great sickness only if
    we learn in full who Laios' killers are, and then
    kill them or send them forth in exile from the land.
    Don't grudge us the prophetic voice of birds or any   310
    other road of divination that you have;[37]
    rescue yourself, rescue this city, rescue me
    from all this taint now emanating from the dead.
    We're in your hands; the finest task is for a man
    to help with every resource lying in his power.   315

TEIRESIAS

    Woe! Woe! How awful to have understanding yet
    not benefit from it. I knew this all too well
    but it escaped me—otherwise I'd not have come.

OIDIPOUS

    What is it? How down-heartedly you have arrived!

TEIRESIAS

    Let me go home. If you're persuaded by me you   320
    will bear your lot most easily, and I bear mine.

---

[37] The most important forms of divination in ancient Greek religion were augury and burnt sacrifice (Introduction, pp. 24-5).

OIDIPOUS

It is not lawful to withhold your voice, nor is
it friendly to this city that has nurtured you.

TEIRESIAS

It is because I can see your words going forth
inopportunely.[38] May I not suffer the same!   325

OIDIPOUS

If you have understanding, by the gods, don't turn
away, since we all bow to you as suppliants.

TEIRESIAS

You all lack understanding, that is why. I won't
reveal my evils ever—not to call them yours.[39]

OIDIPOUS

What did you say? You know but will not tell? Is your   330
intention to betray us and destroy the city?

TEIRESIAS

I shall not grieve myself or you. Why question me
in vain? You will discover nothing by this means.

OIDIPOUS

Oh evilest of evil men, you'd drive the nature
of a rock to anger! Won't you ever speak,   335
but show yourself so rigid and intractable?

TEIRESIAS

You criticize my anger, but you don't perceive
the one you're dwelling with—that's why you're blaming me.[40]

OIDIPOUS

Indeed! Who would not turn to anger hearing words
like these, with which you're now dishonoring this city?   340

TEIRESIAS

If I keep silent, things will still come by themselves.

OIDIPOUS

If they are on their way, should you not speak of them?

---

38   Though Oidipous' edict is for the health of the city, it will produce "inopportune,"
     i.e. disastrous, results for himself. Teiresias does not wish to be the one to reveal
     this outcome.

39   They are Teiresias' evils because he is the only one who has knowledge of them,
     but he does not wish to reveal the extent to which they are really Oidipous' own
     evils.

40   Overtly, Teiresias is referring to Oidipous' anger, which is a feminine noun in
     Greek and can be thought of as "living with" him; covertly, however, his wording
     alludes to Jokasta, of whose true identity Oidipous is ignorant.

TEIRESIAS

I'll tell no more. Rage back at me, if that is what
you want, with all the savage anger that you can.

OIDIPOUS

All right then! I'm in such a temper that I'll leave   345
out nothing that I understand. Know that I think
you are the one who helped conceive this deed, yes, and
performed it, all but killing him with your own hands;
if you had sight, I'd say the deed was yours alone.

TEIRESIAS

Oh really? Then I tell you to abide by your   350
own proclamation, and from this day forth address
no more these people or myself, since it is you
who are the sacrilegious curse upon this land!

OIDIPOUS

Is this the story you've so shamelessly stirred up?
How do you think that you'll escape the consequences?   355

TEIRESIAS

I have escaped them, for I nurse the strength of truth.

OIDIPOUS

Truth taught by whom? Not, certainly, by your own skills!

TEIRESIAS

By you; you urged me to speak out against my will.

OIDIPOUS

Speak what? Repeat it, so that I may learn some more.

TEIRESIAS

Did you not understand before? Is this a test?   360

OIDIPOUS

Not so that I could say I know it; speak again!

TEIRESIAS

I say that that man's killer, whom you seek, is you.

OIDIPOUS

You won't be happy that you voiced disaster twice!

TEIRESIAS

Shall I add something else, to make your anger worse?

OIDIPOUS

As much as you desire; it shall be said in vain.   365

TEIRESIAS

I say you're unaware your dearest ties are most
disgraceful, and don't see what evil you are in.

OIDIPOUS

You think you'll always say this with impunity?

TEIRESIAS

Yes, if there's any power in the strength of truth.

OIDIPOUS

There is—for all but you; it is not yours because   370
you're blind in ears and mind as well as in your eyes.

TEIRESIAS

You miserable man, reproaching me with taunts
That each one here will soon use to reproach yourself.

OIDIPOUS

You nursling of unbroken night, you never could
bring harm to me or anyone who sees the light.   375

TEIRESIAS

It's not your destiny to fall through me; Apollo
is enough; to do this deed is his concern.

OIDIPOUS

And whose "discoveries" were these? Kreon's perhaps?[41]

TEIRESIAS

Kreon is no disaster to you: it is you.

OIDIPOUS

Oh wealth! Oh kingly rule! Oh skill surpassing skill   380
in the competitive and highly envied life—
how great is the resentment stored in you,[42] if it's
for this, my rule—a thing the city placed into
my hands as an unasked-for gift—for this that he,
the trusty Kreon, he who always was my friend,   385
has crept against me secretly, desiring to
depose me, sneaking in this conjuror, this scheme-
weaving deceptive beggar-priest with eyes only
for profit, blind in using his prophetic skill.
Tell me, when have your prophecies been clear and true?   390

---

41 Oidipous is easily suspicious of plots against himself, but his choice of Kreon as
a suspect is not entirely implausible (cf. 555-6).

42 The "skill surpassing skill" refers to the supreme skills needed to be a successful
ruler, but also reminds us more specifically of the special intelligence that sets
Oidipous apart from other mortals. The "competitive and highly envied life"
alludes to a model of heroism prevalent in Greek culture, whereby individuals
sought to outstrip each other in performing exploits and gaining public honors,
power and renown. It was assumed that others would both emulate and envy the
most successful competitors.

Why did you not, when the song-weaving hound was here,[43]
say anything to bring these townspeople release?
And yet her riddle was not one to be explained
by some man passing by—it needed prophecy,
knowledge that you conspicuously failed to get   395
from birds or any god. But then I came along,
know-nothing Oidipous,[44] and brought an end to her,
succeeding by the power of thought—not taught by birds.
And I'm the man you're now attempting to depose,
because you think that you'll stand close to Kreon's throne.   400
You'll both weep for your purge, I think—both you and he
who hatched this plot. Did you not seem to me too old,
you'd learn by suffering what kind of thoughts yours are.

CHORUS

It seems to us, as we surmise, that both his words
and yours were spoken out of anger, Oidipous.   405
We do not need such talk: we need to look into
how best we may resolve the oracles from god.

TEIRESIAS

You may be king, but I've an equal right to answer
equally; in this I too have power, since I
live not as your slave, but as that of Loxias;[45]   410
so I do not depend on Kreon's patronage.[46]
And I say this—since you insulted me as blind:
you're sighted, but don't see what evil you are in,
or where you dwell, or whom you're living with at home.
Do you know where you come from? You are unaware   415
that you're an enemy to your own kin beneath
and on the earth; your father's and your mother's two-
pronged curse with awful foot will one day drive you from

---

43 This may reflect a mythic variant in which the Sphinx partly resembles a dog.
   Alternatively, she may be called a "hound" because she is the agent or servant
   of an angry god (in this case Hera, who had been dishonored by the Thebans).
   Similarly, the Furies (goddesses of revenge) are often represented as bloodhounds
   (cf. Introduction, p. 23).
44 Oidipous here puns on the fanciful derivation of his name from the Greek verb
   "to know" (see n. on 43). His sarcastic self-description is in fact the essential truth
   about the present state of his self-knowledge.
45 Loxias is a common name for Apollo (Introduction, p. 22).
46 By alluding to the need for foreign residents in Athens to be represented in legal
   matters by a native patron, Sophocles subtly distinguishes Teiresias from Oidipous, who arrived in Thebes as a supposed foreigner. The word originally means
   "defender" or "champion" (as it is translated at 304, 882).

this land in darkness, though you now can see aright.[47]
What place won't serve as harbor to your screams, and what   420
Cithaeron won't resound with them,[48] when you have come
to realize what kind of wedding-anchorage
you sailed into within this house, ending a voyage
once fortunate. Nor do you realize that another
crowd of evils will equate you with yourself   425
and with your children.[49] *Now* fling mud at Kreon and
at me for speaking, since no mortal who exists
will ever be wiped out more evilly than you.

OIDIPOUS

Is it endurable to hear these words from him?
To hell with you! Get out of here at once! Go back   430
to where you came from! Just be gone and quit my house!

TEIRESIAS

I would not be here if you had not called for me.

OIDIPOUS

I didn't know that you'd speak foolishness, or I'd
scarcely have sent for you to come here to my house.

TEIRESIAS

I was born foolish—so you think; but those who gave   435
you your own birth, your parents, thought I understood.

OIDIPOUS

What parents? Stay! What mortal gave me my own birth?[50]

TEIRESIAS

This day will give you birth—and will destroy you too.

OIDIPOUS

The words you speak are all too riddling and unclear!

TEIRESIAS

Are you not best by birth at finding out such things?   440

---

47   The personified curse is one of the identities of the Furies (Introduction, p. 23).
Here they are likened to a two-pronged whip, consisting in curses from Oidipous'
two parents.

48   Cithaeron is a mountain near Thebes. The name is used here to evoke mountains
generally, but it also has special significance for Oidipous' story (cf. 1026, 1086-95,
1134-5).

49   He will be "equal to himself" in discovering the true measure of who he is, and his
children's "equal" in being born from the same mother (cf. 1498-9). Some editors
prefer to alter the text to a word meaning "wipe out" instead of "equate."

50   Teiresias' apparently casual mention of Oidipous' parents reminds him of the
insult directed at his legitimacy back in Corinth (779-80).

OIDIPOUS

Insult me in those matters where you'll find me great!

TEIRESIAS

And yet that self-same fortune has destroyed you too.[51]

OIDIPOUS

I'm not concerned, if I have kept this city safe.

TEIRESIAS

Well then, I'll go.

[He turns to the boy who led him in.]

You, child, take me away from here.

OIDIPOUS

Yes, let him take you; here beneath my feet you're making   445
trouble. Go, so that you give me no more grief.

TEIRESIAS

I'll go—when I've said what I came to say: I feel
no dread before your face; you can't destroy me, no!
I say to you: the man you have been seeking for
so long, with threats and proclamations in regard   450
to Laios' murder—he is here; he's said to dwell
here as a foreigner, but soon he'll be revealed
as Theban-born, a circumstance that will not bring
him pleasure: he will travel to a foreign land,
now blind instead of sighted, begging, he who was   455
a wealthy man, using a staff to point the way.
He'll be revealed as living with his children as
brother and father both at once; both son and husband
of the woman who gave birth to him; his father's
fellow-sower and his murderer.[52] Go in   460
and count this up, and if you find me false, *then* say
I have no understanding from my prophet's skill.

[Exeunt Teiresias, led by the boy along the entry-ramp by which he entered, Oidipous into the palace. The chorus now sing and dance the first stasimon ("song in position").]

CHORUS

Who is the man the prophetic rock   *Strophe A*
at Delphi sang of as having fulfilled
the most unspeakable of deeds   465

---

51   I.e. if Oidipous had not solved the riddle of the Sphinx, he would not be in the
present situation.
52   I.e. both he and Laios "sowed" their seed in the same woman.

unspeakable with bloody hands?[53]
The hour has come for him to ply in flight
feet stronger than those of storm-swift horses;
for the offspring of Zeus,
armed with fire and lightning,   470
is leaping on him,
and the unerring, awesome Keres follow after.[54]

A voice just appearing   *Antistrophe A*
shone out from snowy Parnassus
that all should track down this mysterious man.   475
He is ranging through savage forests,
in caves and over rocks,
like a bull limping crippled
with wretched foot,[55]
trying to keep at a distance the oracles   480
from earth's navel;[56]
but they fly around him, ever-living.

With awe he shakes me, with awe,   *Strophe B*
the clever diviner of bird-signs;
I cannot accept what he says, or deny it—   485
I'm at a loss what to say.
I flutter with expectations,[57]
unable to see what is present
or what lies behind my back.[58]
For I've never learned of a quarrel,   490
past or present, existing
between the Labdakids and Polybos' son

---

[53]   Apollo's temple at Delphi was built on a platform of rock.
[54]   The "offspring of Zeus" is Apollo, here serving as his father's agent (cf. n. on 153) and armed with his weapons. The Keres are winged goddesses of death and revenge sometimes identified with the Furies.
[55]   An alternative interpretation of this line is "bereft of companionship, wretched, with wretched foot." The interpretation given in the translation ties the image closely to that of the crippled Oidipous.
[56]   Delphi was traditionally regarded as the location of the center of the earth, which was marked by a large rounded stone in Apollo's temple called the "navel-stone."
[57]   "Expectation" translates the Greek *elpis*. This word is usually rendered in English as "hope," but in Greek it is an ambiguous term, referring to apprehensions as well as hopes about the future (cf. 772 and n. on *Ant.* 236; compare also *Ant.* 330, 365, 392, 615-19).
[58]   Since we cannot see the future, it is often represented in Greek as lying behind us, rather than ahead.

which I might use as a touchstone
that would cause me to go against
Oidipous' repute among all the people,   495
and help the Labdakids
with these mysterious deaths.[59]

Zeus and Apollo have understanding   *Antistrophe B*
and knowledge of mortal affairs;
among men, though, there's no true way to judge   500
if a prophet's worth more than I am.
A man may outstrip cleverness
with cleverness of his own.[60]
But I for one will never assent
to his critics before I see   505
their words prove to be right.
For this much was clearly revealed:
the winged maiden came at him,
and by that touchstone he was seen openly
as both clever and sweet for the city.[61]   510
Never, then, shall the verdict
of my thinking convict him of evil.

[Enter Kreon, along the entry-ramp leading from the city.]

KREON

Men of this city, I am here because I heard
that Oidipous the king has spoken awful words
of accusation at me, which I won't endure.   515
For if he thinks that in the present circumstances
he has suffered something harmful at my hands,
in word or deed, then I no longer yearn to live
a lengthy life, if I must bear such ill-repute.

---

[59] I.e. if the chorus knew of a pre-existing quarrel between the families of Laios and Polybos this might give Teiresias' accusations some credibility, and give themselves a criterion (or "touchstone") for doubting Oidipous' reputation as favorable to Thebes. This would in turn encourage them to "help" the Labdakids (i.e. the family of Laios, son of Labdakos) to solve the mysterious murder by pursuing the prophet's accusation of Oidipous. Note that although Polybos is Oidipous' adopted Corinthian father, the chorus has no reason to doubt that he is his natural father, which would make him unrelated to the Labdakids.

[60] These words suggest two opposed possibilities: that the supreme intelligence of Oidipous surpasses all others (cf. 380-81), and that the special wisdom of the prophet, though not based on rational intelligence, may surpass even the king's.

[61] The "winged maiden" is the Sphinx (Introduction, p. 17).

Such words are damaging to me, not in a simple   520
way but in the greatest sense, if I'm called evil
in the city, and by you and by my friends.

CHORUS

Yes, that reproach was made; but it was forced, perhaps,
by anger, not derived from judgment or from thought.

KREON

Did he declare that it was by my thinking that   525
the prophet was persuaded to assert false claims?

CHORUS

He did; but I don't know what thinking prompted it.

KREON

And when he charged me with this accusation, did
he have his eyes aright and a right-thinking mind?

CHORUS

I do not know; I don't see what the powerful do.   530
But here he comes himself, emerging from the house.

[Enter Oidipous from the palace.]

OIDIPOUS

You there! How could you come here? Is your face so bold
that you have dared to come here to my house, when you
are clearly both the murderer of this man here
and robber of my kingdom in the eyes of all?[62]   535
Come, tell me, by the gods, was it because you saw
me as a fool or coward that you made these plans?
Or did you think I'd not find out about your deed
as it sneaked up on me, or if I learned of it
would not protect myself? Is not your task a foolish   540
one, to hunt for kingship without wealth or friends,
when catching it needs property and mass support?

KREON

You know what you should do? Listen to equal words
in answer to your own; then judge, when you have learned.

OIDIPOUS

Your speaking skill is awesome, but I'm slow to learn—   545
from *you*, since you're a hostile burden, so I've found.

---

[62] "This man here" is a common Greek idiom for referring to oneself, which may
serve to add pathos or enhance the speaker's dignity (cf. 815, 828, 1464). In calling
Kreon his "murderer" and "robber," Oidipous is, of course, exaggerating (though
cf. 669-70). But his choice of language also equates Kreon with Laios' murderer
(cf. 122, 124).

KREON
First hear what I shall say upon this very point.

OIDIPOUS
Upon this very point, don't tell me you're not evil.

KREON
If you believe that wilfulness without good sense
is something worth possessing, you're not thinking right.   550

OIDIPOUS
If *you* believe that you can harm a kinsman and
not pay the penalty, then you're not thinking well.[63]

KREON
Those words were justly spoken, I agree; but tell
me what this suffering you say you've suffered *is*.

OIDIPOUS
Did you, or did you not, persuade me that I should   555
send someone for the reverent man of prophecy?

KREON
I did; and I still think this was the proper plan.

OIDIPOUS
How long a time has passed since this man Laios went...

KREON
And did what kind of deed? I do not understand.

OIDIPOUS
...and vanished from your sight, struck by a deadly blow?   560

KREON
You'd have to measure out a long and ancient time.

OIDIPOUS
And back then was this prophet practising his skill?

KREON
As cleverly as now, and honored equally.

OIDIPOUS
And did he mention me at all, at that time then?

KREON
No; not at least at any time when I stood by.   565

OIDIPOUS
But did you not inquire then who the killer was?

---

63   These two lines, like many others, refer ironically to Oidipous himself, who will
     pay for mistreating his closest kin.

KREON

We did, of course, but did not hear of anything.

OIDIPOUS

If he's so clever, why did he not speak out then?

KREON

I don't know; I keep silent when I lack sound thought.[64]

OIDIPOUS

But this you do know, and, if thinking well, would say.   570

KREON

What's that? If I do know, I won't refuse to speak.

OIDIPOUS

That were he not in league with you, he never would
have said it was by me that Laios was destroyed.

KREON

You know if that is what he said. But I've the right
to learn these things from you as much as you from me.   575

OIDIPOUS

Learn then—you won't convict *me* as a murderer.

KREON

All right: do you not have my sister as your wife?

OIDIPOUS

That statement is impossible to contradict.

KREON

And in your rule, do you not give her equal power?[65]

OIDIPOUS

Yes; anything she ever wants, she gets from me.   580

KREON

And as a third, am I not equal to you both?

OIDIPOUS

Exactly; that's what shows you are an evil friend.

KREON

Not if you reason with yourself as I have done.
Consider, first, if you think anyone would choose
to rule in fear instead of sleeping peacefully—   585

---

64   Expressions with the root *phron-*, meaning "sound thinking," have a broad seman-
tic scope, from intellectual capacity to clinical sanity, moral soundness and good
sense.

65   Oidipous and Jokasta are not joint rulers, but as his wife he consults her and
grants her authority equivalent to his own. Kreon's emphasis on equality is not a
constitutional fact, but a rhetorical ploy to set up the following argument.

provided that his power's the same. It's not my nature
to desire to be a king when I can act
already like a king, and it's the same for any
other man who knows how to be sensible.
Now I gain all things fearlessly from you; were I   590
the ruler, I would often have to act against
my will.[66] How then could kingship be a sweeter thing
for me to have than painless rule and royal power?
I am not yet so self-deceived that I desire
to have more than what is both fine and profits me.   595
Now everyone is glad to see me, now I am
embraced by everyone, now those desiring things
from you seek me out, since success depends on me.
Why then would I exchange this way of life for yours?
A mind that's sound could not become an evil one.   600
I'm not in love with thinking of that kind, nor could
I bear to act that way in league with someone else.
Test me: go back to Delphi and inquire if my
report about the oracle was clear and true;
then, if you catch me having shared in any plan   605
with the diviner, take me off and kill me, not
by one vote, but by two: my own as well as yours.
But don't accuse me without evidence, with unclear
judgment. It's unjust to think without due cause
that evil men are good, or good men evil ones.   610
To cast a good friend out, I say, is equal to
rejecting what one loves the most—one's very life.[67]
As time goes by you will securely recognize
all this; for only time points out the just; but you
may recognize who's evil in a single day.[68]   615

CHORUS

He's spoken well for someone careful not to fall,
my lord; fast thinking does not bring security.

---

[66] Although an absolute ruler can in principle do whatever he wants, a responsible
king will often be constrained by the needs and wishes of his people.

[67] This sentiment draws on two commonplaces of Greek friendship: one's self (or
soul, or life) is one's closest friend, and a true friend is a "second self."

[68] Kreon's central point is that with time his innocence will be revealed. The antitheti-
cal statement, that bad people are often quickly revealed by some word or deed,
is strictly irrelevant in this context, but applies ironically to the case of Oidipous
himself (cf. 438).

OIDIPOUS

When someone making plans against me secretly
moves fast, I must be fast to make my counter-plans.
If I remain inactive, this man's schemes will be   620
accomplished, my mistakes irrevocably made.

KREON

What then is your desire? To cast me from the land?

OIDIPOUS

Far from it! I don't want your exile, but your death!
* * * * * * * * * *

KREON

When you point out what kind of thing resentment is...[69]
* * * * * * * * * *

OIDIPOUS

You speak as if you won't believe my words and yield.   625

KREON

No, for I see you thinking badly.

OIDIPOUS

Well for me!

KREON

You should think equally of me.

OIDIPOUS

You're evil-born.

KREON

What if you do not understand?

OIDIPOUS

Yet I must rule![70]

KREON

Not if your rule's an evil one.

OIDIPOUS

Oh city, city!

KREON

The city's not just yours: I share in it as well.   630

CHORUS

Stop this, my lords! I see Jokasta opportunely
coming from the house; with her arrival you
should set to rights the quarrel that has just flared up.

---

[69] This line makes little sense in context. Some editors posit one or more lines before
or after it which have fallen out of the manuscripts.

[70] Alternatively, this could mean "you must obey."

[Enter Jokasta from the palace.]

JOKASTA

What is this foolish verbal strife, you wretches, which
you have provoked? Aren't you ashamed of stirring up 635
these private evils when the land itself's so sick?
You, go into the house, and Kreon, you to yours;
don't build up nothing into some great cause of grief.

KREON

Blood-sister, Oidipous your husband thinks it right
to do to me one of two awful evil things: 640
to thrust me from my fatherland or have me killed.[71]

OIDIPOUS

Yes, wife; for I have caught him doing evil deeds
against my person with the aid of evil skills.

KREON

May I not prosper! May I perish, cursed, if I
have done to you one thing that you accuse me of! 645

JOKASTA

I beg you by the gods, believe him, Oidipous,
respecting most of all his oath sworn by the gods,
but also me and all these people present here.[72]

*[The chorus and actors now participate in a kommos, or lyric dialogue, interspersed
with trimeters (649-96).]*

CHORUS

My lord, take thought, be willing   *Strophe*
to be persuaded, I beseech—   650

OIDIPOUS

In what do you want me to yield?

CHORUS

This man was no fool in the past;
Now his oath makes him mighty—respect him.

OIDIPOUS

You know what you desire?

CHORUS

                I know.

---

[71] The text here is probably corrupt, but the sense must be something like that given
in the translation.

[72] Although Kreon did not mention the gods explicitly, the curse under which he
has placed himself implies their sanction. It was customary in Athenian trials to
swear an oath to one's own innocence.

OIDIPOUS

                              Explain your words.

CHORUS

Don't cast off a friend in dishonor, one bound by a curse,   655
with an unproven verbal accusation.

OIDIPOUS

Know well that when you seek for this, you're seeking for
my own destruction or my exile from this land.

CHORUS

No, by Helios, god
foremost of all gods![73]   660
May I perish forsaken
by gods and friends
in the greatest extremity,
if such is my thinking!
But alas for me, ill-fated,   665
the land, decaying, tears my heart,
if this quarrel between you two
is to join our ancient evils.

OIDIPOUS

Then he may go—even if I must utterly
die or be thrust, dishonored, from this land by force.   670
I feel compassion for your piteous request—
not his; *him* I'll abhor, wherever he may be.

KREON

Yielding's abhorrent to you, clearly; when you're so
far gone in rage you're burdensome. Such natures are
most grievous for themselves to bear, and justly so.   675

OIDIPOUS

Get out of here! Leave me alone!

KREON

                              I'm on my way.
I've found you ignorant: these people kept me safe.

[Exit Kreon along the side-entrance leading to the city.]

CHORUS

Woman, why do you delay   *Antistrophe*
to take this man into the house?

---

[73] Helios, the sun god, is here called "foremost" of the gods because of his importance
     as a god of oaths (Introduction, p. 22).

JOKASTA

I will after learning what fortune chanced.   680

CHORUS

An ignorant verbal suspicion arose;
and injustice tears the heart.

JOKASTA

This came from both of them?

CHORUS

It did.

JOKASTA

And what was said?

CHORUS

It seems to me enough, with the land in mind,
enough, for this to rest where it broke off.[74]   685

OIDIPOUS

You see where you have come to, excellent in judgment
though you are, trying to dull my heart's keen edge?

CHORUS

My lord, know this—
I've said it more than once—
that I would be revealed   690
to be out of my mind,
resourceless in sound thought,
if I kept my distance from you—
you who, when my dear land
was frantic with despair,   695
wafted it back on the right course.
Now may you again be our good guide!

JOKASTA

Tell me too, by the gods, my lord, the matter that
has caused you to establish and retain such wrath.

OIDIPOUS

I'll speak; for I revere you more than these folk, wife.   700
It's Kreon, and the plans against me that he's hatched.

JOKASTA

Speak clearly of the quarrel that you blame him for.

---

[74] This concern for the land is the play's last allusion to the plague. As the circle draws
in on Oidipous, identifying him as the cause of the land's sickness, the sufferings
of the Thebans become more narrowly projected onto him as an individual, and
references to "the city" markedly decrease.

OIDIPOUS

He says the murderer of Laios is myself.

JOKASTA

He knows this by himself, or taught by someone else?

OIDIPOUS

Neither. He sent an evil-working prophet here,   705
and so he keeps his own mouth fully free from blame.

JOKASTA

Release yourself from fear about the matters that
you're speaking of. Listen to me and learn that there's
no mortal creature sharing in prophetic skill.
I shall reveal to you brief evidence of this: 710
An oracle once came to Laios—I won't say
from Phoibos, but from Phoibos' servants—saying that
his destiny would be to perish at the hand
of any child that would be born to him and me.
And yet, the story goes, some foreign robbers killed   715
him one day at a junction where three highways meet;[75]
as for our child, three days had not passed since his birth
when Laios yoked his feet and threw him out, at someone
else's hand, on the untrodden mountainside.[76]
So Phoibos did not bring to pass that he should be   720
his father's murderer, or Laios suffer at
his own child's hand—the awful thing he feared; yet this
is what the words of prophecy marked out for them.
So pay them no attention; if a god seeks what
he needs, he'll easily uncover it himself.   725

OIDIPOUS

What wandering of spirit, wife, has gripped me since
I heard you speak just now—what turbulence of thought!

JOKASTA

What anxious thought arrests you and inspires these words?

OIDIPOUS

Here's what I thought I heard you saying: Laios was
slaughtered right at a junction where three highways meet.   730

JOKASTA

Yes—that is what was said, nor has the rumor ceased.

---

[75] The word translated "story" (*phatis*) is also used for prophetic "voices" at 151, 310,
322, 1440, and for Oidipous' reputation at 495.

[76] In some versions of the tale, the infant Oidipous is pinned through the ankles, but
these lines imply nothing more specific than feet.

OIDIPOUS

Where is this spot at which he suffered such a thing?

JOKASTA

The land's called Phocis, and the place is where the road
forks, leading folk from Delphi and from Daulia.

OIDIPOUS

And how much time has passed since the event occurred?   735

JOKASTA

The city heard the proclamation just before
you were revealed to us as ruler of this land.

OIDIPOUS

Oh Zeus, what have you planned to do to regarding me?

JOKASTA

What is this, Oidipous, that so disturbs your heart?

OIDIPOUS

Don't ask me yet; but tell me more of Laios—what   740
was his physique, and was he still in manhood's prime?

JOKASTA

His hair was dark, just blooming with a sheen of white;
and in appearance he was not so far from you.

OIDIPOUS

Alas, wretch that I am! I seem to have just cast
an awful curse upon myself in ignorance.   745

JOKASTA

What do you mean? I shudder as I gaze at you!

OIDIPOUS

I'm awfully afraid the prophet may have sight.
Say one more thing, and you will point me to the truth.

JOKASTA

I shudder, but I'll speak—when I have learned your question.

OIDIPOUS

Did he proceed with few attending him, or with   750
the kind of retinue that suits a ruling man?

JOKASTA

The group was five in number altogether, one
a herald; and a single carriage carried Laios.[77]

---

[77] The herald is mentioned because he would have been a conspicuous member of
the party, bearing a herald's staff and preceeding the king's carriage (he is the
"leader" referred to at 804).

OIDIPOUS

Aiai! These things are now transparent! Tell me, wife,
who was the person who reported this to you?   755

JOKASTA

The only one who got back safely: a house-slave.

OIDIPOUS

Tell me, is he by chance still present in the house?

JOKASTA

No longer. When he came back here and saw that you
were holding power, and Laios dead, he touched my hand
in supplication, begging me to send him to   760
the countryside to pasture flocks, so that he might
be out of sight of town as far as possible.
I sent him; since he was deserving, for a slave,
to win this favor or an even greater one.

OIDIPOUS

Then can he somehow come back quickly here to us?   765

JOKASTA

That can be done. But what's the point of this desire?

OIDIPOUS

I'm very much afraid, my wife, that I have said
a lot too much; that's why I want to see this man.

JOKASTA

Then he shall come; but surely I deserve to learn
as well, my lord, what's causing you so much distress.   770

OIDIPOUS

I won't withold it from you, now that I have come
so far in expectation; to whom should I speak,
while going through such fortunes, better than to you?
    My father was king Polybos of Corinth and
my mother Merope, a Dorian. I was   775
thought greatest man among the townsfolk there until
some fortune brought this chance event, deserving of
surprise, but not deserving serious concern:
a man at dinner who had drunk too much called me
over the wine, a bastard, not my father's son.   780
Weighed down in spirit, I restrained myself for that
day—barely—but the next day went to see my mother
and my father. When I questioned them, they came
down hard upon the fellow who had let fly that
reproach; I was delighted; nonetheless the thing   785

kept nagging at me; for the tale spread far and wide.
So then I made my way to Pytho, secretly
from both my mother and my father; Phoibos did
not honor the request I came with, but instead
sent me away with words revealing other awful   790
and unhappy things for miserable me:
I must have intercourse with my own mother, show
to human eyes a race unbearable to see,
and kill the father of my birth. When I heard this,
I fled in exile from the land of Corinth, using
stars to measure out a path that would ensure   795
that I stayed far from there in future, somewhere I
should never see these evil oracles' reproaches
be fulfilled. As I went on my way, I reached
the region where you say this king of yours was killed.
    Now, wife, to you I'll speak the truth. As I came near,   800
upon my travels, to that threefold path, I met
a herald, and a man who rode upon a carriage
drawn by colts, in just the way that you described.
The two of them—the leader and the older man
himself—both tried to drive me from the road by force.[78]   805
The driver, who was trying to push me to one side—
I struck him out of anger. When the older man
saw this, he watched till I was passing by his wagon
then brought down a two-pronged goad right on my head.
The price he paid was more than equal: swiftly hit   810
by this staff in my hand, he was sent rolling headlong
from the carriage all the way onto his back.
I killed the lot of them. If any kinship tie
connects this foreigner with Laios,[79] who could now
be sunk in deeper misery than this man here?   815
What man could be more hateful to divinities,
than he whom no one, foreigner or townsman, may
address or take into his house, but rather all
must thrust him from their homes. And it is I myself—
none other—who has laid this curse upon myself.   820
And with the same two hands that killed him I am now
fouling the dead man's marriage-bed. Am I not evil

---

78   The road here ran through a steep, narrow, wooded valley, down which Oidipous
     was descending while Laios' party drove up it (cf. 1398-9).
79   "This foreigner" refers overtly to the man in the carriage, but on an ironic level it
     might be taken to refer to Oidipous himself.

in my birth, yes, utterly impure, if I
must flee to exile, and yet never see my kin
or step into my fatherland, or else I must   825
be yoked in marriage to my mother, kill my father
Polybos, who nurtured me and gave me birth?
Would someone not speak rightly of this man if he
should judge that it was some savage divinity
who sent me this? Oh never, you pure reverence of   830
the gods, oh never may I see that day! No, may
I disappear from mortal sight before I see
the stain of such dire circumstances come on me.

CHORUS
This makes us shudder, lord; but cling to hope until
you learn what happened from the person who was there.   835

OIDIPOUS
Indeed this is the only scrap of hope that's left
for me, to wait until that man, the herdsman, comes.

JOKASTA
What is your heart's desire for him, when he appears?

OIDIPOUS
I'll tell you: if he's found to give the same account
as you just gave, I have escaped from suffering.   840

JOKASTA
What did you hear me say that was remarkable?

OIDIPOUS
You said he spoke of *men* who killed him, robbers in
the plural; if that's still the number that he says,
I'm not the killer: many cannot equal one.   845
But if he clearly mentions one man traveling
alone, the balance of the deed then tilts my way.[80]

JOKASTA
Know well this *is* the story that he brought to light;
it is impossible that he disown it now,
since all the city heard these things, not I alone.   850
But even if he deviates from what he said
back then, he never will reveal that it is true,

---

[80]   The metaphor is one of a sinking pan on a scale, like the scales that Zeus uses in
the *Iliad* to determine which of two duelling warriors is fated to die (e.g. 22.209-13).
In this case it suggests both the weight of accumulating evidence, and the burden
of responsibility weighing down on Oidipous' head (cf. *Ant.* 1346-7).

my lord, that Laios' murder was predicted right,[81]
for Loxias expressly said that he must die
at my son's hands; yet it was never my unhappy   855
child that killed him, since the infant perished first.
Therefore, as far as prophecy's concerned, I would
in future not look this way as opposed to that.[82]

OIDIPOUS

You reason well. But all the same, send somebody
to bring the laborer—do not omit this task.   860

JOKASTA

I'll do it fast; but let's go back inside the house.
I'd not do anything that was not dear to you.

[Exeunt into the palace. The chorus now sing and dance the second stasimon.]

CHORUS

May destiny be at my side   *Strophe A*
as I bear reverence and purity
in all my words and deeds,   865
under those laws set up, lofty of foot,
born in heaven's bright air,
which have no father but Olympus;[83]
the mortal nature of men did not
give them their birth, nor shall   870
forgetfulness ever put them to sleep;
the god in them is great and untouched by age.[84]
Outrage gives birth to kings;[85]   *Antistrophe A*
surfeited in futile folly
with much that is inopportune,   875
disadvantageous, outrage mounts
to the topmost pinnacle and plunges
down necessity's precipice,

---

81 Literally, "straight" (see n. on 39).

82 These words may be an image from augury (Introduction, p. 25). But they could
also simply mean "I won't give prophecy the time of day." Jokasta is still arguing
against Teiresias' credibility, rather than addressing the more recent evidence.

83 The chorus imagine divine laws, governing human words and deeds, displayed
in the heavenly home of the gods (Olympus) just as the Athenian laws were displayed in public inscriptions (cf. *Ant*. 450-57).

84 "The god" here refers to the divine power that inheres in these laws.

85 The Greek word implies the role of the biological father rather than the mother.
"Outrage" translates the Greek *hybris* (see Introduction, pp. 27-8).

where feet are useless.[86]
Yet I pray that god may never break up   880
the contest that's good for the city;[87]
never shall I cease to have god as my champion.[88]

But if someone travels   *Strophe B*
haughtily in hand or word,[89]
unfearful of Justice, not revering   885
the seats of divinities,
may an evil destiny seize him
for his ill-destined decadence,
unless his profits are reaped justly
and he abstains from irreverence,   890
or if he clings in wicked folly
to that which is untouchable.[90]
What man in that case will succeed
in warding off arrows of rage from his life?
For if such deeds are held in honor   895
why should I dance for the gods?[91]
I will no longer reverently go   *Antistrophe B*
to earth's untouchable navel,
or to the temple at Abai,

---

[86] The personified figure of *hybris* is imagined elevating itself to the pinnacle of a roof or mountain, from which its own momentum casts it down (cf. *Ant.* 127-40). The inability of *hybris* to use its feet suggests both a sardonic reference to falling through the air and the incapacity of someone crushed by such a fall. This is contrasted with the divine laws which are "lofty of foot," i.e. live and move effectively up in heaven.

[87] The chorus here distinguishes the self-seeking of the autocrat from beneficial competitiveness, such as Oidipous' struggle to save the city of Thebes, which characterizes the successful hero and king (cf. n. on 382).

[88] The connection of thought seems to be that divine approval is the factor determining whether competitive striving is beneficial or harmful. Like the corresponding line in the strophe (871), this line asserts the chorus' piety as grounds for their convictions.

[89] The travel metaphor alludes generally to the "road of life," but evokes more specifically the wanderings of Oidipous, and his encounter with Laios, which might be judged as "haughty" on either side, or both. The word translated as "haughtily" literally means "overlooking"—a word applicable to Oidipous' behavior here in a different sense.

[90] Sacred items and places are often represented as "untouchable" by human beings (compare 898 and *OC* 39-40).

[91] Dancing was an important form of divine worship (cf. 1092), and the chorus-members are themselves dancing as they sing these words.

or that of Olympia,[92]   900
if these prophecies don't fit together
for every mortal hand to point to.
Rather, oh Zeus ruling in power,
if you are rightly so addressed,[93] lord of all,
may you and your immortal rule   905
not rest unaware of this.
For people are already dismissing
the oracles about Laios—they decay;
Apollo no longer stands conspicuous in honor;
and godliness has vanished.   910

[Enter Jokasta from the palace, carrying garlands and incense.]

JOKASTA

Lords of this land, the notion came to me to go
in supplication to the temples of the gods,
taking these garlands here and incense in my hands.
For Oidipous excites his heart excessively
with painful thoughts of every kind; he does not use   915
old things as evidence for new ones, like a man
with sense;[94] each speaker sways him—if he speaks of fear.
Since I am getting nowhere by advising him,
I've come to supplicate you with these prayers—for you
are nearest, Lykeian Apollo[95]—so that you   920
may bring us some release untainted by a curse;
for as things are, we shudder, all of us, to see
him stricken from his wits—the helmsman of our ship.

[Enter First Messenger along the entry-ramp leading from the country. He is an old, poor and low-class man, but not a slave.]

MESSENGER 1

Might I learn from you foreigners, perhaps, where stands

---

92 For the "navel" of the earth see n. on 481. Abai was a nearby town northeast of
    Delphi, which also had an important oracle of Apollo. Olympia was an major
    shrine and oracle of Zeus in the Peloponnese.
93 I.e. Zeus must now prove the appropriateness of his title as "ruling in power" by
    exercising that power on behalf of the oracles.
94 I.e. use the oracle given to Laios, which apparently failed, as evidence for the
    unreliability of the more recent oracles given to himself. Or possibly, she means
    that the manner in which he is now using the old as evidence for new is not the
    manner of a rational man.
95 Apollo is "nearest" in more than one sense. An altar of Apollo stood by the door
    of most houses, and may have been represented on stage. And Apollo is the god
    most closely related to the oracles in question.

the house of Oidipous the king? Or best of all,   925
if you know where he is himself, then tell me that.[96]

CHORUS

This is his dwelling, foreigner, and he's inside;
this woman is his wife and mother of his children.[97]

MESSENGER 1

Then may she always prosper, and the ones she lives
with prosper too, since she is that man's wedded wife.[98]   930

JOKASTA

The same to you, for you deserve it, foreigner,
for these kind words of yours. But tell me why you've come—
what you desire, or what you're wishing to report.

MESSENGER 1

Good tidings for your husband, woman, and your house.

JOKASTA

What kind of thing? And from what person have you come?   935

MESSENGER 1

I come from Corinth, and my tale will surely please
you—yes, of course it will. But it may grieve you too.

JOKASTA

What is it? How does it possess such double power?

MESSENGER 1

The local people of that land will set him up
as king of Isthmia—that's what they're saying there.[99]   940

JOKASTA

What? Is old Polybos no longer wielding power?

MESSENGER 1

No longer; death now holds him buried in the tomb.

JOKASTA

What's this you say? Is Oidipous's father dead?

---

[96] Each of these three lines ends with a pun on the name of Oidipous as one who knows, plus a word for "where" (*oim' hopou, Oidipou, oisth' hopou*), producing a rhyming effect that is rare in Greek.

[97] The ironic wording ("wife and mother...of his children") reflects that of the Greek.

[98] The word "wedded" translates a Greek word meaning "complete," indicating that the marriage has been "completed" by the birth of children. This is part of the reason for the messenger's congratulation, and as such, of course, bears heavy irony.

[99] Isthmia is the land governed by Corinth, named for the Isthmus of Corinth, a narrow neck of land connecting mainland Greece to the Peloponnese (see Map 2).

MESSENGER 1

If I'm not speaking truly I deserve to die.

JOKASTA [to one of her attendants]

Go to your master, serving maid, and tell him this   945
as fast as possible.

[Exit servant into the palace.]

You prophecies from gods,
see what you've come to! Oidipous stayed exiled for
so long in terror that he'd kill that man; but now
he's died through some chance fortune, not at this man's hand.

[Enter Oidipous from inside the palace.]

OIDIPOUS

Jokasta, dearest royal wife, why did you send   950
your maid to bring me here to you outside the house?

JOKASTA

First listen to this man; when you have heard him, look
where they have gone, those reverent prophecies from god.

OIDIPOUS

Who is this man? What does he have to say to me?

JOKASTA

He comes from Corinth to report that that Polybos   955
your father is no longer living: he is dead.

OIDIPOUS

What are you saying, foreigner? Tell me yourself.

MESSENGER 1

If I must give you first a clear report of this
event, know well that he is really dead and gone.

OIDIPOUS

Destroyed by treachery, or did some sickness strike?   960

MESSENGER 1

A slight tilt sends an old man's body to its rest.[100]

OIDIPOUS

Poor wretch, he perished from some sickness, so it seems.

MESSENGER 1

That and the length of time that he had measured out.

OIDIPOUS

Alas, alas! Why should one look, then, oh my wife,

---

[100] The image is again that of a balance (cf. n. on 847). But "tilting" is also a medical
term, referring to a slight shift in a patient's condition.

to the prophetic hearth of Pytho or the birds   965
screeching above us, whose interpreters declared
that I was going to kill my father?[101] He is dead,
concealed beneath the earth, while I am here and have
not touched my sword—unless he perished out of longing
for me; that's one way I might have caused his death.   970
In any case, the present prophecies now lie
in Hades, worthless, taken there by Polybos.[102]

JOKASTA

Is that not just what I've been saying all along?

OIDIPOUS

You said it, yes; but I was led astray by fear.

JOKASTA

From now on don't take any of these things to heart.   975

OIDIPOUS

But how should I not shudder at my mother's bed?

JOKASTA

What should a human being fear, who is in fortune's
power and can't know clearly what's to come?[103] It's best
to take life as it comes, as far as possible.
So don't be fearful of your mother's marriage-bed;   980
for many mortal men have shared their mother's bed
in dreams as well;[104] the person who treats all such things
as meaning nothing bears this life most easily.

OIDIPOUS

All this would be well said by you, if she who bore
me weren't alive still; as it is, she lives, so I   985
must shudder by necessity, though you speak well.

---

101 The "Pythian hearth" was a hearth kept constantly alight in Apollo's temple at
Delphi, on which laurel-leaves were burned before the priestess gave her prophecies. The word "screech" suggests that the birds' cries are unintelligible, or in this
context, meaningless (cf. *Ant.* 1001 and Introduction, p. 25).

102 If Polybos had died out of longing for his adopted son, then the oracle would have
been fulfilled without any responsibility on Oidipous' part. If not, Oidipous in no
way caused his father's death. Either way, the oracle is now "dead" in the sense
that its threat has supposedly been averted.

103 I.e. since the future is unpredictable, we should not fear any specific event that
has been prophesied.

104 Dreams, as well as oracles, were regarded as omens of the future. A dream might
also be seen as an innocuous fulfilment of the oracle (Introduction, p. 25).

JOKASTA
Your father's funeral's a mighty ray of hope.[105]

OIDIPOUS
It is; but I still fear the woman who's alive.

MESSENGER 1
Who is this woman that you're also fearful of?

OIDIPOUS
It's Merope, old man, who lived with Polybos.   990

MESSENGER 1
And what's the reason that you have this fear of her?

OIDIPOUS
An awful god-sent prophecy, oh foreigner.

MESSENGER 1
Can it be spoken? Or may no one else be told?

OIDIPOUS
It's certainly permitted. Loxias once said
I must have intercourse with my own mother and   995
shed with my hands my father's blood. That's why I've made
my home so far away from Corinth for so long.
Good fortune has been mine; and yet it is most sweet
to look upon the eyes of those who gave one birth.[106]

MESSENGER 1
And so you left that city shuddering at this?   1000

OIDIPOUS
I'd no desire to spill my father's blood, old man.

MESSENGER 1
Then since I've come here with good will towards you, lord,
why don't I instantly release you from this fear?

OIDIPOUS
Indeed, you'd win from me the thanks that you deserve.

MESSENGER 1
Indeed, that's mainly what I came here for, to reap   1005
some kind of benefit when you came home again.

---

105 Literally, "a great eye." The eye was regarded as the most precious part of the body, and was thought of as emitting a ray of light. It therefore came to stand for the light of hope or safety (cf. 81), or anything precious, especially a dearly loved family member (compare 999). The latter meaning gives the expression extra poignance in this context, where anxiety about the oracles has rendered the death of a close family member joyful instead of sad.
106 "Eyes" is often used in this way to mean "face." But in this particular play such expressions have a special resonance.

OIDIPOUS

I'll never go to join the ones who gave me birth!

MESSENGER 1

You don't know what you're doing, child, that's very clear…

OIDIPOUS

How's that, old man? Tell me your meaning, by the gods.

MESSENGER 1

…if on account of this you flee from going home.   1010

OIDIPOUS

I dread that Phoibos' words may turn out clear and true.

MESSENGER 1

That you may get some taint from those who gave you birth?

OIDIPOUS

Yes, this, old man—this keeps me constantly afraid.

MESSENGER 1

Then do you know you're justly terrified of nothing?

OIDIPOUS

How so, if I was really born these parents' child?   1015

MESSENGER 1

Because king Polybos was not your kin at all.

OIDIPOUS

What? Was not Polybos the father of my birth?

MESSENGER 1

No more than this man here, but equally with me.

OIDIPOUS

How could a nothing equal him who gave me birth?

MESSENGER 1

Because that man begot you no more than myself.   1020

OIDIPOUS

What was his reason, then, for calling me his child?

MESSENGER 1

Know that he got you from my hands once as a gift.

OIDIPOUS

Yet he so greatly loved me—from another's hand?

MESSENGER 1

His prior childlessness persuaded him to this.

OIDIPOUS

And did you chance upon this gift, or pay for me?   1025

MESSENGER 1

I found you in Cithaeron's winding wooded glens.

OIDIPOUS

And for what reason were you traveling in those parts?

MESSENGER 1

I supervised a flock that grazed the mountainside.

OIDIPOUS

You mean you were a shepherd, wandering for hire?[107]

MESSENGER 1

And at that time, my child, I was your savior too.   1030

OIDIPOUS

What was the anguish that your hands preserved me from?

MESSENGER 1

A grief to which your feet could serve as witnesses.

OIDIPOUS

Alas, why does this ancient evil cross your lips?

MESSENGER 1

When I released you, both your feet were pierced right through.

OIDIPOUS

A dread reproach I took up from my swaddling bands.[108]   1035

MESSENGER 1

From this chance fortune you were named the one you are.[109]

OIDIPOUS

Which of my parents did this? Tell me, by the gods!

MESSENGER 1

I don't know; he who gave you to me would know more.

OIDIPOUS

It was not you who chanced on me, but someone else?

MESSENGER 1

Another shepherd gave you to me as a gift.   1040

OIDIPOUS

Who was the fellow? Can you make this clear in words?

---

[107] The shepherd is a hired laborer, who in the eyes of a nobleman would rank little more than a slave. Hence Oidipous' tone is one of some contempt, and the shepherd's response slightly reproachful.

[108] Swaddling bands were cloths in which infants were tightly confined for about two months after birth. The expression is similar to the English "from the cradle." Ironically, the verb translated "took up" is the same verb used for a father accepting a newborn baby into the family.

[109] The name Oidipous was popularly supposed to be derived from two words meaning "swollen" and "foot."

MESSENGER 1

I think that he was named as one of Laios' men.

OIDIPOUS

You mean the king who ruled this land once, long ago?

MESSENGER 1

Yes; that's the man this fellow served as herdsman for.

OIDIPOUS

And is the fellow still alive, for me to see?   1045

MESSENGER 1

You local people of this land would know that best.

OIDIPOUS

Does anyone among you know the herdsman that
he speaks of, having seen him either here or in
the countryside? If so, inform me, since the time
is opportune for all of this to be found out.   1050

CHORUS

I think he is none other than the countryman
whom you were seeking earlier to see. But she,
Jokasta here, could tell you best if that is so.

OIDIPOUS

You know that shepherd, wife, whom we just now desired
to come here? Is it he of whom this fellow speaks?   1055

JOKASTA

What of it? Pay it no attention. Do not even
wish to call to mind mere foolish, futile words.

OIDIPOUS

It cannot be that I should get such evidence
as this and not reveal the truth about my birth.

JOKASTA

No, by the gods! If you have any care for your   1060
own life, don't search this out! My sickness is enough.[110]

OIDIPOUS

Take heart! If I'm revealed a triple slave,[111] my mother
thrice enslaved, *you* won't be shown as evil-born.

JOKASTA

Yet be persuaded, I beseech you—don't do this!

---

[110] Jokasta is referring to her own distress at perceiving the truth, but Oidipous
assumes she is simply upset about his supposed low birth.

[111] This might mean "utterly a slave," or "a third-generation slave." For the ambigui-
ties in the meaning of *kakos* see n. on *OC* 87.

OIDIPOUS

You can't persuade me not to clearly learn the truth.   1065

JOKASTA

I speak the best for you—I understand things well.[112]

OIDIPOUS

This "best for you"'s been grieving me for some time now.

JOKASTA

Ill-destined, may you never find out who you are!

OIDIPOUS

Won't someone go and bring that herdsman here to me?

And let this woman here enjoy her wealthy birth.   1070

JOKASTA

Ah! Ah! Unhappy one! This is the only word

I can address you with—that's all, for evermore.

[Jokasta rushes off into the palace.]

CHORUS

Why has your wife departed from us, Oidipous,

rushing away in savage pain? I am afraid

that from her silence something evil will break forth.[113]   1075

OIDIPOUS

Break forth what will! I shall pursue my wish to see

the seed from which I spring, however slight its rank.

She may perhaps feel shame—since, like a woman, she

thinks big—to find out that I am of wretched birth.[114]

But *I* won't be dishonored, since I count myself   1080

a child of Fortune with her beneficial gifts.

This is the mother I was born from, and my kin

the months have marked me out to be both small and great.[115]

So born, I never could turn out to be another

person and not learn in full about my birth.   1085

---

112   This is a good example of the ambiguity of *phron-* words (see n. on 569). Jokasta
      means that she is concerned for Oidipous' well-being, but she also understands
      things on an intellectual level better than he does.
113   The image is that of the calm before a storm (cf. 1280/and *Ant.* 1244-52).
114   Despite his unusually warm and intimate relationship with his wife, Oidipous
      shares the general cultural contempt for women.
115   Like Oidipous, the months are "children" of Fortune, since they bring various
      events with the waxing and waning of the moon. The passage of time, as mea-
      sured by the months he has lived, has "marked him out" as "small and great"
      both literally (as a newborn and an adult) and figuratively (as a humiliated infant
      and a great king).

[The chorus now sing and dance the brief third stasimon, during which Oidipous and the first Messenger both remain on stage.]

CHORUS

If I am a prophet indeed   *Strophe A*
and knowing in judgment,
this will happen to you,
by Olympus, oh Cithaeron:
tomorrow's full moon will exalt you   1090
as Oidipous' compatriot
and nurse and mother, and we
shall honor you in dance
for rendering such service
to my king.[116] Oh Phoibos,   1095
you to whom we cry aloud,
may this prove pleasing to you!

Who bore you, my child,   *Antistrophe A*
which of the long-lived nymphs,
consorting with your father,   1100
mountain-roving Pan?[117]
Or was it some bedmate of Loxias,
who loves all the upland pastures?[118]
Or was it the lord of Cyllene,
or the Bacchic god who dwells   1105
up on the mountain-peaks,
who received you as a lucky find
from one of the glancing-eyed Nymphs
with whom he so often plays?[119]

[Enter Shepherd, along the entry-ramp leading from the countryside.]

---

[116] I.e. Cithaeron, the putative location of Oidipous' conception and birth, will be honored by an all-night festival. Such events were not uncommon (cf. *Ant*. 153, 1153) The mention of the full moon provides a thematic link with Oidipous' invocation of the months as his kin (1083), but may also allude to the fact that the dramatic festival was followed by a festival held at the full moon (called the Pandia).

[117] The nymphs are not immortal, like the gods, but they do live longer than human beings. They are often found in the company of Pan, a nature-god with a goat's feet and horns who lives in caves.

[118] The word translated "pasture" (*agronomos*) echoes a title of Apollo (=Loxias), who is often found in the countryside and serves as as a shepherd in several myths.

[119] The lord of Cyllene, a mountain in Arcadia (Map 1), is Hermes, who is also the god of herdsmen. Dionysos (the "Bacchic god") is another nature-god linked with mountains and nymphs.

OIDIPOUS

If I must make a calculation, elders, though   1110
I've never dealt with him I think I see the herdsman
we have sought so long. This man here matches him
in his old age, which measures just as long for both;
besides, I recognize those leading him as slaves
of my own house. But you're no doubt ahead of me   1115
in knowledge, since you've seen the herdsman in the past.

CHORUS

Know well I recognize him; he was one of Laios'
men, and for a herdsman, trusty as the next.

OIDIPOUS

I ask you first, Corinthian foreigner, is this
the fellow that you meant?

MESSENGER 1

                                        The very one you see.   1120

OIDIPOUS [to the Shepherd, whose eyes are downcast]

You there, old man, look here and speak in answer to
the questions that I ask. Were you once Laios' slave?

SHEPHERD

Yes, I was his—not bought, but nurtured in his house.

OIDIPOUS

In what work were you occupied, or way of life?

SHEPHERD

Most of my life I've followed after flocks of sheep.   1125

OIDIPOUS

And in what region did you mostly tend your herds?

SHEPHERD

There was Cithaeron, and the lands nearby as well.

OIDIPOUS [pointing to the Corinthian messenger]

And do you know this man from meeting him round there?

SHEPHERD

What was he doing? Who's the man you're speaking of?

OIDIPOUS

This one here. Have you ever dealt with him at all?   1130

SHEPHERD

Not so that I could say at once from memory.

MESSENGER 1

That's not surprising, master. But I'll help him, though
he doesn't know me, to remember clear and true.

I'm sure he really knows that when we grazed around
Cithaeron, he with his two flocks and I with one,[120]   1135
    * * * * * * * * * * *

I kept him company for three whole periods
of time, each six months long, from spring to Arktouros;[121]
in winter I would drive my sheep back to their barns,
and he his flocks to Laios' homesteads. Come, did any
of this happen as I say it did, or not?   1140

SHEPHERD

You speak the truth, although that time is long ago.

MESSENGER 1

Come on then, tell us: at that time, you know you gave
a child to me, to raise and nurture as my own?

SHEPHERD

What if I did? Why are you asking me all this?

MESSENGER 1

This is the man, my friend, who was that infant then.   1145

SHEPHERD

To hell with you! Won't you be silent once for all?

OIDIPOUS

No! Don't chastise this man, old fellow; it's your words
that need chastisement rather than what he has said.

SHEPHERD

In what way, best of masters, have I been at fault?

OIDIPOUS

Not speaking of the child that this man asks about.   1150

SHEPHERD

Because he talks in ignorance and wastes his pains.

OIDIPOUS

If you won't speak to please me, you will speak in tears.

SHEPHERD

In god's name do not torture me. I'm an old man!

OIDIPOUS

Someone twist back his arms, as fast as possible!

SHEPHERD

What for, unhappy man? Desiring to learn what?   1155

---

120 Many editors believe a line is missing here, since the Greek makes imperfect sense
  as it stands.
121 Arktouros is the brightest star in the constellation Boötes (the plowman). It
  appeared in classical Greece in mid-September.

OIDIPOUS

Did you give to this man the child of which he asks?

SHEPHERD

I did; if only I had perished on that day!

OIDIPOUS

You'll come to that if you don't give a just reply.

SHEPHERD

I'm much more certainly destroyed if I do tell.

OIDIPOUS

This man is bent on spinning out delays, it seems.   1160

SHEPHERD

No! I already said that I gave him the child.

OIDIPOUS

Where did you get it? From your house, or someone else?

SHEPHERD

Not my own child! I took it in from somebody.

OIDIPOUS

From which among these citizens, and from what house?

SHEPHERD

No, by the gods! No, master! Don't ask any more!   1165

OIDIPOUS

You are destroyed if I must ask you this again.

SHEPHERD

Well then, it was in Laios' house the child was born.

OIDIPOUS

A slave? Or was the infant kin to him by birth?

SHEPHERD

Alas, I'm just about to say the awful truth!

OIDIPOUS

And I to hear it; nonetheless it must be heard.   1170

SHEPHERD

All right: the child was called his own; but she who is
inside, your wife, could best tell you the truth of this.[122]

OIDIPOUS

Was she the one who gave him to you?

---

[122] The word order reflects the original, in which the shepherd seems uncertain how to
refer to Jokasta, of whose true relationship to Oidipous he is now aware. "Inside"
locates her in the definitive feminine sphere of the house, but is also somewhat
ominous in light of 1071-2.

SHEPHERD

Yes, my lord.

OIDIPOUS

What was her purpose?

SHEPHERD

That I do away with him.

OIDIPOUS

Her own child, wretch?

SHEPHERD

She dreaded evil prophecies.   1175

OIDIPOUS

What kind?

SHEPHERD

They said he'd kill the one who fathered him.

OIDIPOUS

Then why did you instead leave him with this old man?

SHEPHERD

From pity, master, thinking he would take him to
another land, where he was from; and yet he saved
him for the greatest evils; for if you are who   1180
he says you are, know this: ill-destined was your birth.

OIDIPOUS

Ah! Ah! It has all come out clear and true! Oh light,
may I now look my last on you,[123] revealed as born
from those I should not be, as intimate with those
I should not be, as killing those I should not kill.   1185

*[Exeunt, Oidipous into the palace, Corinthian Messenger and Shepherd to the
countryside. The chorus dance and sing the fourth stasimon.]*

CHORUS

Ah, generations of mortals,   *Strophe A*
how I count your lives
as equal to nothingness![124]
For who, what man gains more of happiness

---

123 This sounds like a warning of suicide, since tragic characters often say farewell
    to the daylight when they are heading towards certain death (e.g. *Ant.* 806-10,
    879-81). Oidipous' demand for a sword (1255-6) raises similar expectations (cf.
    Ant. 1232-9).

124 This could mean that human life is intrinsically worthless, or that the happiness
    of a human life cannot be judged until after one is dead—a frequent sentiment in
    Greek texts (see e.g. 1528-30).

than just enough to think he's so,   1190
then sink like the setting sun?
Taking your fate from god,
yours, as my exemplar,
yours, poor wretched Oidipous,
I count no mortal thing as blessed.[125]   1195

You shot your arrow beyond the limit,[126]   *Antistrophe A*
winning power over a prosperity
not blessed with happiness in every way;
You destroyed—oh Zeus!—
the hook-taloned maiden, singer of oracles,   1200
and stood up as a rampart
against death for my land;
since then you have been called my king
and been honored most greatly
as ruler of great Thebes.   1205

But now who is more miserable to hear of?   *Strophe B*
Who is at home with greater pains, or more savage
doom, his life turned upside-down?
Ah, famous royal Oidipous,
for whom the same great harbor sufficed   1210
both for the child and for the father
to fall into as bridegroom,[127] how,
oh how could the furrows your father plowed
endure you so long in silence?

All-seeing time has found you out against your will;[128]   *Antistrophe B*
it long ago passed judgment on the non-marriage   1216
marriage, which made begetter and begotten one.
Ah, child, oh child of Laios! If only,

---

[125] "Fate from god" translates *daimōn*, a word I have elsewhere translated as "divinity." It refers loosely to all kinds of divine forces, including, as here, the divinely sent destiny that shapes a person's life.

[126] This image refers to Oidipous' supreme, almost superhuman success in outwitting the Sphinx. At the same time, the idea of going beyond a boundary or limitation is an ominous one (cf. 124, 873-8).

[127] The "harbor" is Jokasta's womb (cf. 421-3).

[128] Time is often personified and invested with divine omniscience and justice (compare 614, *OC* 1453-5). Oidipous did, of course, desire to find out the truth. But the discovery was "against his will" in the sense that no one could actually want to learn such facts about himself.

if only I had never seen you![129]
How I lament for you above all others,   1220
pouring cries forth from my mouth!
To speak aright, it was from you that I drew breath,
from you I closed my eyes in sleep.[130]

[The Second Messenger enters from the palace and addresses the chorus.]

MESSENGER 2

Oh you always most greatly honored in this land,
what deeds you'll hear about, what sights you'll see, what sorrow
you will shoulder—if you still pay due attention   1225
to the house of Labdakos, as kinsmen should.[131]
The Ister or the Phasis,[132] so I think, could not
wash clean this dwelling-place, such evils it conceals,
and some of them will shortly be revealed to light—
things willed, not done against the will. Disasters that   1230
are shown to be self-chosen bring the greatest pain.[133]

CHORUS

What we already knew about was fully burdened
with lament. What do you have to add to that?

MESSENGER 2

The quickest thing to speak and learn about is death:
she's dead, Jokasta, our own royal, godlike queen.[134]   1235

CHORUS

Alas, poor wretched one! What was responsible?

---

129 This is not simply an expression of selfishness on the part of the chorus, who remain
devoted to Oidipous. Rather, it expresses the wish that none of this should ever
have happened, and in particular, that Laios' child should never have survived
to stand before them. Similarly 1348.

130 The interpretation of these lines is controversial. The most likely meaning is: you
have brought me both life (by killing the Sphinx) and the "sleep" of death (i.e. the
plague, or the metaphorical death of despair). Alternatively, the whole sentence
might mean simply "you were everything to me."

131 The chorus are Oidipous' kinsmen since, as noblemen, they too are descended
from the Kadmean stock to which the royal house belongs.

132 The Ister and Phasis are two great rivers at the edges of the Greek world. The
Ister is the modern Danube. The Phasis, beyond the Black Sea, was viewed as the
boundary between Europe and Asia.

133 In the chorus's opinion, self-inflicted suffering is the most painful because it cannot
be blamed on an external cause. Other characters, such as Oidipous himself, would
not necessarily agree with this sentiment.

134 Because Jokasta's name is delayed, for a split second the chorus and audience
may think that it is Oidipous who is dead, as the wording of his last exit led us to
expect (see n. on 1183). "Godlike" is a traditional epithet of royalty.

MESSENGER 2

She did it to herself. The deed's most grievous part
is absent, since the vision of it is not here.
But still, as far as memory can report, you shall
discover what she suffered—miserable one.   1240
  When she had passed inside the palace entry-way,
frantic with raging grief, she rushed straight to her bridal
bed, tearing her hair with fingers of both hands.
Once in her room, she slammed the doors and called aloud
to Laios, now long since a corpse, reminding him   1245
about the seed he sowed so long ago, which brought
him death and left herself, who bore that child, for his
own son to father misbegotten children on.
She mourned the bed where she, unhappy one, gave birth
twice over: husband from her husband, children from   1250
her child. And then she perished, but I don't know how,
for Oidipous struck his way in there, screaming; this
kept us from seeing out her evil to the end;[135]
so it was him we stared at as he roamed the house.
He ranged about, imploring us to bring a sword   1255
to him and tell him where to find his non-wife wife,
the twice-plowed field that bore his children and himself.
And in his frenzy some divinity pointed
the way—for it was none of us, the men nearby.
He gave an awful cry, then leaped against the double   1260
doors, as if he had a guide, bent both the panels
inward from their frame, and fell into the room.
We saw the woman in there dangling, with her neck
entangled in the twisted noose from which she swung.
On seeing her, the poor man bellowed awfully   1265
and loosed the knot that held her dangling. When she lay,
poor wretch, upon the ground, next came an awful sight.
He tore off from her dress the pair of gold-wrought pins
that kept it in due order,[136] raised them up and struck
them in his eyeballs in their sockets, crying out   1270
that they should never see him or the evils he

---

[135] Since Jokasta has locked her bedroom doors from the inside, the Messenger must
mean that he and the other attendants were distracted by Oidipous' entrance into
the house from listening further to Jokasta or trying to enter the chamber and find
out what was happening. But his language suggests rather that of the theatrical
spectator who is prevented from viewing a performance to the end.

[136] A woman's clothing was secured on both shoulders with brooches, similar in
construction to modern safety-pins, but much larger.

had suffered and had done, but should in future look
in darkness on the people he should not have seen,
and fail to recognize those he'd desired to find.
While chanting things like this, he lifted up the pins   1275
and gouged his eyes with them, not once but many times.[137]
The bleeding eye-balls drenched his cheeks, not just emitting
slowly oozing drops of blood, but drenching him
with the black downpour of a storm of bloody hail.
Such are the evils that have broken forth from two,   1280
not one: the mingled evils of a man and wife.
Their past prosperity from long ago was justly
blessed; but now, upon this day, there is no groaning
cry, no doom, disgrace or death, no evil thing
that can be named, which does not keep them company.   1285

CHORUS

Poor wretch—and have his evils slackened off by now?

MESSENGER 2

He screams for someone to throw wide the doors and show
to all the Kadmeans his father's killer and
his mother's... I can't utter his unholy words;
he means to throw himself forth from the land, and not   1290
stay in this house, accursed as he has cursed himself.[138]
But he needs someone to support and guide him, since
the sickness that afflicts him is too great to bear.
He will display this to your eyes as well; for see,
the gates are opening; soon you will gaze upon   1295
a sight of such a kind that even one who felt
abhorrence for the man would surely pity him.[139]

[Oidipous enters from the palace, wearing a new mask that shows his blindness.
After fourteen lines of anapests (1298-1311) and a single trimeter (1312) he and the
chorus participate in a kommos (lyric dialogue) which includes both lyric and iambic
lines.]

CHORUS

Oh suffering awful for humankind
to see, most awful of all that I've ever

---

[137] The verb "chanting" conveys both repetition and the power of a curse or ritual
act (cf. *Ant.* 658, 1304-5).

[138] The curse will contaminate Oidipous' family and house if he remains there (cf.
236-42).

[139] This could mean either that even an enemy who hated Oidipous would pity him,
or that he would be pitied even by someone appalled by his deeds and the sight
he presents.

encountered! What mad frenzy, wretch,   1300
came over you? What divinity has
leapt further than furthest against you in your
divinely sent and wretched destiny?
Woe, woe, unhappy one! I can't even
look at you, though there are many things I   1305
want to ask, to discover, to gaze at—
such is the shuddering you inspire.

OIDIPOUS

Aiai! Aiai! Unhappy me!
Where on earth am I carried to, wretch that I am?[140]
Where does my voice rush fluttering off to?   1310
Ah, divinity, where have you leapt to?[141]

CHORUS

To somewhere awful, neither heard nor looked upon.

OIDIPOUS

Ah, my cloud of darkness   *Strophe A*
horrific, overwhelming, unspeakable,   1315
invincible, wafted by an evil wind!
Alas!
Alas once more! How they have pierced me, both at once,
the stinging of these goads and memory of my evils![142]

CHORUS

It's no surprise that in such great disasters you   1320
should sorrow doubly, cry out doubly at your evils.

OIDIPOUS

Ah friend!   *Antistrophe A*
You are my steadfast attendant! For you
still stay to tend me, blind as I am!
Alas, alas!   1325
I am not unaware of you; although I am
in darkness, I still clearly recognize your voice.

---

140 Oidipous' use of the passive indicates his helplessness as a blind man. But it also suggests the other wanderings, metaphorical and literal, of a life that has been directed by forces of which he was unaware.

141 Fate or misfortune is often imagined as "leaping" on the head of its victims (cf. 263, 1300-1302, *Ant.* 1344-7). In this case, however, Oidipous imagines his fate as having leapt not upon his head, but into a distant (i.e. extreme and alien) location.

142 "Stinging" refers to the sting of the gadfly, which was so painful that it was thought to cause madness. The "goads" are the two pins with which Oidipous pierced his eyes, but the word also recalls the two-pronged goad with which Laios struck him (809), and his parents' "two-pronged" curse (417-19).

CHORUS

You who have done these awful deeds, how could you bear
to quench your vision thus? What god incited you?

OIDIPOUS

It was Apollo, my friends, Apollo,   *Strophe B*
who fulfilled my evil, these my evil sufferings.[143]   1331
But the murderous hand that struck me
was no one's but my own,
wretch that I am!
Why should I see, when there   1335
was nothing sweet for me to see if I had sight?

CHORUS

That's how it was, just as you say.

OIDIPOUS

What sight for me to see
could be cherished?
What address could be heard   1340
with pleasure, friends?
Lead me from this place
as fast as possible!
Lead me away, friends, utterly lost,
most utterly accursed,   1345
and also to the gods
most utterly hateful of mortals!

CHORUS

Oh how I wish I'd never known you, wretched in
your mind and in your circumstances equally.

OIDIPOUS

May the wanderer perish, whoever he was,   *Antistrophe B*
who took from my feet the savage shackles,   1351
rescued me from death
and saved me—
doing me no favor;
for if I'd died then I'd not have   1355
brought all this grief to both my dear ones and myself.

CHORUS

I too would have wished this to be so.

OIDIPOUS

Then I'd not have come here

---

[143] On the meaning of this passage see Introduction, pp. 26-7.

as my father's murderer,
and mortals would not call me   1360
bridegroom of her who bore me.
As it is, I'm god-forsaken,
child of impiety, sharing fatherhood
with him who gave me birth,
wretch that I am!   1365
If any evil outranks evil,
that is the allotment of Oidipous.

CHORUS

I don't know how to say you planned this well; you would
do better to exist no longer than live blind.

OIDIPOUS

Don't try to tell me that what I have done was not
done for the best! Don't give me any more advice!   1370
If I had sight, I don't know with what eyes I could
have looked upon my father when I went to Hades,
and my poor wretched mother; I've done deeds to both
of them so dire that hanging is too good for me.
Or did my children—born as they were born—provide   1375
a vision that I might desire to gaze upon?
No, never! Never with these eyes of mine at least.
Nor did the town, its ramparts or its images
and temples of divinities, which I, most finely
nurtured of all men in Thebes, I wretched one,   1380
deprived myself of, when I did myself proclaim
that all should thrust out the irreverent one, who was
revealed by gods to be impure and Laios' kin.
After declaring such a stain upon myself
was I to look with eyes aright at these folk here?[144]   1385
No! Rather, if there was some way to block the flow
of hearing through my ears, I would not have held back
from closing off my miserable body in
this way as well, to make me deaf as well as blind—
it's sweet for thought to dwell apart from evil things.   1390
    Ah why, Cithaeron, did you take me in? Oh why

---

[144] To look someone in the eye is a sign of frankness, honesty, and/or a sound mind, suggesting that one has nothing to be ashamed of (cf. 528, 523-5). To do so when one is disgraced may be considered an affront to the person in question. In this case, of course, Oidipous is also referring to his inability to look at anyone at all, owing to his blindness (cf. 419), which itself expresses the intensity of his sense of shame.

did you not kill me straight away, so that I never
could display my origins to human kind?
Oh Polybos, and Corinth, so-called fatherland
of long ago, you nursed me as a thing of beauty   1395
festering with evil underneath the skin;
now I'm found out as evil and of evil birth.
Oh you three paths, you hidden glade, you woods, you narrow
place where three roads meet, who drank in at my hands
the blood that flows in my own veins, my father's blood,   1400
do you remember still what deeds I did there in
your presence, and what further actions I performed
when I came here? Oh marriage, marriage, you both gave
me birth, and after I was born from you again
raised up my seed, displaying to the world fathers   1405
as brothers, children shedding kindred blood, brides as
both wives and mothers, all the utterly disgraceful
deeds that can occur among the human race.
    But it's not fine to speak of things not fine to do.
So by the gods, hide me as fast as possible   1410
outside this land, or murder me, or throw me in
the sea, where you may never look on me again.
Come, don't disdain to touch a miserable man;
let me persuade you, do not dread me; for my evils
can't be borne by any mortal but myself.[145]   1415

CHORUS

Just when you need him for the deeds and plans that you
are begging for, here's Kreon; he's the only person
left to take your place as guardian of this land.

OIDIPOUS

Alas, how shall I speak to him? What cause has he
to trust me in all justice? I have been found out   1420
as evil to him in the past in every way.

[Enter Kreon along the entry ramp leading from the city.]

KREON

I have not come here, Oidipous, to laugh at you,
nor to reproach you with the evils of the past.

[He addresses the chorus and attendants.]

You, even if you've lost all sense of shame before
mere mortal creatures, then at least respect the flame   1425

---

[145] On this line see Introduction, p. 28.

that feeds all things, lord Helios, and don't display
uncovered such a curse as this, which neither earth
nor sacred rain nor light is willing to take in.[146]
Come now, take him from here, as fast as possible,
inside the house; for reverence requires that only   1430
kindred see and hear the evils of their kin.

OIDIPOUS

It's not what I expected, that you'd come here, best
of men, to me the evilest; so by the gods
let me persuade you—for your own sake, not for mine.

KREON

What's this request you beg for so insistently?   1435

OIDIPOUS

Throw me, as fast as possible, out of this land,
somewhere no mortal can address or look on me.

KREON

I would have done so—know this well—if I did not
desire to learn first from the god what must be done.

OIDIPOUS

His voice said clearly and in full that I, the father-   1440
killer, the irreverent one, should be destroyed.

KREON

That's what was said; but standing where we do in need
it's better that we learn for certain what to do.

OIDIPOUS

You will inquire for such a miserable man?

KREON

I will; perhaps this time you too may trust the god.   1445

OIDIPOUS

I will; but it is you I now enjoin and urge:
arrange what burial you want for her within
the house; it's right that you fulfill this for your kin.[147]
But as for me, let this my fathers' town not be
deemed worthy to have me as an inhabitant   1450
while I'm alive; but let me dwell up in the mountains
in my own place, called Cithaeron, which my mother

---

[146] Kreon invokes all the constituent elements of the universe: earth, "light" or air,
fire, and water (symbolized by rain). This signifies the rejection of Oidipous by
the whole physical world, as well as the land of Thebes.

[147] Oidipous avoids mentioning his mother-wife by name (contrast 950). After the
announcement of her death (1235), Jokasta's name is not spoken again.

and my father, while still living, chose as my
appointed place of burial, so that my death
may come from those attempting to destroy me then.
Yet I know this: no sickness and no other cause   1455
could kill me; I would never have been saved from death
back then, if not to meet some awful evil end.[148]
    But let my destiny go where it will; as for
my children, though, do not preoccupy yourself,
Kreon, about the boys; they're men, so they will never   1460
lack for livelihood wherever they may be;
but my two piteous and miserable girls,
whose food was always set at my own table, so
that they were never parted from this man, but always
shared, the two of them, in what I touched—with these   1465
two do concern yourself; above all, let me touch
them with my hands and shed tears for our evil lot.[149]
Come, my lord![150]
Come, noble in your birth! If my hands held them I
would think I had them as I did when I could see.   1470

[Enter Antigone and Ismene from within the house, weeping and led by an
attendant.[151]]

What is that?
Oh gods, can it be true? Can I be hearing them,
my dear ones, streaming tears? Has Kreon pitied me
and sent to me my offspring, these two dearest ones?
Am I right?   1475

KREON

You're right. I brought about this visit, knowing you
would still delight in them as you have done so long.

OIDIPOUS

May fortune favor you! May some divinity

---

[148] Oidipous senses that even if he is once more abandoned on Cithaeron, as his parents wished, he will once again be saved from a normal death, because his story so far has been so remarkable. His death, as dramatized in *OC*, is far from "evil," but it is certainly extraordinary.

[149] In classical Athens, young girls would not dine with their father. The description reflects a conception of the heroic age as freer in such matters. But it also suggests a special intensity in Oidipous' relationship to his daughters.

[150] Oidipous' iambic trimeters are punctuated three times (1468, 1471, 1475) by short exclamatory phrases, in a rare technique expressive of high emotion.

[151] The exact moment of their entrance is uncertain. Some editors think they enter with Kreon and are silent until now. Alternatively, Kreon may have sent an attendant for them earlier.

chance to protect you better than myself, for this,
their road to me. Where are you, children? Come to me!   1480
Come to your brother's hands, which did a favor to
the eyes, once shining, of the father who begot
you both, by making them see thus—the father now
revealed as having sown you, children, in the place
where he was sown, unseeing and unquestioning.   1485
I weep for you two also—since I lack the strength
to look at you—my mind upon the bitter life
that still remains for you to live at human hands.
What gatherings of townsfolk will you now attend,
what public festivals, without returning home   1490
in tears, instead of gazing at the spectacle?[152]
And when you reach the proper age for marriage, who
will be the one, my children? Who will run the risk
of taking on reproaches of the kind that will
inflict disaster on your parents and yourselves?   1495
What evil is not here? Your father murdered his
own father; plowed the one who bore him, in the place
where he himself was sown, and thus in that same place
from which he had his birth begot you equally.
Reproached for all these things, who then will marry you?   1500
The man does not exist, my children; clearly you
must waste away in barren, childless spinsterhood.
    Son of Menoikeus, you're the only father left
to these two girls, since both of us who gave them birth
have perished; father, don't stand by and watch them, your   1505
own kinsfolk, wandering as vagrant beggars without
husbands; do not make their evils equal mine.
Take pity on them, seeing them bereft so young
of everything except for what you have to give.
Touch me, consenting, with your hand, oh noble one.[153]   1510
    For you two, children, if you understood, I would
have much advice; but as it is, make this your prayer:

---

[152]   Even in classical Athens, where women were barred from participation in political
        life, they might attend certain public religious festivals, some of which included
        such "spectacles" as processions, and indeed the drama itself (Introduction, pp. 6-7).
        Such festivals were an integral part of the life of the city-state and also the family,
        which would be disgraced if its members were excluded from participating.
[153]   The blind Oidipous cannot see whether Kreon is nodding in assent (the literal
        meaning of the verb), so he asks for a touch instead. His request also suggests the
        clasping of right hands as a token of agreement (cf. OC 1631-3). A touch of the
        hand might also signify affection (cf. 1466-7).

to live where opportunity permits, and meet
a better life than me, the father of your birth.

*[The remainder of the play is in trochaic tetrameters, an unusual meter for tragedy,
with slightly longer lines than iambic trimeters; they are translated here with eight
iambic beats.]*

KREON

You have gone far enough in shedding tears; now go
inside the house.   1515

OIDIPOUS

Though it's not sweet, I must obey.[154]

KREON

What's opportune is always fine.

OIDIPOUS

Then do you know what terms I'll go on?

KREON

Speak, then I shall hear and know.

OIDIPOUS

Send me forth homeless from this land.

KREON

You ask what is the god's to give.

OIDIPOUS

I've come to be most hateful to the gods.

KREON

Then you'll soon get your wish.

OIDIPOUS

Is that a "yes"?

KREON

I do not like to say in vain what I don't think.[155]   1520

OIDIPOUS

Then lead me now away from here.

KREON:

Go now, but let your children go.

OIDIPOUS

No, don't take them away from me!

KREON

Don't wish for power in everything;

---

[154]   The word "obey" is in Greek the same as "be persuaded" (cf. 650, 1064).
[155]   This could imply either "Yes" or "No" in answer to Oidipous' question.

the power that once was yours did not attend you through the course of
life.

*[Exeunt Oidipous into the palace, led by attendants, the other characters along the
entry ramp leading to the city. The chorus conclude the play with a final reflection
addressed to each other,[156] then exeunt in the direction of the city.]*

CHORUS

Oh you who make your home in Thebes, our fatherland, see
Oidipous!

Behold the overwhelming wave of awful circumstances he   1525
has entered, he who knew the famous riddles and who was a man
most powerful, whose fortune everyone among the citizens
looked on with envy. Therefore one should never say a mortal man
is prosperous while he still waits to look upon his final day,
until he passes life's last limit having suffered no distress.   1530

---

[156] For various technical reasons, many scholars believe this final choral tag is spurious.

OIDIPOUS AT COLONUS

CHARACTERS

OIDIPOUS, former king of Thebes
ANTIGONE, daughter of Oidipous
STRANGER, a resident of Colonus
CHORUS of fifteen aged noblemen of Colonus
ISMENE, daughter of Oidipous
THESEUS, king of Athens
KREON, Oidipous' brother-in-law, king of Thebes
POLYNEICES, son of Oidipous
MESSENGER, an attendant of Theseus
Guards and attendants of Theseus; Kreon's armed escort

Setting: A grove sacred to the goddesses known as the Eumenides ("Kindly Ones"), at Colonus, a rural village near Athens.[1] Within the sacred precinct is a large rock, which forms a seat, and an opening through which one may exit into the grove at the rear. Just outside the precinct is a low ledge of natural rock.

[Enter Oidipous, a blind old man, guided by his young daughter Antigone. They are dressed as beggars, and Oidipous carries a staff and a beggar's pouch. They enter along one of the side-entrances, which throughout the play will represent the road from Thebes. Oidipous addresses his daughter in iambic trimeters, the meter of dialogue (Introduction, p. 15).]

OIDIPOUS

Antigone, child of a blind old man,[2] what region
have we come to, or the city of what men?
Who'll take in Oidipous the wanderer upon

---

[1] The Greek *polis* or city-state included not just the city proper, but the rural lands and villages surrounding it, which in the case of Athens make up the territory known as Attica. Colonus (Sophocles' birthplace) was about a mile and a quarter northwest of Athens (see Map 2). It was politically part of Athens, and its people were Athenian citizens (cf. 67).

[2] Oidipous blinded himself out of horror when he discovered that he had unwittingly murdered his father and married his mother. These events are dramatized in *OT* (Introduction, pp. 17-18).

this day, providing some scant offering of gifts?
I beg for just a little, and I get still less   5
than little—and yet that's sufficient for my needs.
For suffering and time, my long companion, and
a third thing, my nobility, have taught me how
to be content. But child, if you see anywhere
to sit, a public place or some grove of the gods,   10
stop me and settle me, that we may make inquiry
where we are: for we have come as strangers who
must learn from townsfolk and fulfill what we are told.

ANTIGONE
Father, long-suffering Oidipous, the city's crown
of ramparts is—to judge by eye—still far away.[3]   15
But this place here is clearly sacred—I surmise—
luxuriant with laurels, olives, vines; a throng
of feathered nightingales sing blessedly within.[4]
So rest your limbs and sit here, on this unhewn rock:
the road you've traveled down is long for an old man.   20

OIDIPOUS
Then help me sit, and guard me—blind man that I am.

ANTIGONE
That's something time's already taught me how to do.

[She seats him on the large rock within the sacred precinct.]

OIDIPOUS
Can you explain to me where we have settled down?

ANTIGONE
I know we are at Athens but don't know this place.

OIDIPOUS
Yes, every traveler told us *that* at any rate.   25

ANTIGONE
Well then, shall I go off and learn what spot this is?

OIDIPOUS
Yes, child, if it is somewhere that is habitable.

---

3   The most prominent feature of these "ramparts" was the Athenian Acropolis, which rose up behind the spectators in the theater of Dionysos. It served as a fortress when the city was under attack.
4   It has been pointed out that nightingales arrive in Greece for the summer at about the same time as the spring festival of Dionysos, when the play was first performed.

ANTIGONE

It's certainly inhabited.

[Enter a local stranger along the other side-entrance, which represents the road from the adjacent village of Colonus and from Athens.]

But I don't think
there's any need: I see a man not far from us.

OIDIPOUS

Is he proceeding forward, setting out this way?   30

ANTIGONE

No, he's already present. Speak whatever words
you think are opportune, because the man is here.

OIDIPOUS

Oh stranger, hearing from this girl, who sees for both
herself and me, that you have come as an auspicious
messenger, to tell us what we find unclear...   35

STRANGER

Before inquiring any further, leave that seat!
You occupy a place where it's impure to tread.

OIDIPOUS

What is this place, and to what god does it belong?

STRANGER

Untouched and uninhabited! It's occupied
by fearful goddesses, daughters of Earth and Dark.[5]   40

OIDIPOUS

Tell me what solemn name to use for them in prayer.

STRANGER

The people here would call them the Eumenides,
all-seeing; but they favor other names elsewhere.

OIDIPOUS

Then may they welcome graciously their suppliant,
for I shall never leave this seat of mine again.[6]   45

STRANGER

What does this mean?

---

[5] I.e. the Eumenides (see Introduction, p. 23.)

[6] On supplication see Introduction, p. 21. The word "seat," used repeatedly for Oidipous' location at the grove, and for Polyneices' later supplication at Poseidon's altar, is a quasi-technical term in this context.

OIDIPOUS

The watchword of my circumstances.[7]

STRANGER

I do not dare to make you leave without the city's
sanction; I must tell them first what you are doing.

OIDIPOUS

Now stranger, by the gods, do not dishonor me,
despite my vagrant state, but tell me what I ask.   50

STRANGER

Reveal your question: I shall not dishonor you.

OIDIPOUS

What kind of place is this that we have stepped into?

STRANGER

You'll hear and understand all that I know myself.
This place is sacred as a whole; solemn Poseidon
occupies it;[8] here is also the fire-bearing   55
god, Titan Prometheus;[9] but the spot you're trampling
on is called the bronze-stepped threshold of this land,
mainstay of Athens;[10] and the fields that lie nearby
boast as their founding lord that horseman over there,
Kolonos;[11] he's the man that all the people are   60
called after, so the common name they bear is his.
Such is this region, stranger, honored not in legend

---

7   This phrase is as mysterious in Greek as in English. We shall shortly discover that
Apollo's oracle prophesied rest and death for Oidipous at a shrine of the "solemn
goddesses" (84-93). So when Oidipous hears to whom the grove is sacred, he
recognizes it as the "watchword," established by Apollo, that marks the end of
his sufferings.

8   Poseidon, god of the sea and of horses, had an altar at Colonus. It is not part of
the dramatic scene, but provides a convenient off-stage location for Theseus, who
must remain available for quick entrances (cf. 887-9, 1491-5).

9   Prometheus was the son of the Titan Iapetos. He stole fire from the gods to give
to mortals, and was represented in art as carrying a torch.

10   The place is named after a nearby spot (not represented on stage), probably a
cave or fissure in the earth, believed to be an entrance (hence "threshold") to the
underworld. This is where Oidipous will finally meet his end (1590-91). It is the
"mainstay" of Athens both because it represents the ancient earth on which the
city stands, and because it is a sacred spot providing religious protection.

11   Kolonos (from whom the place-name Colonus is derived) was the eponymous
founding hero of the region. The stranger points in the direction of his statue, either
on or (more likely) off the stage. Though heroes were powerful deceased mortals,
as distinct from gods, they might receive divine honors, so the stranger refers to
Colonos by extension as a "god" in 65. On hero-cult in general see Introduction,
pp. 29-30.

but more highly, by our constant company.

OIDIPOUS

So there are people dwelling in this area?

STRANGER

Most certainly, taking their name from this god here. 65

OIDIPOUS

And are they ruled, or do the people have their say?[12]

STRANGER

The town's king is the ruler of this land as well.

OIDIPOUS

Who is this man, who holds the power in speech and strength?

STRANGER

He is called Theseus, child of our old king, Aigeus.

OIDIPOUS

Could one of you go to him as a messenger? 70

STRANGER

Why? To report, or to arrange something for you?

OIDIPOUS

That he may win great profit through a little aid.

STRANGER

And from a man who has no sight what aid can come?

OIDIPOUS

The words I have to speak will be all seeing ones.[13]

STRANGER

I tell you, stranger, so that you may not slip up— 75
for you are noble, from your looks, but for your fate
from god[14]—stay here where you appeared, until I go
and tell this to the local people, those who live
round here, not in the town. They are the ones who will
decide if you should stay, or travel on again. 80

---

[12] Oidipous is asking whether the government is a monarchy or a democracy.

[13] This mysterious phrase echoes the description of the Eumenides as "all-seeing" (43). The blind were thought especially capable of prophecy and divine inspiration (cf. Introduction, p. 25). Thus Oidipous' words will display the power of sight that his eyes lack.

[14] The expression "fate from god" is used here and in a few other places (1337, 1370, 1443, 1750) for the Greek word *daimōn*, which literally means "divinity" (as I have translated it elsewhere). Since disasters as well as blessings come from the gods, this word can be used for bad or good fortune, and is used here by the stranger for Oidipous' manifest blindness and poverty.

[Exit Stranger along the side-entrance by which he arrived.]

OIDIPOUS

Child, has the stranger gone away from us again?

ANTIGONE

He's gone. So you can now say everything you wish
in peace, father, for I alone am here nearby.

[Oidipous raises his hands in prayer to the Eumenides.]

OIDIPOUS

Oh dread-eyed ladies, since yours is the seat where I
first let my limbs relax on coming to this land,   85
be not unfeeling to myself or Phoibos,[15] who,
when he gave me those many evil prophecies,[16]
said this, when a long time had passed, would be my rest:
that when I reached at last a land where I would find
the hospitable seat of solemn goddesses,   90
there would I round the post of my long-suffering life,[17]
dwelling with profit to the ones who took me in,
and doom to those who sent me forth, driving me out.
He pledged to me that signs would come of these events—
an earthquake, or some thunder, or a flash from Zeus.[18]   95
And now I recognize that it was certainly
a trusty omen sent by you that guided me
along this road and to this grove. For otherwise
I never would have met you first while traveling—
I sober and you wineless[19]—nor would I have sat   100
upon this solemn uncarved step. But, goddesses,
in keeping with Apollo's oracle, now grant
some closure and conclusion to my life—unless
you think I fall short through my endless servitude

---

15 Phoibos is the god Apollo, who prophesied Oidipous' terrible fate (Introduction,
     pp. 17 and 21-2).

16 "Evil" translates *kakos*, a very common word for any kind of harm or "badness."
     The ambiguities of this word often cannot be disentangled. To bring out its fre-
     quency and thematic range, I have mostly translated it as "evil," even though this
     sometimes sounds a little archaic or strange. When used for people, it is a strong
     term of condemnation.

17 The metaphor refers to the turning point in a chariot race, after which the contes-
     tants headed for the finishing line.

18 On Zeus see Introduction, p. 21.

19 Unlike most Greek divinities, the Eumenides never received wine as an offering
     (cf. 481). Oidipous is called "sober" because of the austerity of his recent life, but
     the word also suggests his special affinity with these goddesses (Introduction, pp.
     30-31).

to anguish most extreme of any mortal man. 105
Come, oh sweet daughters of primeval Darkness! Come,
oh greatest Pallas' city,[20] which they call her own,
Athens, the city honored highest of them all!
Pity this miserable shadow of the man
called Oidipous—for this is not what I once was. 110

ANTIGONE

Silence! Some people aged by time are coming here,
approaching to spy out the seat you've occupied.

OIDIPOUS

I shall be silent. As for you, conceal me off
the road, out of the way within the grove, until
I can learn thoroughly what they will have to say; 115
for learning brings us safety in the things we do.

[Exeunt Oidipous and Antigone into the grove. Enter the chorus of fifteen aged noblemen of Colonus, singing and dancing to their entry-song or parodos, along the side-entrance representing the road from Colonus, and into the orchestra.[21]]

CHORUS *Strophe A*

Look! Who was he, then?
Where is he dwelling?
Where has he sped to, out of the way,
he of all most outrageous, of all? 120
Glance about! Look for him!
Search all around! A wanderer,
the old man is some wanderer,
and not from these parts,
or he would never have stepped 125
within the untrodden grove
of these unconquerable maidens,
whose name we're terrified to say,
whom we pass by without glancing,
without speaking, without words, 130
moving our lips silently
to express reverent thoughts.
But now there's word that one
has come who shows no awe;
as I look round the whole 135
of the sacred space, I still

---

[20] Pallas is a frequent name for Athena, patron goddess of Athens.
[21] This parodos takes the unusual form of a lengthy lyric dialogue (117-253). The structure is complex and somewhat irregular, and anapests are interspersed at 138-48, 170-75, 188-91 (Introduction, p. 15).

cannot discern where he's dwelling.

[Enter Oidipous and Antigone from the grove. They converse with the chorus in song.]

OIDIPOUS

I am that man! For I see by voice,
as the saying goes.

CHORUS

Oh! Oh!   140
Dreadful to see and dreadful to hear!

OIDIPOUS

Don't, I supplicate, see me as lawless!

CHORUS

Zeus the Protector, who is the old man?

OIDIPOUS

One not entirely to be called blessed for the
first of destinies, you who are guardians   145
over this land. But that's clear. Otherwise
I would not move thus with another's eyes,
or be anchored, great as I am, on the small.

CHORUS   *Antistrophe A*

Ah! Ah! Your sightless eyes,
were they thus from birth?   150
You've had a wretched life,
and a long one, I surmise.
But you won't, if I can help it,
bring down these further curses.
For you are transgressing,   155
transgressing! But—lest you intrude
within this grassy voiceless glade,
where a bowl of water runs together
with the flow of honeyed drink-offerings
(take good care to avoid   160
these things, ill-fated stranger)—
move away, step back!
A long path bars you from us—
do you hear, long-suffering vagrant?
If you have any word to offer   165
for conversation with me,
step back from where no one may step;
where it is lawful for all to do so,
there speak; until then, refrain.

OIDIPOUS

Daughter, what counsel should we turn to? 170

ANTIGONE

Father, we must have equal concern with the
townsfolk, yielding and listening as need be.

OIDIPOUS

Put your hand on me, then.

ANTIGONE

I'm touching you now.

OIDIPOUS

Strangers, may I not suffer injustice,
if I trust you and move away. 175

CHORUS *Strophe B*

Never, old man, be sure,
shall anyone take you away
from these seats against your will.[22]

[Guided by Antigone, Oidipous moves forward a short distance.]

OIDIPOUS

Further, then?

CHORUS

Step further forward.

[They move forward a little more.]

OIDIPOUS

Further?

CHORUS

Lead him on, girl— 180
forward. For you understand.

ANTIGONE

Come, follow this way; follow
on your blind feet, father, where I lead you.[23]

CHORUS

Endure, as a stranger in a strange land,
long-suffering one, to loathe 185
whatever the city does not hold dear,
and to revere what is dear to it.

---

22 The chorus are emphatically guaranteeing that Oidipous may remain safely in
the vicinity of the grove, with its rocky "seats," even after he has left the sacred
area with the rock where he was sitting earlier.

23 A few lines may be missing from the text at about this point.

OIDIPOUS
> Then take me, child,
> to a place where, entering reverence,[24] we
> will be able to speak and able to listen.   190
> Let us not wage war on necessity.

[Antigone leads her father outside the sacred precinct to a natural ledge of rock, which is big enough to serve as a low seat, but is distinct from the larger rock within the sacred area where Oidipous sat earlier.]

CHORUS   Antistrophe B
> There! Direct your feet no further
> from that ledge of natural rock.

OIDIPOUS
> Like this?

CHORUS
> That's enough, as you can hear.

OIDIPOUS
> Shall I sit down?

CHORUS
> Yes, turn and sit   195
> on the front of the stony ledge, crouching low.

ANTIGONE
> Father, this task is mine. Peacefully...

OIDIPOUS
> Oh alas! Alas!

ANTIGONE
> ... fit step to step,
> leaning your aged body   200
> upon my loving arm.

OIDIPOUS
> Alas for my malignant doom!

[Antigone settles her father on his new seat.]

CHORUS
> Long-suffering man, now you're comfortable,
> tell us, what mortal are you by birth?
> Who are you, led along in such pain? What   205
> fatherland might I discover to be yours?

OIDIPOUS
> Strangers, I'm citiless. But don't ...

---

24   I.e. entering an area where it is not impious to tread.

CHORUS

What's this that you're prohibiting, old man?   *Epode*

OIDIPOUS

Don't! Don't! Don't ask me
who I am! Don't probe   210
by seeking further!

CHORUS

What is this?

OIDIPOUS

Dreadful is my birth!

CHORUS

Tell!

OIDIPOUS

Child—alas!—what am I to say?

CHORUS

Of what seed are you—speak,
stranger!—on your father's side?   215

OIDIPOUS

Alas, what will I suffer, my child?

ANTIGONE

Speak, since you're stepping to the brink.

OIDIPOUS

Then I shall speak: I've no way to conceal it.

CHORUS

These are long delays. Now be quick!

OIDIPOUS

Do you know one born from Laios?[25]

CHORUS

Oh! Oh!Oh!   220

OIDIPOUS

And the family of the Labdakids?[26]

CHORUS

Oh Zeus!

OIDIPOUS

The miserable Oidipous?

---

[25] Laios was Oidipous' father, whom he killed in ignorance of their relationship (Introduction, pp. 17-18).
[26] Labdakos was Laios' father. His descendants are called the Labdakids.

CHORUS

What? Is *that* who you are?

OIDIPOUS

Don't feel dread at my words!

CHORUS

Oh! Oh! Oh!

OIDIPOUS

Ill-fated am I!

CHORUS

Oh! Oh!

OIDIPOUS

Daughter, what's going to happen now?   225

CHORUS

Out! Go far away from this land!

OIDIPOUS

But how will you redeem your promises?

CHORUS

Fated payment comes to no one
who pays back what he suffered first.[27]
One deceit matched to other   230
deceits gives pain, not favor,
to keep in return.
Away again from these seats!
Be gone once more from my land in haste,
lest you impose some further debt   235
of suffering on my city![28]

ANTIGONE

Respectful-minded strangers,[29]
since you could not endure
my old father here—after hearing

---

27   The chorus claim to be justified in injuring Oidipous because he injured them first
     by not revealing his identity. The language of payment and repayment is often
     used in Greek to express the idea of retaliatory justice (e.g. 994-5) or, conversely,
     reciprocal favors and friendship (e.g. 635, 1203).
28   The chorus fear that Oidipous' polluting presence will force them to "pay" a "debt"
     of suffering to the gods (cf. Introduction, p. 28).
29   "Respect" (*aidōs*) is an important concept in popular Greek ethics. It implies a
     sensitivity to the due claims of others, whether divine or mortal. Antigone refers
     here to the chorus' religious reasons for rejecting Oidipous. But she will also beg
     for the "respect" due to suppliants (247), as Polyneices does later (1268).

tell of his unwilling deeds[30]— 240
at least, I supplicate you, strangers,
pity my wretched self. For I beseech you
on behalf of my long-suffering father—
beseech you, looking into your eyes
with eyes not blind, like one born of 245
your own blood—that this miserable man
may meet respect; on you as on a god
we, long-suffering, depend. Come, grant
this unexpected favor, I beseech you
by whatever you hold dear at home— 250
child, marriage-bed, property, or god.
For you will not see any mortal who,
if a god leads him on, can escape.[31]

[The parodos ends, and the meter returns to the iambic trimeters used for spoken dialogue.]

CHORUS

Know, child of Oidipous, that we do pity you
and this man for your circumstances equally; 255
But, terrified at what the gods may send, we lack
the strength to say more than the words that we just spoke.

OIDIPOUS

What is the use of glory then? What is the use
of fine repute that flows away in vain? They say
that Athens is most reverent, that it alone 260
is able to protect a stranger when he is
beset by evils, it alone can bring him aid.
Where are those claims in my case? After making me
rise from these steps you're driving me away, in dread
of nothing but my name—not, certainly, my body 265
or my deeds; for know this much, my deeds were suffered
more than perpetrated—were it right to speak
about my mother and my father, which is why
you fear me so; this I know well. Yet how am I
by nature evil? I who acted in return 270
for what I suffered, so that even if I'd done
it consciously, I'd not be evil even then.

---

[30] Oidipous' past deeds were "unwilling" or "against his will" (521, 964, 977, 987) because although he willingly killed Laios and married Jokasta, he was ignorant at the time of their relationship to himself, and therefore did not "willingly" murder his father or marry his mother.

[31] On this idea see Introduction, p. 26.

In fact, I reached that point unknowingly, while those
who made me suffer, they destroyed me knowingly.[32]
Therefore I supplicate you, strangers, by the gods,   275
just as you made me move away, so too protect
me, and by no means, while you're honoring the gods,
deny the gods their due. You should consider that
they look upon those mortals who are reverent,
they also look on the irreverent ones, nor ever   280
yet has an impious man escaped from them.
With their help, then, don't cloud the blessedness of Athens
by becoming servants to impious deeds.
But, just as you took in this suppliant under pledge,
so rescue me and be my guard. Do not, seeing   285
this face so hard to look upon, dishonor me.
For I have come as someone sacred, reverent,
and bringing benefit to this town's people. When
the one who has authority is here, whoever
is your leader, you'll hear all and understand;   290
meanwhile, by no means make yourself an evil man.

CHORUS

A great necessity obliges me, old man,
to view your arguments with awe; for they have been
expressed in no slight words. For me it will suffice
that this decision should remain with our land's lords.   295

OIDIPOUS

Where, strangers, is the king who rules over this land?

CHORUS

He's at his father's town within the land; the person
who first sent me here has gone to summon him.

OIDIPOUS

And do you think that he'll concern himself or think
about the blind man, so that he'll come here himself?   300

CHORUS

Most certainly he will, once he has heard your name.

OIDIPOUS

But who is there who will report that word to him?

CHORUS

The path is long; but many travelers' tales are fond

---

[32] Oidipous' parents attempted to destroy him as a baby, in order to avoid the terrible
      prophecies. But he may also be referring to the intentional cruelty of his enemies
      at Thebes, who "destroyed" him by casting him into exile (cf. 985-7).

of wandering, and when he hears them, he'll be here—
have confidence! Your name, old man, is so widespread 305
among all people that—even if he is slow
with sleep—on hearing who you are he'll quickly come.

OIDIPOUS

May he arrive then with good fortune for his city
and for me; what good man is not his own friend?

[Antigone catches sight of a figure in the distance. Her excited speech is in iambic trimeters, the meter of spoken verse, but is punctuated by shorter, non-iambic lines at 315 and 318.]

ANTIGONE

Oh Zeus! What should I say, father, where turn my thoughts? 310

OIDIPOUS

What's happening, Antigone my child?

ANTIGONE

                            I see
a woman moving closer to us, mounted on
a colt from Aetna;[33] on her head she wears a hat
from Thessaly,[34] to keep the sunshine from her face.
What should I say? 315
Is it? Or isn't it? Is my mind wandering?
It is, yes... No, it's not ... I don't know what to say.
I'm overcome!
It's no one else! Bright glances from her eyes as she
approaches greet me, indicating clearly that 320
this is the person of Ismene, no one else!

OIDIPOUS

What did you say, my child?

ANTIGONE

                        I see your daughter, my
blood-sister! Soon we'll recognize her by her voice.

[Enter Ismene from the direction of Thebes.[35]]

ISMENE

Father and sister, sweetest pair of names to me!
I found you with such difficulty: now once more 325

---

[33] Aetna is in Sicily, an island famous for its horses.
[34] This is a kind of broad-brimmed felt traveling hat.
[35] We do not know whether a real horse was used for Ismene's entrance, or it was left to the audience's imagination. Most likely, however, she enters on foot. We may imagine that she has left her horse with the attendant mentioned at 334.

it's difficult to see you through my tears of pain![36]

OIDIPOUS

Child, you have come?

ISMENE

Father ill-starred to look upon!

OIDIPOUS

Child, you've appeared?

ISMENE

Not without anguish to myself.

OIDIPOUS

Come touch me, daughter!

ISMENE

I am holding both of you.

OIDIPOUS

My seed, blood-sisters![37]

ISMENE

Oh what miserable nurture![38]   330

OIDIPOUS

Of her and me?

ISMENE

And my ill-fated self, the third.

OIDIPOUS

Why did you come, child?

ISMENE

Father, from concern for you.

OIDIPOUS

Was it from yearning?

ISMENE

And to bring you a report
in person, with the only house-slave I could trust.

OIDIPOUS

Where are the young men, your blood-brothers, for such pains?   335

ISMENE

They're where they are; their present lot is full of dread.

---

36 Ismene's joy is mixed with pain at the wretched condition in which she has found
    her father and sister.
37 The ambiguity of these words reminds us that Oidipous' daughters are also his
    sisters.
38 Ismene is exclaiming at the wretched sustenance of her father and sister. "Nurture,"
    especially that of Oidipous, is an important theme in the play.

OIDIPOUS

Those two! In every way they are exactly like
the customs that hold sway in Egypt, in their nature
and their attitude toward life's nurturance.[39]
For there it is the males who sit at home and weave, 340
their consorts who provide life's nurture from outside.
So too with you, my children: those to whom these pains
were fitting stay at home like maidens in the house,
while you two in their place bear painfully, for my
unhappy self, my evils. For Antigone, 345
since leaving youthful nurture and acquiring strength
of body, has been wandering, ill-fated one,
with me, an old man's guide;[40] a vagrant going often
through the savage forest, barefoot and unfed;
often in pouring rain and burning sun, enduring 350
anguish, she ranks life at home in second place,
if only her poor father may have nurturance.
And you, child,[41] came out to your father in the past
with all the prophecies concerning me,[42] in secret
from the Kadmeans,[43] and were a trusty guardian 355
of my cause, when I was driven from the land.
And now again, Ismene, what's the tale you've come
to bring your father? On what errand have you stirred
from home? You've not come empty-handed— that I clearly
know. Can you be bringing me some dreadful news? 360

ISMENE

The sufferings I suffered, father, seeking out
where you were dwelling for your nurture—those I shall
pass over and let go. I do not wish to grieve
twice over, feeling pain and then recounting it.
But I have come to tell you of the evils that 365

---

[39] This passage was probably suggested to Sophocles by the discussion of Egyptian customs at Herodotus 2.35. It is a fantastical piece of anthropology, totally reversing Greek gender norms.

[40] The word Oidipous uses here (*gerontagōgei*) echoes the common Greek word for a schoolboy's attendant (*paidagōgos*), thus underlining the reversal of natural roles in the relationship between father and daughter.

[41] I.e. Ismene, who has been living at Thebes but has still done all she can to help her exiled father.

[42] It appears that various prophecies have been made concerning Oidipous during his exile. Ismene brings news of the most recent and significant one (387-94), and Polyneices mentions another (1300).

[43] "Kadmean" means "Theban," after Kadmos, the founder of Thebes.

are now surrounding both your two ill-fated sons.
It pleased them formerly to leave the throne to Kreon
and not stain the city, as they looked with reason
on the ancient ruin of the family,
on how it overwhelmed your miserable house;   370
but evil strife has come now, from some god and their
own wicked minds, and entered the thrice-miserable
pair, making them grasp at rule and kingly power.[44]
The younger one, the lesser-born in years, has now
deprived the first-born, Polyneices, of the throne,   375
and driven him in exile from his fatherland.
The latter, so the general story goes among
us, went in exile to the Argive valley where
he's mustering new marriage ties and friends with shields,[45]
resolved that he will either occupy the plain   380
of Kadmos in due honor, or rise to the sky.[46]
This is not just an empty string of words, father,
but dreadful deeds. As for your pains, however, at
what point the gods will pity them, I cannot learn.

OIDIPOUS

Have you obtained some hope, then, that the gods will have   385
regard for me, so that I may one day be saved?

ISMENE

Yes, father, judging from the recent prophecies.

OIDIPOUS

Which ones? What have the oracles pronounced, my child?

ISMENE

That you'll be sought for one day by the people living

---

44   "King" is used in this translation for *tyrannos* and related words. Although *tyrannos* gives us the word "tyrant," it does not mean a tyrant in our sense, but any absolute ruler, whether benign or tyrannical (it is used, for example, of Oidipous in *OT*, and Kreon uses it of himself at 851). This kind of rule was, however, often regarded with suspicion, especially by the democratic Athenians, and *tyrannos* can have pejorative overtones. Note that such language is never used of Theseus or Athens in this play, but only of rule over Thebes (373, 419, 449, 1338). In other places, the word "king" translates various different Greek words for a monarch.

45   Polyneices married the daughter of the king of Argos, thus making the Argives his allies. The rest of his allies are listed at 1313-22.

46   The text is problematic here. On this interpretation, it means that Polyneices thinks he will either win "sky-high" glory, or die and be buried honorably in the land of Thebes (a theme obviously relevant to *Antigone* as well as this play). Compare 1306-7.

there,[47] in life and death, for their protection's sake.   390

OIDIPOUS

But who could prosper on account of such a man?

ISMENE

Their power is coming to depend on you, it's said.

OIDIPOUS

When I no more exist, is *that* when I'm a man?[48]

ISMENE

Before, the gods destroyed you; now they raise you upright.

OIDIPOUS

It's poor to raise in old age one who fell in youth.   395

ISMENE

Yet know that on account of this Kreon will come
to you in just a little time—not long at all.

OIDIPOUS

To do what deed, my daughter? Tell me what this means.

ISMENE

To settle you near Kadmos' land and keep you in
their power, not letting you set foot within its bounds.   400

OIDIPOUS

How can I help them if I lie outside their gates?

ISMENE

Your grave, if it's not treated well, will burden them.[49]

OIDIPOUS

One might learn this much by one's wits, without a god.

ISMENE

This is the reason why they want to settle you
close to the land, where you won't be in your own power.   405

OIDIPOUS

And will they shade my body with the dust of Thebes?[50]

---

[47] I.e. at Thebes.

[48] Oidipous expresses his abject condition by declaring that he no longer exists (cf. 109-10). He takes a dim view of the divine process that has reduced him to such a state before making him once more "a man" by giving him power over the lives of others.

[49] Ritual offerings were regularly made to placate the dead. The tomb of a hero, if neglected, was especially dangerous (see Introduction, p. 30).

[50] Oidipous is asking whether he is to be buried in Theban soil.

ISMENE

The blood of your own race will not permit this, father.[51]

OIDIPOUS

In that case they won't ever get me in their power!

ISMENE

One day, then, this will burden all the Kadmeans.

OIDIPOUS

When what conjunction of events appears, my child?   410

ISMENE

Caused by your anger, when they halt there at your tomb.

OIDIPOUS

From whom, child, did you hear what you are telling me?

ISMENE

Some men who came as envoys from the Delphic hearth.[52]

OIDIPOUS

Did Phoibos really say these things concerning me?

ISMENE

So said those men returning to the plain of Thebes.   415

OIDIPOUS

Has either of my sons, then, heard about these things?

ISMENE

Yes, both of them alike; both understand them well.

OIDIPOUS

And those most evil ones, on hearing of these things,
placed kingly power above their yearning for myself?[53]

ISMENE

I grieve to hear this, but must bear it nonetheless.   420

OIDIPOUS

Then never may the gods extinguish their predestined
strife! And may the final outcome for them both
come to depend on me in this, the battle that
they're set on now and raising up their spears to fight;
then neither will the one who has now got the scepter   425
and the throne remain, nor will the one who's gone

---

51 Ismene is referring as delicately as possible to Oidipous' parricide, which allegedly
    prevents him from being buried in Theban soil.
52 It was common practice for a city to send envoys to consult oracles, especially
    Apollo's oracle at Delphi, about matters of public importance.
53 Oidipous' sons showed that they valued the throne above their father by neglect-
    ing him until they discovered that their rule depended on him.

ever return. For when I, who begot them, was
thrust in dishonor from my fatherland, those two
did not prevent it or defend me, but I was
sent forth by them, uprooted and proclaimed an exile.   430
    Now, you may say that it was reasonable for
the city to bestow that gift on me, since at
the time I wanted it. Not so! On that first day,
when my heart seethed, and death was sweetest to me—to
be stoned to death with rocks—at that time nobody   435
appeared to help fulfill my passionate desire;
but after time had passed, when all my anguish had
been softened and I learned my raging heart had run
too far, chastising to excess my prior faults,
then, after so much time, the city drove me from   440
the land by force, and they, their father's sons, who had
the power to help their father, were not willing to
take action, and for lack of one small word from them
I've roamed abroad, an exiled beggar, ever since;
from these two maidens I have had—as far as nature   445
grants them—nurturance of life, security
within the land, the aid that kinship should provide;
but those two chose above the father of their birth
a throne, and sceptered sway, and kingship in the land.
So they shall never gain an ally in this man!   450
And benefit shall never come to them from that
Kadmean rule! So much I know, from hearing this
girl's prophecies and ruminating on the age-
old sayings Phoibos has fulfilled for me at last.
    Therefore let them send Kreon forth to seek me out,   455
and any other person who has strength within
that city. If you're willing to protect me, with
the help of these, your solemn guardian goddesses,
then, strangers, you will gain a great protector for
this city, and bring pain upon my enemies.   460

CHORUS

You're worthy of our pity, Oidipous, both you
and these two children here. And since in speaking you
include yourself as a protector of this land,
I wish to counsel you to your advantage now.

OIDIPOUS

Oh dearest host, I shall fulfill all your advice.   465

CHORUS

Perform a cleansing rite for these divinities
to whom you came at first and trampled on their soil.

OIDIPOUS

Explain it, strangers. In what way must this be done?

CHORUS

First carry sacred offerings of liquid from
an ever-flowing spring; touch them with holy hands.   470

OIDIPOUS

And after I have taken this untainted stream?

CHORUS

There are some mixing-bowls—the handiwork of a
skilled craftsman; wreathe their rims and handles on each side.

OIDIPOUS

With twigs, or woolen cloths, or in what other way?

CHORUS

Taking the freshly shorn-off fleece of a young lamb.   475

OIDIPOUS

All right. But how must I conclude what happens next?

CHORUS

Pour out the liquids, standing facing towards the dawn.[54]

OIDIPOUS

Am I to pour them from the bowls of which you spoke?

CHORUS

Yes, in three streams; empty the last one thoroughly.

OIDIPOUS

What should I fill it with? Explain that to me too.   480

CHORUS

Water and honey; but do not add any wine.[55]

OIDIPOUS

And when the dark-leaved earth receives these offerings?

CHORUS

Place thrice nine sprigs of olive-wood upon it with
both hands, and then invoke their favor with this prayer...

---

[54] This refers not to the time of day but to the east (representing light and purity).
Offerings to "earth" divinities like the Eumenides were never made until after
midday.

[55] The Eumenides never received offerings of wine (cf. 100). Honey is a traditional
offering to the dead. Wool, water, and the olive were all thought to have purifying
power.

OIDIPOUS

I wish to hear this: it's the most important part. 485

CHORUS

... just as we call them Kindly Ones,[56] so too with kindly
breasts to take in and protect the suppliant.
So should you beg them—you or someone in your place—
speaking inaudibly, not crying out aloud.
Then move away and don't turn back.[57] If you do this 490
I'd stand beside you, stranger, in all confidence;
but otherwise I would feel dread on your account.[58]

OIDIPOUS

My children, do you hear these local strangers' words?

ANTIGONE

We heard; command us to perform what must be done.

OIDIPOUS

I cannot walk this road, for I'm disabled by 495
two evil things—my weakness and my lack of sight.
Let one of you two go and do this; for I think
one living thing suffices for a multitude
to make this payment, if that one is well-disposed.
Take action, you two, quickly! But do not leave me 500
alone. My body does not have the strength to move
along if I'm bereft of help or have no guide.

ISMENE

I'll go there and fulfill the rite. But where's the spot
where I must do this service? This I wish to learn.

CHORUS

It's on the far side of this grove, stranger. If you 505
lack anything, the one who dwells there will explain.

ISMENE

I'll go and do it. You, Antigone, stay here
and be our father's guard: for parents' sake, though one
may labor painfully, one must not mind the pain.

[Exit Ismene into the grove. The chorus and Oidipous now sing a lyric dialogue.]

CHORUS *Strophe A*

It's dreadful, stranger, to wake the evil now long at rest.

---

56 This is the literal meaning of "Eumenides" (Introduction, p. 23).
57 After offerings to "earth" divinities one had to avert one's eyes.
58 The chorus are concerned for Oidipous' welfare (cf. 464), but they also fear the
   goddesses' anger on their own behalf.

Yet I long passionately to inquire...   511

OIDIPOUS

What is this?

CHORUS

...about the wretched grief, revealed
as ineluctable, that you confronted.

OIDIPOUS

In the name of your own hospitality,   515
don't shamelessly expose my sufferings!

CHORUS

But stranger, I desire to hear it told aright,
this widespread tale that is far from fading.

OIDIPOUS

Alas!

CHORUS

Be content, I supplicate.

OIDIPOUS

Woe! Woe!

CHORUS

Be persuaded, as I was in all *you* desired.   520

OIDIPOUS   *Antistrophe A*

I bore evil, strangers, bore it against my will—god be my
   witness!
None of those things was my own choice.

CHORUS

But why, then?

OIDIPOUS

The city bound me, knowing nothing, by an evil bed   525
to a marriage that was doom.

CHORUS

Was it really with your mother, as I hear,
that you filled your infamous marriage bed?

OIDIPOUS

Alas! It is death to hear those words,
stranger! But these two girls, my own...   530

CHORUS

What are you saying?

OIDIPOUS

... children, but a two-fold doom...

CHORUS

Oh Zeus!

OIDIPOUS

... sprang from our common mother's labor-pains.

CHORUS   *Strophe B*

So they are both your offspring and...

OIDIPOUS

Yes, sisters in common with their father!   535

CHORUS

Oh!

OIDIPOUS

Oh indeed! The wheeling
onslaught of countless evils!

CHORUS

You suffered...

OIDIPOUS

I suffered burdens accursed.

CHORUS

You did...

OIDIPOUS

I *did* nothing!

CHORUS

What then?

OIDIPOUS

I accepted
a gift. How I wish—my long-suffering heart!—   540
I had never taken that reward for my help.[59]

CHORUS   *Antistrophe B*

What then, unhappy man? Did you murder...

OIDIPOUS

What is this? What do you want to learn?

CHORUS

...your own father?

OIDIPOUS

Ah! A second

---

[59]   Oidipous received the throne of Thebes and the hand of Jokasta as a reward for
saving the city from the Sphinx (Introduction, p. 18).

stroke! Sickness upon sickness![60]

CHORUS

You killed...

OIDIPOUS

I killed. But I have...   545

CHORUS

What's this?

OIDIPOUS

... a just defense.

CHORUS

What then?

OIDIPOUS

I'll tell you.

I murdered and destroyed him, caught by doom,
but clean under the law: I came to this in ignorance.

*[Enter Theseus from the direction of Athens. The lyric dialogue ends, and the meter
returns to iambic trimeters.]*

CHORUS

But see, our lord has now arrived, the offspring of
Aigeus, Theseus, who was sent for at your word.   550

THESEUS

Hearing from many people in the time gone by
about the way your eyes were bloodily destroyed,
I recognized you, child of Laios; now too, when
I see you on this road, I further understand.
Both your attire and your unhappy face make clear   555
to me that you are who you are. In pity, then,
I want to ask, ill-fated Oidipous, with what
entreaty for the city or myself you stopped
here, you and the ill-fated maiden by your side.
Explain to me. For you would have to speak of some   560
most dreadful deed to make me stand aside from you,
I who know well that I was raised a stranger too,
like you, and wrestled in a strange land with more dangers
threatening my life than any other man,[61]

---

60   "Sickness" is a common metaphor for mental anguish (cf. 598, 765).
61   Theseus was "reared as a stranger" because he was raised by his mother, Aithra,
     at her home in Troezen in the Peloponnese (see Map 2), without knowing that
     his father was king of Athens. On reaching adulthood he traveled to his father's
     home, performing many heroic deeds along the way (the "dangers threatening
     my life"). Similarly Oidipous was raised in Corinth by his adopted father Polybos,

so that I'd never turn aside from helping to 565
protect someone who is a stranger, like you now.
For I know well that I'm a man, and that I have
no greater share than you do of tomorrow's day.

OIDIPOUS

Theseus, by making this short speech your nobleness
allows me to have need of little speech myself. 570
For who I am, and from what father born, and from
what land arrived, all this you've accurately said,
so that no more remains for me to tell except
what I desire from you, and then my words are done.

THESEUS

Explain this to me now, that I may learn it all. 575

OIDIPOUS

I come to give to you my miserable body
as a gift—not excellent to look at, yet
the profit that it brings is better than fine looks.

THESEUS

What kind of profit do you claim that you have brought?

OIDIPOUS

You'll learn of it in time, but not, I think, just yet. 580

THESEUS

At what time, then, will what you offer be made clear?

OIDIPOUS

When I am dead and you consign me to the tomb.

THESEUS

You beg life's final rites, then, and what comes between
you have forgotten, or it has no worth for you.

OIDIPOUS

Just so; for with these things I reap the others too.[62] 585

THESEUS

This favor that you beg of me is slight in scope.

OIDIPOUS

Look out, though! This is no small struggle, no indeed!

---

not knowing that his biological father Laios was king of Thebes. On discovering
his true identity he suffered great misery, including his present wanderings as a
stranger. Theseus manages to emphasize tactfully the experiences that unite them
without touching on the qualitative difference in their misfortunes.

[62] I.e., if he is promised burial in Attica the remainder of his life is also secure, since
Theseus must protect him from any threat.

THESEUS

Is it your offspring that you're speaking of, or what?

OIDIPOUS

They wish to take me by necessity to Thebes.

THESEUS

If that is what you want, exile is no fine thing.   590

OIDIPOUS

When I did want it, they would not let me return.

THESEUS

Rage is not beneficial among evils, fool.

OIDIPOUS

Learn from me first, and then advise; for now, refrain.

THESEUS

Explain. For I must form a judgment prior to speech.

OIDIPOUS

I've suffered dreadful evils, Theseus, piled on evils.   595

THESEUS

You mean the age-old circumstances of your kin?

OIDIPOUS

Not that; for each and every Greek cries that aloud.

THESEUS

What is your sickness, then, beyond the human scale?

OIDIPOUS

This is my situation: I was driven from
my land by my own seed, and I can never go   600
back there again, because I am a parricide.

THESEUS

How can they send you back, if you're to dwell apart?

OIDIPOUS

Divine pronouncements place necessity on them.

THESEUS

What is the suffering they dread from oracles?

OIDIPOUS

In this land, by necessity, they'll be struck down.   605

THESEUS

How could my dealings with them turn to bitterness?

OIDIPOUS

Oh dearest offspring of Aigeus, for the gods
alone there is no growing old, nor ever death;
but time, all-powerful, confounds all other things.

The strength within the land decays, the body's strength   610
decays; trust dies, distrustfulness springs into life,
the breath of friendship does not stay the same, either
from man to man or from one city to the next.
For some folk now, for others at a later time,
delightful things turn bitter and then dear again.   615
So too with Thebes: if everything between you now
is fine and tranquil weather, yet still countless time,
as it goes by, gives birth to countless nights and days,
in which they'll scatter with a spear the pledges that
are now in harmony, because of some small thing.   620
When that time comes, my sleeping and concealed cold corpse
shall one day drink up their hot blood, if Zeus is still
Zeus and if Phoibos, son of Zeus, speaks clear and true.
    But since it does not please me to recount what should
rest undisturbed, let me stop where I started out.[63]   625
But only guard your trust, and you will never say
you took in Oidipous to dwell here uselessly
within this region—if the gods don't play me false.

CHORUS

My lord, this man has long appeared as one who will
fulfill these words and others like them for this land.   630

THESEUS

Who would cast out the kindness,[64] then, of such a man?
For first, a common hearth of spear-friendship with us
is open to him at all times.[65] Second, he has
arrived here as a suppliant of the gods, and pays
no little tribute to this land and me. Revering   635
this, I'll never cast his favor out, but let
him dwell within our land here as a citizen.

[He addresses the chorus.]

    If it is pleasing to the stranger to stay here,
I shall appoint you as his guard, or he may come
with me. I give you, Oidipous, the choice of what   640
is pleasing to you. I'll agree with what you choose.

---

[63] The precise details of Oidipous' death must remain secret (cf. 1522-9). Where he
      "started out" was with a promise of benefit to Athens (576-8).
[64] This word (*eumeneia*) is often used for the good will of the gods, and echoes the
      name of the Eumenides (see Introduction, p. 23 and cf. 486-7).
[65] Theseus is referring to a pre-existing military alliance between the royal houses
      of Athens and Thebes.

OIDIPOUS
Zeus, may you give good fortune to such men as this!

THESEUS
What's your desire, then? To come with me to my house?

OIDIPOUS
If it were lawful for me. But the place is here...

THESEUS
Where you'll do what? I shall not stand against your will.   645

OIDIPOUS
... where I shall overpower those who cast me out.

THESEUS
The gift you speak of from your presence would be great.

OIDIPOUS
If what *you* say stands firm, fulfilled for me by you.

THESEUS
Have confidence in this man here; I won't betray you.[66]

OIDIPOUS
I shall not place you under oath, like someone evil.   650

THESEUS
You would obtain no more by that than by my word.

OIDIPOUS
What will you do then?

THESEUS
                              Just what are you shrinking from?

OIDIPOUS
Men will arrive...

THESEUS
                              These folk will make that their concern.

OIDIPOUS
Look out, in leaving...

THESEUS
                              Don't explain what I must do.

OIDIPOUS
It's necessary for one who shrinks ...

THESEUS
                              My heart shrinks not.   655

---

[66] "This man" is a common Greek idiom for referring to oneself (cf. e.g. 450, 1328, 1546, 1617-18 and n. on *OT* 535).

OIDIPOUS
You do not know the threats...

THESEUS

I do know that no man
will take you from this place by force against my will.
For threateners have often uttered many words of threat
in vain from rage; but when the mind regains control
over itself, those empty threatenings are gone. 660
So too with them, perhaps: though they made bold to speak
those dreadful words of taking you away, I know
their voyage to get here will be long and hard to sail.[67]
Now I advise you to be confident, even
apart from my resolve, if Phoibos sent you here; 665
but even if I'm absent, still I know my name
will guard you so that you won't suffer evil things.

[Exit Theseus, in the direction of Colonus and Athens. The chorus now dance and sing their first stasimon ("song in position") (668-719).[68]]

CHORUS *Strophe A*

In this land of fine horses, stranger,
you've reached the best shelter on earth,
white Colonus;[69] here may be found 670
most often the clear-toned nightingale,
plaintively piping within green glades,
occupying the wine-dark ivy
and the leaves of the god
where none may tread, 675
with their countless berries,
sheltered from sun,
and from every stormy wind.[70]
Here the Bacchic reveler ever steps,
Dionysos, attended by nurses divine.[71] 680

---

[67] This is a metaphor, since the journey from Thebes to Athens is over land (see Map 2). Sailing is a common source of metaphor among the Greeks (a sea-faring people), especially for risky undertakings (cf. 1746).

[68] The song marks and celebrates the moment of Oidipous' formal acceptance by Theseus as an Athenian citizen (637). The first strophic pair is devoted to Colonus, and the second to Attica more generally.

[69] This adjective refers to the fact that the soil at Colonus was light in color.

[70] The "god" in this sentence is Dionysos, to whom ivy, grape-vines and other plants were sacred (Introduction, p. 22).

[71] The infant Dionysos was nursed by nymphs, who remained his companions in the Bacchic revelry that was distinctive of him and his cult.

Under the heavenly dew   *Antistrophe A*
ever flourishes, day by day,
the finely-clustered narcissus,
ancient crown of the two great goddesses,
and the gold-beaming crocus;[72]   685
the sleepless springs never dwindle,
distributing Cephisus' stream,[73]
but each day in untainted flood
it reaches always, with swift fertility,
the plains of the broad-breasted earth.   690
The choruses of Muses
do not abhor this land,
nor Aphrodite of the golden reins.[74]

And there is something I've   *Strophe B*
not heard of in Asia's land,[75]   695
or springing up in the great Dorian isle
of Pelops,[76] a self-generating growth,
unconquered by any hand,
bringing fear to hostile spears,[77]
which flourishes most greatly in this land: 700
the leaf of the grey, child-nurturing olive.
This no one, young or dwelling with old age,
shall efface with ravaging hand.
For it's watched over by the eye,

---

[72] The narcissus was sacred to Demeter and Persephone, the two great goddesses of the underworld, and was associated with death. The crocus and the nightingale (mentioned in the strophe) also symbolize death, as befits the place where Oidipous will die.

[73] The Cephisus is a river flowing to the west of Athens, near Colonus (see Map 2).

[74] Aphrodite, goddess of erotic desire, was sometimes portrayed as driving a golden chariot drawn by birds (sparrows, doves, or swans).

[75] To the ancient Greeks, "Asia" signified what is now known as the Middle East.

[76] "Isle of Pelops" is the literal meaning of "Peloponnese," the southern Greek peninsula largely inhabited by Dorian Greeks. Olives did grow here and in "Asia," but the first tree did not "spring up" there (see next note).

[77] Attic legend had it that the first olive tree sprang from the Acropolis in Athens at the command of Athena. Certain olive trees were sacred, including one on the Acropolis, which was said to have returned miraculously to life after burning during the Persian Wars (hence "self-generating"). It was also said that invaders had spared the sacred olives because they were under the protection of Athena (hence "source of fear"). "Unconquered by any hand" could allude to either or both of these stories.

ever-seeing, of Zeus Morios,[78]   705
and by grey-eyed Athena.

Another tale of highest praise   *Antistrophe B*
have I for this my mother-city:
gifts of the great divinity,[79]
greatest boast of our land,   710
the splendor of horses, of colts, of the sea.
You, child of Kronos,[80]
enthroned our city on this boast;
you, Lord Poseidon,
invented the horse-taming bridle,   715
here in these streets first.
And the fine oar-blade flies splendidly by,
leaping to follow the dances
of the Nereids' hundred feet.[81]

*[The chorus end their song and dance. Enter Kreon, with an armed escort, from the
direction of Thebes.]*

ANTIGONE
Oh soil most eulogized with praise, the time has come   720
when you must manifest those shining words in deeds.

OIDIPOUS
What fresh thing is upon us, child?

ANTIGONE
                                        Here's Kreon coming
close upon us, father, with an escort too.

OIDIPOUS
Old men, my dearest friends, from you now may the final
source of my protection be made manifest.   725

CHORUS
Have confidence, it shall be there; even if I
am old, this land's strength is not weakened by old age.

KREON
Oh men of noble birth, who make your dwelling in
this land, I see within your eyes a sudden fear

---

[78] "Morios" is the title of Zeus in his capacity as protector of the sacred olives.
[79] This "great divinity" is Poseidon, god of the sea and of horses.
[80] Poseidon was son of Kronos and Rhea, who, according to Hesiod, were also the
    parents of Zeus, Hades and Hera.
[81] The fifty sea-nymphs known as Nereids are the daughters of the sea-god Nereus.
    They are sometimes portrayed as escorting ships through the waves.

that has sprung up at my arrival in this place.   730
But do not shrink from me, or let fly evil words.
I have not come here wishing to take action, since
I'm old, and understand the city I have reached
is mighty in its strength, if any is in Greece.
But I 've been sent, at my age, to persuade this man   735
to follow me to Kadmean soil—not sent by just
one man, but under orders from the townsfolk as
a whole, since it devolved on me by kinship to
mourn this man's troubles most of all the citizens.
Hear me, long-suffering Oidipous, and come back to   740
your home. The whole of Kadmos' people calls on you,
with justice, and myself the most of all, just as,
unless my nature is the evillest of human
beings, it is I who grieve the most, old man,
at these your evils, seeing you, unhappy one,   745
a stranger going always as a vagrant lacking
livelihood, with one attendant, who—oh woe
is me!—I never thought would fall into a state
as shocking as this girl, ill-fated one, has fallen
into, always tending you and your blind face,   750
living a beggar's life, at her age, and not married
yet, but there for any passing man to seize.[82]
Is this reproach not miserable—woe is me!—
that I have cast at you and me and all our kin?
     But since one can't conceal what is exposed, let me   755
persuade you, Oidipous, by your paternal gods:
come willingly to your paternal town and home,
bidding this city here a friend's farewell, for it
deserves it; but more reverence is justly due
to your home-city, as your nurse from long ago.   760

OIDIPOUS

Oh you who would dare anything! Who would devise
a crafty scheme from any argument that's just!
Why are you trying this? Why do you want to capture
me again, when that would grieve me most of all?
For in the past, when I was sickened by my home-   765
grown evils, and expulsion from the land was my
delight, you did not want to grant this favor to

---

[82]   The extreme length and complexity of this sentence contribute to the artifice of
Kreon's rhetoric. Note that the final words ironically foreshadow his own behavior
(see 818-19).

me though I wanted it;[83] but when I'd had my fill
of rage, and it was sweet to pass my life at home,
that's when you thrust me forth and cast me out, nor was   770
this "kinship" dear to you in any way back *then*.
And now too, when you see this city at my side
is well-disposed to me, with this whole race,[84] you try
to drag me back, using soft words to say harsh things.
Where's the delight in being loved against one's will?   775
It's just as if you begged someone insistently
for something and he gave you nothing, not wanting
to bring you aid; but when your heart was full of your
desire, *that's* when he gave it, when the favor brought
no favor. Would you not find such a pleasure vain?   780
This is the kind of thing you're offering to me—
things good in words, but evil when it comes to deeds.
I'll tell these people too, to make your evil clear:
you've come to take me, not to take me home, but so
that you can make me dwell nearby, and thus your city   785
may escape unharmed by evils from this land.
But that is not your lot, this is: my vengeful spirit
dwelling in the land back there for evermore;
and this is what awaits my children: they will get
just this much of my native land—to die in it.[85]   790
     Do I not understand the way things are at Thebes
better than you? Much better, in so far as what
I hear has clearer and more truthful sources: Phoibos
and his father, Zeus himself. Your specious lips
have come here honed to a sharp edge.[86] Yet by these words   795
of yours you'll get more evil than protection. But
I know I'm not persuading you, so go away,
and leave us to live here: even like this, our life
would not be evil, if we could delight in it.

---

83 These events are dramatized at the end of *OT*. Oidipous' account here makes his
    subsequent exile appear arbitrary and cruel. But exile was the traditional penalty
    for bloodshed (cf. 407), and in the earlier play Oidipous himself curses the killer
    of Laios with exile (*OT* 236-51).
84 "Race" translates *genos*, a word that also means "kin," and was used by Kreon in
    his appeal to Oidipous (738, 754). Its use here suggests that the Athenians have
    replaced the race and family that disowned Oidipous, making Kreon's overtures
    futile.
85 Oidipous is clearly speaking of his sons, not his daughters. But we may recall that
    Antigone too dies at Thebes, as an indirect result of her father's curse.
86 In the Greek there is a pun on the word *stoma*, which can mean both "mouth" and
    "edge."

KREON

Who suffers more misfortune, do you think, from your   800
behavior in this conversation, you or me?

OIDIPOUS

The sweetest thing for me would be for you to fail
in trying to persuade both me and these men here.

KREON

Ill-fated one, won't you grow sense, even with time?
In old age must you still be nurtured as a blight?   805

OIDIPOUS

Your tongue is awesome in its skill; but I don't know
of any just man who speaks well on every case.

KREON

To speak much and speak opportunely aren't the same.

OIDIPOUS

As if the words *you* spoke were brief and opportune.

KREON

No, not to someone with as little sense as you.   810

OIDIPOUS

Be gone!—I'll speak for these men too—and don't blockade
me with a guard here in the place where I must dwell.

KREON

I call these men, not you, to witness what you answer
to your friends. But if I ever capture you...

OIDIPOUS

But with these allies, who could capture me by force?   815

KREON

Even without that you will suffer pain indeed!

OIDIPOUS

What action lies behind this threat that you have made?

KREON

Of your two children I've already seized and sent
away the first; soon I shall take the other too![87]

OIDIPOUS

Alas!

---

87   We may imagine that Kreon secretly kidnapped Ismene from the grove before
his entrance. Alternatively he may have silently sent a guard to do so earlier in
this scene, but this is nowhere signaled in the text and might spoil the surprise of
Kreon's announcement here.

KREON
>   Soon your "alas!" will have still greater cause!   820

OIDIPOUS
>   You have my child?

KREON
>   And this one too before long!

OIDIPOUS
>   Strangers! What will you do? Will you betray me and
>   not drive forth this irreverent man, out of your land?

CHORUS
>   Out of here quickly, stranger! What you're doing now
>   is an injustice; so is what you did before.   825

[Kreon addresses his men.]

KREON
>   Now is your opportunity to take this girl—
>   against her will, if she won't travel willingly.

[Kreon and his men approach Antigone.]

ANTIGONE
>   Oh woe is me! Where can I flee? What god or mortal
>   will protect me?

CHORUS
>   Stranger, what is this you're doing?

KREON
>   I shall not touch this man, but only her who's mine.[88]   830

[He seizes Antigone.]

OIDIPOUS
>   Lords of the land!

CHORUS
>   Stranger, you're doing unjust deeds!

KREON
>   They're just!

CHORUS
>   How are they just?

KREON
>   I'm taking what is mine.

---

88 In *OT*, Oidipous leaves his daughters in Thebes under Kreon's protection (1503-
10). This might justify the latter in calling them "mine." But in *OC* he can scarcely
lay such a claim to Antigone, who has been wandering with her father for many
years.

[The scene is punctuated by a lyric dialogue, in which the strophe (833-43) is separated from the antistrophe (876-86) by some thirty lines of spoken dialogue (844-75). The division of many of the lines between more than one speaker gives an impression of excited confusion, which is enhanced in the lyrics by the use of dochmiacs, a metre often used to express emotional agitation.]

OIDIPOUS   *Strophe*

 Oh city!

CHORUS

 What are you doing, stranger? Let her go!

 Soon you'll come to the test of blows!   835

KREON

 Keep away!

CHORUS

     Not from you, while this is your plan!

KREON

 You'll fight my city, if you make trouble for me!

OIDIPOUS

 Didn't I say this would happen?

CHORUS

       Release the child

 from your hands, quickly!

KREON

      Don't command without power.

CHORUS

 I tell you, set her free!

[Kreon hands Antigone over to his men, to whom his next few words are addressed.]

KREON

     And I tell you, start traveling!   840

[Kreon's men start dragging Antigone towards the road to Thebes.]

CHORUS

 Come here! Come, come, oh people of this place!

 The city is being destroyed, my city, by strength![89]

 Come here, I beg you!

---

[89] Athens is not literally under attack, but its authority is being undermined by the violation of sanctuary and abduction of a suppliant (cf. 879).

ANTIGONE

I'm dragged unhappily away! Oh strangers, strangers![90]

OIDIPOUS

Where are you, child?

ANTIGONE

                                        I'm traveling away by force!   845

OIDIPOUS

Hold out your hands, my child!

ANTIGONE

                                        I do not have the strength!

KREON [to his men]

Why aren't you taking her away?

OIDIPOUS

                                        Woe! Woe is me!

[Exeunt Kreon's men, with Antigone, in the direction of Thebes.]

KREON

You won't be traveling with *those* two scepters to
support you any more.[91] But, since you want to conquer
both your fatherland and friends, at whose command   850
I do these deeds—despite the fact that I am king[92]—
then conquer us: in time, I know, you'll recognize
that you're not doing fine things for yourself, not now
or in the past when you, despite your friends, gave favor
to the anger that has always blighted you.[93]   855

[Kreon starts to follow his men, but the chorus confront him.]

---

90   These words are addressed to the chorus. The Greek word *xenos*, translated
     throughout as "stranger," can also mean "host," "guest," or "guest-friend."
     Those who welcome a stranger initiate guest-friendship, a relationship based on
     mutual hospitality. The word "stranger" may thus be an assertion of friendship,
     depending on the context (cf. e.g. 822, 1119, 1206, 1552).
91   Since a scepter is in origin a staff or walking-stick, the same word is used in Greek
     for both (cf. Introduction, p. 12). There is a nice dramatic irony in Kreon's words,
     since as it turns out, Oidipous will not need the support of these "scepters" any
     longer.
92   It is not clear who is presently ruling at Thebes. Kreon held power after Oidipous
     blinded himself, but Eteokles recently took the throne from Polyneices (375-6). We
     should not press the point. What matters for this scene is that Kreon represents
     the powers that be at Thebes, whether or not he is currently its formal king.
93   In *OT*, Oidipous is portrayed as a quick-tempered man who turns angrily on
     various friends, including Kreon. The most clearly self-destructive consequences
     are the killing of his father Laios (*OT* 806-813) and his consequent self-blinding
     (1268-70; cf. *OC* 433-9, 1195-1200).

CHORUS

Stop, stranger, where you are!

KREON

I tell you, do not touch me!

CHORUS

While I'm deprived of those two, I won't let you go.

KREON

Then soon you'll pay my city a still greater price;
for I shall not lay hands on those two girls alone.

CHORUS

What will you turn to?

KREON

I shall catch and take this man.   860

CHORUS

You're saying something dreadful!

KREON

It shall soon be done
as well, unless the ruler of this land prevents me.

OIDIPOUS

Oh shameless voice, will you indeed lay hands on *me*?

KREON

Silence, I tell you!

OIDIPOUS

No! May these divinities
not stop me speaking out this further curse,[94] on you,   865
most evil one, who've wrenched away and carried off
my unarmed eye by force, before my sightless eyes.
Therefore may Helios, the god who looks upon
all things,[95] grant me that both you and your family
experience some day an old age such as mine.[96]   870

---

[94]   Oidipous has already cursed his sons (421-7). For this further curse on Kreon he
seeks the approval of the goddesses of the grove (cf. Introduction, p. 23). Note
that in such contexts Oidipous avoids calling them by the benevolent name of
Eumenides (cf. 1010, 1391).

[95]   Helios is the god of the sun (Introduction, p. 22).

[96]   Curses were believed to be powerful weapons, and were much used against personal enemies. It is common to wish on one's enemies the same evils that they have
inflicted on oneself, as Oidipous does here. *Ant.* dramatizes some of the disasters that
befell Kreon in his later years, including the suicides of his wife and son. Curses are
not always effective, in life or literature, but Oidipous' curses have a special power,
since he is an emerging cult hero.

KREON
> Do you see this, oh local people of this land?

OIDIPOUS
> They see both me and you, and understand that having
> suffered deeds I am requiting you with words.

KREON
> I shall restrain my rage no longer, but shall take
> this man by force, though I'm alone and slowed by time.   875

OIDIPOUS   *Antistrophe*
> Oh woe is me!

CHORUS
> What audacity you've come with,
> if you think you'll fulfill this, stranger!

KREON
> I do think so!

CHORUS
> Then I consider this a city no more!

KREON
> In just causes even the small conquers the great.   880

OIDIPOUS
> Do you hear the words he utters?

CHORUS
>   But Zeus won't fulfill them,
> that I know.

KREON
>   Zeus might know that, but you don't.

CHORUS
> Is this not an outrage?

KREON
>   An outrage, but you must put up with it!

CHORUS
> *Oh!* All people! *Oh!* Chieftains of the land!
> Come quickly, come!   885
> These men are going too far!

[Enter Theseus, with attendants, from the direction of Colonus.]

THESEUS
> What is this outcry? What's the matter? What fear made
> you stop me sacrificing at the altar to
> the sea-god who protects Colonus? Speak, that I
> may know why I displeased my feet by rushing here.   890

OIDIPOUS

Oh dearest friend—for I have recognized your voice—
I've suffered dreadful things at this man's hand just now.

THESEUS

What things? Who is it that has troubled you? Speak on!

OIDIPOUS

Kreon, whom you see here, has wrenched from me and carried
off the only pair of children that I have.[97]   895

THESEUS

What did you say?

OIDIPOUS

You've heard exactly what I suffered.

THESEUS [to his retinue]

Go to that altar, one of you attendants, quickly
as you can, and lay necessity on all
the people—with and without horses—to make haste
with slack rein from the sacrifice, to where the two   900
roads used by travelers unite,[98] so that the girls
may not pass through, and I may not, subdued by force,
be to this stranger here a thing of mockery.
Go quickly, as I order you!

[He turns towards Kreon.]

As for this man,
if I had reached the pitch of anger he deserves,   905
I would not let him go unwounded from my hand;
but as it is, he shall be disciplined with those
same laws—and only those—that he brought here himself.

[He addresses Kreon.]

For you shall never leave this land until you bring
those girls and set them clearly here before my sight.   910
You've perpetrated deeds that are unworthy of
myself, and those who gave you birth, and your own land,
by entering a city that abides by justice
and determines nothing without law, and then—
flouting this land's authorities and falling on   915
it thus—possessing forcibly what you desired.
You must have thought my city was devoid of men,
or was enslaved somehow, and that I equalled nothing.

---

97 Oidipous no longer counts his sons as his children (cf. 1323-4, 1369, 1383).
98 It is impossible to determine the exact location of this crossroads, where the sub-
sequent battle is supposed to take place.

And yet it was not Thebes that raised you to be evil.
It does not love to nurture unjust men, nor would 920
it praise you, if it should discover that you're robbing
what belongs to me and to the gods, taking
by force a band of miserable suppliants.
I would not step into *your* land—not even in
the most just cause of all—without permission from 925
the ruler of the land, whoever that man was,
to take or plunder anything; I'd understand
how strangers should conduct themselves with citizens.
But you're disgracing your own city, which does not
deserve it, and the growing length of time, which makes 930
you old, is also emptying your mind of sense.
     All right then. As I said before, so I declare
now too: let someone bring the children here as quickly
as they can, unless you want to dwell within
this land by force against your will. These things I say 935
to you come from my mind as well as from my tongue.

CHORUS

See what you've come to, stranger? From your origins
you *look* just, but you're found out *doing* evil deeds.

KREON

I don't say that this city has no men, son of
Aigeus, and my deed was not ill-counseled as 940
you say; I did it recognizing that no zeal
would ever fall upon its citizens for my
blood-kin, to nurture them by force against my will.
I also knew that they would not take in a man
impure, a parricide, one in whose company 945
was found a most unholy marriage, since I knew
they had the hill of Ares in their land, with
its good counsel, which is such that it does not allow
vagrants like this to dwell together with this city.[99]
That's what I trusted in, embarking on this hunt. 950
And I would not have done so, if he had not called
down bitter curses on myself and on my kin.
I thought fit to take action in return for that,

---

[99] Kreon is referring to the Council of the Areopagus (literally, "hill of Ares"), a very
ancient Athenian court with jurisdiction over murder and religious pollution,
which met on a rocky hill near the Acropolis. He is wrong, however, in thinking
that the Areopagus would oblige Athens to reject a suppliant like Oidipous (see
Introduction, p. 29).

since I had suffered: rage has no old age except
for death; only the dead are touched by no distress.   955
   So you'll do what you want, since I'm alone, which makes
me feeble, even if the words I speak are just.
Against your deeds, however, I shall try, despite
my age, to take some action one day in return.

OIDIPOUS

Shameless audacity! Whose old age do you think   960
you are outraging, mine or yours, by casting from
your lips against me murders, marriages and those
appalling circumstances that I bore—oh woe
is me!—against my will. So it was pleasing to
the gods, perhaps in ancient wrath against my kin.[100]   965
For you could find no fault in me myself to be
reproached, nothing that I was paying for when I
commited those great faults against myself and mine.
Explain this: if some prophecy from oracles
came to my father, to be killed by his own child,   970
how could you justly use that in reproaching *me*,
who had not yet sprung into birth from father or
from mother, but was unbegotten at that time?
And if again once I was born—unhappy me!—
I came to blows with my own father, killing him,   975
but did not know what I was doing or to whom,
how could you fairly blame me for this unwilled deed?
And are you not ashamed, you wretch, at forcing me
to speak about the marriage of my mother—your
own sister!—which I 'll now describe? For I shall not   980
stay silent, when you've gone so far, unholy lips!
She bore me, yes, she bore me—oh alas for my
evils!—both of us ignorant, and after bearing
me she bore my children, to her own reproach.
But one thing I know well, that you are willfully   985
maligning me and her, while I both married her
unwillingly, and am unwilling to say this.
No, I shall not be called an evil man, not for
this marriage or my father's murder, which you always
bring against me and so bitterly reproach.   990
Of all my questions, answer me just one: if someone
stood by you—the just man!—and tried here and now

---

[100]   On Oidipous' family curse see Introduction, p. 27.

to kill you, would you ask if he, the killer, was
your father or repay him fast? I think that if
you love to live you would repay the one who was   995
responsible, not scrutinizing what was just.
Such were the evils I stepped into, with the gods
my leaders; so I think even my father's spirit
would not contradict me if it came to life.
But you—for you're not just, but think it fine to say   1000
all things, what may be said and what's unspeakable—
you are reproaching me for this before these folk.
    You also like to flatter Theseus to his face,
and Athens for the fine way it is governed; yet
among so many praises you forget one thing: 1005
if there is any land that understands how to
revere the gods with honors, this one does so best,
from which you, stealing me, a suppliant old man,
have tried to take me, having carried off my girls.
Now, in return for that, I call these goddesses,   1010
I supplicate, assailing them with prayers to come
as my defending allies, so that you may learn
what kind of men afford protection to this city.

CHORUS
The stranger is a good man, lord. His circumstances
have been ruinous, but they deserve defense.   1015

THESEUS
Enough words! Those who did the deed are hurrying
away, while we who suffered it are standing still.

KREON
What then do you command a helpless man to do?

THESEUS
Start off along the road they took, with me and no
one else to serve as escort; for I know full well   1020
you did not come unarmed or unequipped to such
a point of outrage in your present daring deed,
but there's someone you trusted in when doing it.
This must I search out carefully, and not permit
my city to be weaker than a single man.   1025
Proceed now to a place where, if you have the children
in this region, you can point them out to me;
but if your men are fleeing with them in their power,
there's no need for our pains; others will hasten, and
they won't escape to thank the gods outside this land.   1030

Lead on now! Know that you, the captor, have been caught;
fortune has captured you, the hunter: things acquired
unjustly through deceptiveness are not kept safe.
Does this make any sense to you, or are my words
as vain as any spoken when you planned this scheme?   1035

KREON

Nothing that you say here is mine to criticize;
at home, however, we'll know too what we must do.

THESEUS

Go on now, with your threats! You stay here, Oidipous,
and take your ease, relying on my trusty pledge
that—if I don't die first—I shall not stop until   1040
I place your children under your authority.

OIDIPOUS

May benefit reward you for your nobleness,
Theseus, and for your just concern on our behalf.

[Exeunt Theseus, his attendants, and Kreon, in the direction of Thebes. The chorus dance and sing the second stasimon.[101]]

CHORUS   *Strophe A*

    If only I were there!—
    where hostile men,   1045
    wheeling at bay,
    will mingle soon
    with bronze-shouting Ares,[102]
    on the Pythian or the torch-lit shores,[103]
    where the Ladies nurse the solemn rites   1050
    for mortals on whose tongue
    a golden lock has been imposed
    by the attendant Eumolpidae.[104]
    It is there, I think, that Theseus,
    he who rouses the battle,   1055

---

[101] This song imaginatively recreates the confrontation between Kreon's and Theseus' men, while it takes place off-stage (cf. Introduction, p. 14).

[102] The name of Ares, god of war, is often used for warfare.

[103] The "Pythian shores" are near Daphne, about six miles from Colonus, where there was a temple of Apollo, one of whose titles was "Pythian." The "torch-lit shores" are about five miles further on, at Eleusis (see Map 2), the site of an annual torch-lit procession in honor of the two great goddesses of the underworld, Demeter and Persephone, who were often called simply "the Ladies." Their rites, known as the Mysteries, held out the prospect of blissful immortality, and were a secret to all but their initiates.

[104] The priest who carried out the initiation and imposed the pledge of silence was always a member of the family of the Eumolpidae.

will join with self-sufficient aid
the traveling pair of virgin sisters—
somewhere in that region.

Perhaps they're approaching the place   *Antistrophe A*
to the west of the snowy rock,[105]   1060
from the pastures of Oea, on colts,
or fleeing with swift chariots
in rivalry. He will be caught!
Dread is the spirit of Ares
in the people of this place,   1065
dread the prime of Theseus' men!
Every bridle flashes,
and every mounted fighter
rushes with slackened rein,
all who honor Athena,   1070
goddess of horses,[106]
and the earth-embracing sea-god,
Rhea's dear son.[107]

Are they in action, or about to be?   *Strophe B*
My judgment woos me to think   1075
that the suffering soon will cease
of those two girls who have endured
dread things from their own blood-kin.
Zeus will fulfill, fulfill something this day.
I prophesy a noble struggle!   1080
I wish I were a storm-swift dove,
speedy and strong, who could gaze
at the struggle from an airy cloud
lifting up my eye.

Oh lord of the gods, all-ruling, all-seeing Zeus,   *Antistrophe B*
grant that the guardians of this land   1086
may fulfill their ambush,
succeeding in their hunt
with conquering strength,
you and your solemn child, Pallas Athena.   1090

---

[105] The text is difficult here, but the "snowy rock" is probably Mount Aigaleos, to the
        west of which lay the Athenian rural district or deme of Oea (see Map 2).

[106] As goddess of horses, Athena shared an altar at Colonus with Poseidon in his
        capacity as god of horses. This is presumably the altar where Theseus has been
        sacrificing.

[107] I.e. Poseidon. On his parentage see above, n. on 712.

And I long for Apollo the hunter,
and his sister who follows after
the densely-dappled swift-footed deer,[108]
to come as a double defense
to this land and its citizens.   1095

[*Enter Theseus and his attendants, with Antigone and Ismene, from the direction of Thebes.*]

CHORUS

Oh vagrant stranger, you won't tell this watchman that
his prophecies were false: I see the girls close by,
escorted by attendants back this way to us.

OIDIPOUS

Where? Where? What's that? What did you say?

ANTIGONE

                                        Oh father, father!
Which of the gods might grant that you could see this best   1100
of men, who has escorted us back here to you?

OIDIPOUS

My child, are you both really here?

ANTIGONE

                                        Yes, saved by these
hands here, of Theseus and his dearest followers.

OIDIPOUS

Come to your father, children! Give your bodies to
me to embrace, which have returned beyond all hope!   1105

ANTIGONE

You'll get this favor; it is one we yearn to grant.

OIDIPOUS

Where are you, where?

ANTIGONE

                        We're here, together, close to you.

[*Oidipous and his daughters embrace one another.*]

OIDIPOUS

Oh dearest offshoots!

ANTIGONE

                        To their parents all are dear.

---

[108]   In addition to various other functions, Apollo was god of the bow and Artemis, his sister, was goddess of hunting.

OIDIPOUS

Oh scepters, my supports!

ANTIGONE

               Ill-fated, you and us!

OIDIPOUS

I have my dearest ones! Death would no longer make   1110
me wholly miserable, with you two standing near.
Press close on either side of me, my children, growing
one with him from whom you grew, and give me rest,
once desolate, from that unhappy wandering.[109]
And tell me what was done, speaking as briefly as   1115
you can, since little speech suffices girls your age.

ANTIGONE

This is the man who saved us, father. You must hear
from him who did the deed; so my part will be brief.

OIDIPOUS

Stranger, don't be surprised at my persistence, if
I speak at length to my two children, who've appeared   1120
to me beyond all hope. I understand that my
delight in them has reappeared to me from you
and no one else. You of all mortals are the one
who saved them. May the gods reward you as I wish,
both you yourself and this your land: in you alone   1125
of human beings have I found due reverence,
and fairness, and an absence of false-speaking lips.
It is as one who knows these things that I requite
them with these words. For what I have, I have through you,
no other mortal. Hold out your right hand, my lord,   1130
that I may—if it's lawful—touch and kiss your face.
    What am I saying? How could I, one who was born
to misery, want you to touch a man in whom
no stain of evil does not dwell? I do not want
this, nor shall I allow it. Only mortals who   1135
have known such suffering can share in it. I greet
you where you stand; in future show concern for me
in justice, as you've done up to this hour today.

THESEUS

I'm not surprised if you have drawn your words out at

---

[109] The text is obscure here. "Wandering" is a common metaphor for mental anguish.
But it is hard to avoid associating it with the literal wanderings of Oidipous or his
daughters, either in the past, or in the recent kidnapping.

some length, in your delight at these two children here,   1140
nor if you chose to hear their words before my own.
I don't feel this as burdensome at all; for it
is not by means of words that I endeavor to
make my life radiant, but rather by my deeds.
Here is the proof: in none of what I swore to you   1145
did I prove false, old man. For here I am, bringing
these girls alive, unscathed by all those threatenings.
What need to boast in vain of how the fight was won?
You'll learn it for yourself from these girls' company.
    But share with me your judgment of a word that fell   1150
upon my ear just now as I proceeded here—
it is not much to tell, but worthy of surprise,
and human beings should dishonor no event.

OIDIPOUS

What is this word, Aigeus' child? Explain, for I
know nothing of the matter you inquire about.   1155

THESEUS

They say that some man, not your fellow-citizen
but kin to you, has fallen suppliant and taken
up his seat there at the altar of Poseidon,
where I was making sacrifice when I set out.

OIDIPOUS

Where is he from? What is his suppliant's desire?   1160

THESEUS

I only know one thing: it is with you, they tell
me, that he begs to speak just briefly—nothing grand.

OIDIPOUS

What word? That sacred seat is of no small account.

THESEUS

They say he only begs to come and speak with you,
then leave from here unharmed by traveling this road.   1165

OIDIPOUS

Who can he be, who sits in supplication thus?

THESEUS

See if at Argos you have any kin who might
desire to win a favor of this kind from you.

OIDIPOUS

My dearest friend, stop where you are!

THESEUS

What's troubling you?

OIDIPOUS

Do not entreat me...

THESEUS

To perform what deed? Speak on.   1170

OIDIPOUS

From hearing this I know well who the suppliant is.

THESEUS

Whoever is he, that he's worthy of my blame?

OIDIPOUS

My son, who is abhorrent to me, lord; whose words
of all men's I would feel the most distress to hear.

THESEUS

What? Can't you listen, and not do what you do not   1175
desire? Why does it pain you just to hear this man?

OIDIPOUS

His voice, lord, has become most hateful to his father.
Don't make it necessary that I yield in this!

THESEUS

Reflect if supplication makes it necessary—
to safeguard your consideration for the god.   1180

ANTIGONE

Father, let me persuade you, though I'm young to give
you counsel. Let this man provide the favor that
he wishes both to his own mind and to the god;
yield to us both, by granting that our brother come.
He won't, by speaking to your disadvantage, wrench   1185
you forcibly from your resolve—of that you may
be confident. In hearing words what is the harm?
Indeed, words show up actions evilly devised.
You gave him birth; so even if he does to you,
father, most impious deeds of men most evil, it's   1190
not lawful that you do him evil in return.
Respect him. Evil offspring and sharp rage belong
to others too, but when they hear advice their nature's
charmed to acquiescence by the spells of friends.
Reflect not on your present troubles, but on those   1195
you suffered in connection with your father and
your mother. If you look on those, you'll recognize,
I know, that evil is the end of evil rage.

Your reasons for such thinking are not slight ones, you
who are deprived thus of your eyesight. Yield to us!   1200
It's no fine thing that those with just desires should be
insistent, or that someone treated well should fail
to understand how to repay what he's received.

OIDIPOUS

You conquer me, child, winning by your words a pleasure
burdensome to me.[110] Let it be as you please.   1205
Just one thing, stranger—if that man does come here, then
let no one ever get my life into his power.

THESEUS

It's my desire to hear such things just once, old man,
not twice. I do not want to boast; but know that you
are safe, if some one of the gods protects me too.   1210

[*Exit Theseus, in the direction of Colonus.*[111] *The chorus sing the third stasimon,
consisting of one strophic pair with an extra stanza or epode.*]

CHORUS   *Strophe*

    Whoever desires a greater share
    of life, neglecting moderation,
    will in my view be shown up clearly
    as a guardian of stupidity.
    For the long days accumulate   1215
    many things closer to pain,
    nor can you detect delight,
    when someone falls into a life
    longer than needful.
    But the Helper ends it equally,[112]   1220
    when Hades' destiny appears,[113]
    without wedding-song,
    without lyre or dance—
    death at the end.

    Not to be born conquers all reckoning.[114]   *Antistrophe*

---

110 The "you" here is plural, referring to both Antigone and Theseus. Note that this
    passage proves Kreon wrong in his view that Oidipous wants to "conquer" his
    friends (849-52).

111 Theseus returns to the altar of Poseidon, to summon Polyneices and to resume
    the sacrifice interrupted at 887 (cf. 1491-5). This keeps him conveniently available
    for a hasty return at 1500.

112 The "Helper" is death, who delivers all alike from life's sufferings.

113 Hades stands for death (cf. 1440), as Ares does for war (cf. 1047).

114 This is perhaps the most famous statement of a notoriously pessimistic Greek
    proverb.

But once one has appeared,   1225
to go as fast as possible
to the place from which one came,[115]
is second best by far.
While youth is present,
with its empty thoughtlessness,   1230
what trouble wanders far away?
What hardship is not within?
Murders, factions, strife,
battles and resentment!
And the final allotment is old age,   1235
criticized, powerless, unsociable, friendless,
where the evilest of evils dwell together.

So it is with this long-suffering man—not me alone.   *Epode*
As a north-facing headland, wave-lashed all around,   1240
is battered by storms,
so this man's head is battered
by breaking waves of dreadful doom,
his constant companions,
some from the sinking of the sun,   1245
some from its rising,
some at its mid-day beam,
some from the night-shrouded Rhipai.[116]

[Enter Polyneices, from the direction of Colonus.]

ANTIGONE

Here is our stranger, so it seems. At least he comes
alone, without men, father, and his eyes are pouring   1250
tears in streams while he is traveling this way.

OIDIPOUS

Who is he?

ANTIGONE

It's the person that we had in mind
from the beginning: Polyneices—here he is.

---

115 "That place" is the underworld, since humans were sometimes portrayed in myth
     as born from the earth.

116 The Rhipai are mythological mountains in the far north, imagined as permanently
     darkened by stormy gloom. The chorus thus cover the four points of the compass.
     At the same time, the list evokes the passage of a day from morning to night. This
     connects it with the analogy between a human life and a single day, which is
     especially important for the story of Oidipous, because of the riddle of the Sphinx
     (cf. Introduction, p. 17).

POLYNEICES

Alas, what shall I do? Shall I weep first for my
own evils, girls, or shed tears at the sight of my   1255
old father's evils?—he whom I have found here in
a strange land with the two of you, an outcast, in
such clothes as these, whose aged and unlovely filth
is dwelling intimately with this aged man,
wasting his sides, while in the breeze the unkempt hair   1260
upon his head, bereft of eyes, is fluttering;
akin to this, it seems, is what he carries with
him for the nurture of his woeful stomach's needs.[117]
[He turns to address his father directly.]
All this I—ruinous as I am!—learn far too late.
And I bear witness that I've been the evillest   1265
of human beings in your nurture. Find out what
I am from no one else. But even Zeus has sitting
with him on his throne Respect, in all his deeds,
so let her stand beside you, father, also;[118] for
my faults can still be remedied, but not increased.   1270
[He pauses, but Oidipous does not reply.]
Why are you silent?
Speak father! Do not turn away! Have you no answer
for me? Will you send me off dishonored by
your silence,[119] without even telling me what's caused
your wrath?[120]

[Oidipous remains silent, and Polyneices turns back to his sisters.]

Oh my blood-sisters, this man's seed, do you   1275
at least attempt to move our father's lips, hard to
approach and to address, that he may not dismiss
me thus dishonored—as a suppliant of the god—
by saying not one word in answer to my speech.

ANTIGONE

Tell him yourself, long-suffering one, of the desire   1280

---

[117] Oidipous carries a beggar's pouch or wallet to hold the food he has managed to
      beg.
[118] Polyneices personifies *aidōs*, "respect," as an attendant of Zeus. On *aidōs* see above,
      n. on 237. For the personification cf. 1381-2 and 1767.
[119] An answer is part of the "honor" due to Polyneices as a suppliant, since his request
      was to converse with Oidipous (1162, 1164). But both Antigone and Theseus make
      it clear that the suppliancy does not oblige Oidipous to accede to his son's request
      for help (1175-6, 1185-6).
[120] The word translated "wrath" (*mēnis*) is often used for the superhuman wrath of
      gods and cult heroes (cf. 965, 1328).

that brings you here. Abundant words, which give delight
or show distress or stir up pity in some way,
sometimes impart a voice to those whose voice was mute.

POLYNEICES

Then I'll speak out—you guide me well—relying first
upon the god himself as my defender, from   1285
whose shrine the ruler of this land had me rise up
and come here, granting me the right to speak and listen
and depart again along this road unharmed.
I wish to get what I was promised, strangers, from
yourselves, and these two sisters and my father too.   1290
    But now I want to tell you, father, why I've come.
I have been driven from my fatherland and made
an exile, just because I saw fit, as the elder-
born, to take my seat as monarch on your throne.[121]
And in return, Eteokles, the younger-born,   1295
has thrust me from the land, not using words to conquer
me, or testing me with blows and deeds, but through
persuasion of the city[122]—things for which I say
it's your Erinys that is most responsible;[123]
and I have heard this kind of thing from prophets too.   1300
So when I came to Dorian Argos,[124] I acquired
Adrastos as my father-in-law and I made
sworn allies out of all those called preeminent
and honored highly for their spears in Apis' land,[125]
so that with them I might recruit my band of seven   1305
spears to march on Thebes,[126] and either die in a
just cause, or cast the ones who did this from the land.
    All right. What is the reason that I've now come here?
To bring you prayerful entreaties, father, both

---

[121] Polyneices' claim to the throne is weakened by the fact that primogeniture was
       not customary in classical Greece (Introduction, p. 19).
[122] Polyneices suggests that his brother won power by manipulating the people. But
       some of Sophocles' largely democratic audience might have approved of Eteokles'
       methods.
[123] On the Erinyes as avenging spirits see Introduction, p. 23. Here the reference may
       be to the ancestral curse on the house of Oidipous, or to his personal curse upon
       his sons (though Polyneices has not actually witnessed such a curse), or both (since
       the one is manifested through the other).
[124] Argos is in the Peloponnese, whose inhabitants were mostly Dorians (cf. 696-7).
[125] Apis is a name for the Peloponnese (from a mythical king of that name).
[126] Polyneices and his six allies, whom he goes on to list, are the famous "Seven against
       Thebes," who attacked Thebes at its seven gates and tried unsuccessfully to put
       Polyneices on the throne (cf. Ant. 100-154).

from me and from my allies, who have now been set   1310
in place, with seven companies and seven spears,
surrounding all the plain of Thebes. One of them is
spear-hurling Amphiareus, first in power with
the spear, and first in understanding paths of birds;[127]
second is Tydeus, the Aetolian offspring   1315
of Oeneus; third's Eteoklos, Argive by birth;
Hippomedon was sent as fourth by Talaos
his father; fifth, Kapaneus, has been boasting that
he'll crush the town of Thebes and burn it to the ground;[128]
Parthenopaios the Arcadian is sixth   1320
to rush forth, named after the maiden who in time
became his mother—Atalanta's trusty son;[129]
and I, your son, or if not yours, begotten by
an evil destiny, but called your son at least—
I lead the fearless Argive army towards Thebes.   1325
    We supplicate you all together, father, by
these children and by your own life; we beg you to
yield in the heavy wrath that's burdening this man
as I set out for vengeance on my brother, who
has thrust me out and robbed me of my fatherland.   1330
For if there's anything to trust in oracles,
they said power would attend whichever side you joined.
Now by the springs and gods belonging to our race,[130]
I beg you, be persuaded by my words and yield,
since I'm a beggar and a stranger, just like you;   1335
both you and I must flatter others for a home,
both having been allotted the same fate from god.
But he, the king at home, is revelling—oh woe
is me!—in common mockery of both of us.
If you will only stand beside my purpose, then   1340
without much time or trouble I shall shatter him.
I'll take you then and settle you in your own house,

---

127 Amphiareus was an augur, a prophet who foretold the future by observing the
    flight of birds. He foresaw the death of the seven leaders, including himself, in
    the attack on Thebes.
128 Kapaneus was noted for his arrogance, for which he was struck down in the battle
    by a thunderbolt from Zeus (cf. *Ant.* 127-33).
129 Atalanta, who was raised in the woods by a she-bear, would only marry a man
    who could defeat her in a foot race. By this means she postponed marriage until
    Meilanion defeated her by a ruse. Their son's name comes from the word *parthenos*,
    which means "maiden."
130 Since fresh water is essential to human life, springs were often considered symbolic
    of the land. They were protected by nymphs.

myself as well, when I have cast him out by force.
If that is your will too, I'll have my boast; without
you I don't even have the strength to save myself.   1345

CHORUS

Because of him who sent him, Oidipous, say what
is advantageous to this man, then send him back.

OIDIPOUS

Oh men who serve as guardians of this land, were it
not Theseus who had sent him to me, thinking it
was just that he should hear some word from me, never   1350
would he have heard my voice. But as it is he will
depart thus dignified, when he has heard from me
such words as never shall bring gladness to his life.

[He turns to address Polyneices.]

When you, oh you most evil one, possessed the scepter
and the throne at Thebes, which your blood-brother now   1355
possesses, you yourself drove out your father here,[131]
making me citiless and causing me to wear
these garments that you weep to look on, now you've come
into such evils as myself. But these things are
not to be wept at but endured by me while I   1360
still live, thinking of you as of my murderer.
You are the one who gave me anguish as my nurse;
you thrust me out; *you* are the reason I'm a vagrant
begging others for my daily livelihood.
If I 'd not given life to these two girls to be   1365
my nurses, I would not exist, for all *you* did;
but as it is these keep me safe, these nurture me,
these men, not women, when it comes to sharing pain;
but you two had your birth from someone else, not me.

So fate from god is looking on you, but not yet   1370
as it will soon, if those battalions really move
against the town of Thebes. For there's no way that you
shall crush that city, but before that you shall fall
defiled with blood, and your blood-brother equally.[132]
Such curses have I hurled at both of you before,[133]   1375

---

[131] Previously Oidipous accused his sons of failing to speak out against the exile (427-30), and blamed Kreon for perpetrating it (770). But he holds Polyneices equally responsible, especially for failing to recall him when he had the opportunity.

[132] "Defiled" has a double meaning: the brothers will not only be bloodied, but polluted by fratricide.

[133] Cf. 421-7 and see Introduction, p. 19.

and now I call them as my allies, so that you
may both think fit to reverence those who gave you birth,
and not dishonor, just because he's blind, the father
who begot you; for these girls did not act so.
Therefore these curses overpower your supplication   1380
and your throne, if Justice named of old indeed
exists, seated at Zeus's side by ancient law.[134]
     Be gone! I spit you from me fatherless, most evil
of all evil ones! And take with you these curses
that I call on you: you shall not overpower   1385
with spears the land of your own race, or ever win
return to Argos' valley, but with kindred hand
you shall both die and kill the one who drove you out.
Such are my curses! And I call on the abhorrent
darkness of paternal Tartaros to take   1390
you to his home.[135] I call on these divinities.[136]
I call on Ares, who has cast into you both
this dreadful hatred. Hear this and proceed! Go and
report to all the Kadmeans, and likewise to
the trusty allies on your own side, just what kind   1395
of honor Oidipous apportions to his sons.

CHORUS

Your past roads did not give me pleasure, Polyneices;
now go away again as fast as possible.

POLYNEICES

Alas for the path I took here and the way I failed!
Alas too for my comrades! What an end awaits   1400
us to the road that we set out on—woe is me!—
from Argos, such that I can't even speak of it
to any of my comrades, or turn back again,
but must go forth to meet this fortune speechlessly.
Do you at least, blood-sisters, children of this man,[137] 1405
since you have heard the harsh words of our father here
as he was cursing, do not you two, by the gods—
if these our father's curses are fulfilled, and you

---

[134] Justice is often personified as a goddess who carries out the will of Zeus. This is Oidipous' response to Polyneices' personification of Respect (1267-8).

[135] Tartaros is the part of the underworld where the exceptionally wicked are punished for their crimes. The significance of the adjective "paternal" is unclear, but it may hint at the fact that Oidipous, Polyneices' father, is soon to be a resident of the underworld.

[136] The reference is to the goddesses of the grove (see n. on 865).

[137] Note the irony of the ambiguous wording, as at 330.

obtain some home-coming—do not dishonor me,
but place me in a tomb with funeral offerings.[138]   1410
And then the praise that both of you are winning now
from this man for your pains will be accompanied
by still more praise that is no less, for serving me.

ANTIGONE

I supplicate you, Polyneices, be persuaded.

POLYNEICES

In what respect, dearest Antigone? Speak on.   1415

ANTIGONE

Turn round your army, back—as fast as possible!—
to Argos; don't destroy the city and yourself.

POLYNEICES

But that's impossible. How could I once again
lead that same army, once I have been terrified?

ANTIGONE

Why do you need to feel such rage again, my boy?   1420
What profit comes from ravaging your fatherland?

POLYNEICES

To be an exile is disgraceful, and for me,
the elder, to be laughed at by my brother so.

ANTIGONE

You see, then, how you're making this man's prophecies
come out right, who cries death for both of you from both?   1425

POLYNEICES

Yes: that's what he desires; but I must not give in.

ANTIGONE

Alas! Oh woe is me! But who will dare to follow
you, when he has heard what this man prophesied?

POLYNEICES

I won't report the detrimental news at all;
good generals tell what's better, not what disappoints.   1430

ANTIGONE

So you're determined, boy, that it shall be this way?

POLYNEICES

I am; don't try to hold me back. This road will be
my own concern—a road made evil and ill-destined
by our father here and his Erinyes.

---

[138] This alludes to the plot of *Ant.* (Introduction, pp. 8-9). The dislocated style of the
sentence reflects Polyneices' despair.

But as for you two, if you do fulfill for me   1435
what I have asked—in death, since you can't help me any
more while I'm alive—may Zeus reward you well.
Now let me go, and farewell to you both. You'll see
no more of me while I have sight.[139]

ANTIGONE

Oh woe is me!

POLYNEICES

Do not lament me.

ANTIGONE

Who'd *not* weep as you set out,
my brother, to a Hades that you can foresee?[140]   1440

POLYNEICES

If I must die, I shall.

ANTIGONE

Let me persuade you! Don't!

POLYNEICES

Do not persuade where you must not.

ANTIGONE

Then woe is me,
if I'm to be bereft of you.

POLYNEICES

It's up to fate
from god, to turn out either way. For you two, though,
I pray the gods you never meet with evil: you're   1445
unworthy of misfortune in the eyes of all.

*[Exit Polyneices, in the direction of Thebes. The chorus sing two strophic pairs of
lyrics, punctuated by three symmetrical groups of five spoken lines from Oidipous
and Antigone (1457-61, 1472-6, 1486-90).]*

CHORUS   *Strophe A*

New evils have come from somewhere new,
new and heavy-destined,
from the blind stranger—
unless destiny is reaching some goal.   1450
For I cannot call vain
any purpose of divinities.

---

139   "Having sight," or "seeing the light," is often used to mean "alive" (cf. 1549-50),
       since the dead descend to the darkness of Hades. Here the idiom evokes the theme
       of sight and blindness running through the play.
140   As in 1221, the name of the god Hades stands for death.

Time sees, sees all things always,
casting some things down,
the next day raising others up again.   1455

[A peal of thunder is heard.[141]]

Thunder crashing in the sky! Oh Zeus![142]

OIDIPOUS

Oh children, children! If there's anybody present,[143]
could he bring Theseus here, in all ways best of men?

ANTIGONE

Father, what is the reason why you're calling him?

OIDIPOUS

This thunder winging down from Zeus will take me soon   1460
to Hades. Send for him as fast as possible!

[A second peal is heard.]

CHORUS   *Antistrophe A*

See! A great crash, unutterable,
cast by Zeus, bursts forth;
dread stiffens the very tips
of the hairs on my head.   1465
My heart cowers: in the heavens
again a flash of lightning flares!
What end will it produce?
I dread this! It never rushes forth
without momentous outcome.   1470
Oh great sky! Oh Zeus!

OIDIPOUS

The end of life, my children, prophesied for this
man here has come; no longer can I turn away.

ANTIGONE

How do you know? From what have you determined this?

OIDIPOUS

I know it very well. Let someone go as fast   1475
as possible and fetch this land's lord here to me.

---

[141] Thunder and lightning were among the signs of Oidipous' end foretold by Apollo
(94-5). The Greek theatre did have a device for simulating these phenomena, but
it is uncertain whether it had come into use yet in 401 BCE. If not, then the noise
was left to the spectators' imagination.

[142] The chorus appeal to Zeus as the sender of thunder and lightning.

[143] Oidipous means anyone besides his daughters and the chorus. His blindness
prevents him from knowing if a suitable messenger is available. In the event,
Theseus is not fetched by anyone but arrives in response to the uproar (1500).

[A third peal of thunder is heard.]

CHORUS   *Strophe B*

    Ah! Ah! See, yet again!
    A piercing din surrounds us!
    Be gracious, divinity, gracious,
    if indeed you are bringing   1480
    gloom to the land, our mother.[144]
    May I find you propitious, and not,
    from seeing a man accursed,
    share a favor that profits me not.[145]
    Lord Zeus, to you I speak!   1485

OIDIPOUS

    Is the man near yet? Will he reach me, children, while
    I'm still alive, still able to direct my mind?

ANTIGONE

    Why do you want to hold fast to a trusty mind?

OIDIPOUS

    To give fulfillment of the favor that I promised
    in return for my good treatment at that time.   1490

CHORUS   *Antistrophe B*

    Oh! Oh! Child, come, come![146]
    If at the edge of the hollow,[147]
    for Poseidon, god of the sea,
    you hallow the altar with sacrifice, come!
    For the stranger deems you worthy,   1495
    you and your city and friends,
    that he should provide a just favor
    because he was treated well.
    Hurry, rush, oh lord!

[Enter Theseus with attendants, from the direction of the village.]

THESEUS

    What is this uproar that resounds again from you   1500
    in common, clearly from yourselves and manifestly
    from the stranger too? Is it some thunderbolt

---

144   According to local legend, the people of Attica were born from the land. More
     generally, the earth was the mythic mother of all life.
145   The chorus are worried about the nature of the "favor" they will receive in return
     for helping Oidipous (cf. 1497).
146   It is the prerogative of the chorus' age to call Theseus "child," but it also shows
     affection for their king.
147   The text here is corrupt, but it certainly refers to the location of the sacrifice.

from Zeus, or shower of clattering hail? When god sends such
a storm as this one, anything may be surmised.

OIDIPOUS

My lord, you have appeared to one who yearned for you;   1505
some god has made good fortune for you by this road.

THESEUS

What new thing, child of Laios, has occurred this time?

OIDIPOUS

My life is sinking down;[148] I do not want to die
false in my promises to you and to this city.

THESEUS

What evidence assures you that your doom is near?   1510

OIDIPOUS

The gods themselves as heralds are my messengers,
playing me false in none of the appointed signs.

THESEUS

How are you saying this is clear to you, old man?

OIDIPOUS

By the incessant thunderclaps and many lightning-
bolts that flash from the unconquered hand of Zeus.   1515

THESEUS

I am persuaded. For I see you prophesying
much that is not false. Tell me what must be done.

OIDIPOUS

Child of Aigeus, I'll explain to you the things
your city will have stored away for it, unpained
by age. Soon I myself shall guide the way, untouched   1520
by any guide, towards the place where I must die.
Never tell any human being where this is—
where it's concealed, or in what area it lies,
that it may render you protection evermore,
better than many shields, or neighbors' borrowed spears.   1525
The things that are taboo, which must not be disturbed
by words, you'll learn yourself when you go there alone;
I would not speak of them to any one of these
townsfolk, or to my children, though I cherish them.
But you yourself protect them evermore, and when   1530
you reach life's end, reveal them to the foremost man
alone; let him show his successor, and so on.

---

148   The metaphor is that of a pair of scales (see n. on *OT* 847).

And thus this city where you dwell will stay unravaged
by the sown men.[149] Countless cities, even those
well governed, easily commit outrageous acts.   1535
For though the gods see well, they do so late, when one
lets go of their concerns and turns to frenzied deeds.
Child of Aigeus, never wish to suffer this.
    This much I am explaining to a man who knows.
But since the sign from god is pressing me, let us   1540
proceed now to that place and hesitate no more.

[Oidipous starts to walk, unaided and confident, from the stage.]

My children, follow me this way. For I have been
revealed as your new guide, as you two were for me.
Go onward! Do not touch me. Let me find myself
the sacred tomb in which it is the destiny   1545
of this man here to be concealed within this land.
This way, here, come this way! Hermes the escort leads
me this way,[150] and the goddess of the underworld.[151]
Oh light that is no light, once you were mine, but now
this is the the last time that my body touches you.[152]   1550
I go now to conceal the ending of my life
with Hades. May you, dearest of all strangers, and
this land of yours, and your attendants all be blessed,
and in prosperity remember me when I
am dead, enjoying your good fortune evermore.   1555

*[Exit Oidipous in the direction of Colonus, followed by his daughters, Theseus and
his retinue.[153] The chorus sing the fourth and final stasimon.]*

CHORUS   *Strophe*

    If it is lawful for me to revere

---

149   The Thebans are the "sown men" because in myth their ancestors sprang from
       dragon's teeth sown by Kadmos, the city's founder (cf. *Ant*. 1125).
150   Hermes was the herald and messenger of the gods. One of his functions was to
       escort the souls of the dead to the underworld.
151   This refers to Persephone, queen of the underworld.
152   In Greek tragedy dying characters often say farewell to the sunlight
       (cf. n. on 1438 and *OT* 1182-3 with note). Oidipous has not seen the light since he
       blinded himself, but this is the last time he will feel it on his skin.
153   Some have thought that Oidipous exits into the grove, since his death clearly
       takes place in the vicinity of the shrine. But this would involve a large number of
       people, including insignificant attendants, entering the sacred precinct, which is
       supposed to remain untrodden by ordinary mortals. Moreover a procession along
       the side-entrance towards Colonus, led by the newly confident Oidipous, would
       make an impressive theatrical contrast with his faltering first entrance from the
       other side, guided by Antigone.

with prayer the unseen goddess,[154] and you,
lord of those shrouded in night,
Aidoneus, Aidoneus,[155]
grant me that the stranger   1560
may reach without any pain
and without a grievous doom
the all-concealing plain of the dead
down below and the Stygian home.[156]
For despite the many troubles   1565
that have come on him in vain,
a just divinity may raise him up again.

Oh you, earth goddesses,[157] and you,   *Antistrophe*
unconquered body of the beast,[158]
you who sleep at the gate
that welcomes many strangers,   1570
whining from your cave,
the untamed guard of Hades,
as the story has always held.
Oh child of Earth and Tartaros,[159]
I pray that he walk clear   1575
of the stranger who's setting out
to the plains of the underworld.
On you I call, everlasting sleep!

[One of Theseus' attendants enters hastily along the side-entrance by which Oidipous departed.]

MESSENGER

Men of this city! I'll succeed in speaking most
concisely if I say that Oidipous is dead.   1580
But as for what was done, of this the tale cannot
be briefly told, nor were the deeds that happened brief.

---

154 The "unseen goddess" is Persephone. The unusual adjective may be explained by
     the fact that Hades, the name of her husband, literally means "unseen" (cf. 1681).
     It also suits the play's preoccupation with what cannot or should not be looked
     upon.
155 This is a longer version, sometimes found in poetry, of the name of Hades.
156 Stygian means "infernal," from the river Styx in the underworld.
157 I.e. the Eumenides (cf. Introduction, p. 23).
158 The "beast" is Kerberos, the three-headed dog who guards the underworld. He
     was said to fawn on those who entered but devour anyone who tried to leave.
159 This is probably Death, though elsewhere he is the child of Night (Hesiod, *Theogony*
     211). Death is also the "everlasting sleep" invoked at 1578.

CHORUS

He's dead, then, the unhappy man?

MESSENGER

                  Yes; understand

that he's departed from the life he always led.[160]

CHORUS

How? Was it by a painless fortune from the gods?　　　　　　1585

MESSENGER

Now this indeed is worthy of amazement; for

you also, who were present, know the way he moved

away from here, guided by none among his friends,

but he himself providing guidance for us all;

but when he came to the precipitous threshold　　　　　　　1590

rooted within the earth with steps of bronze,[161] he stopped

on one of many paths that forked away from there,[162]

near to the hollow bowl where lies the pact of Theseus

and Peirithous, trustworthy evermore.[163]

Standing between this bowl and the Thorician rock,　　　　　1595

near to the hollow pear-tree and the tomb of stone,[164]

he sat down; then he loosed his filthy garments. Next

he called his children and commanded them to bring

fresh water, both for washing and for offerings.

The two of them went over to the hill of green　　　　　　　1600

Demeter, which was in our view,[165] and in a short

time fetched their father what he ordered and attended

160　The text of this line is corrupt, but it certainly refers somehow to Oidipous' death.

161　On the "bronze threshold" see n. on 57.

162　The language here recalls the famous "forked path" where Oidipous met and killed his father (*OT* 733).

163　Theseus and his friend Peirithous made a pledge of friendship before venturing into the underworld to kidnap Persephone. They were caught, but Theseus (and in some versions Perithous as well) was later rescued by Herakles. The place may have been marked by a monumental bowl of bronze or stone, or the "bowl" may be a hollow or cave in the rock.

164　The audience would have recognized the significance of these local landmarks, which is lost to us. The precise geographical description adds to the miraculous effect of the blind man's progress. The actual spot where Oidipous disappears must, however, have remained mysterious, since its secrecy is so heavily emphasized.

165　Demeter is "verdant" because she is a goddess of vegetation and growth. She is also a goddess of the underworld, which makes her an appropriate patron for this spot.

him with washing and the customary clothes.[166]
    But when his pleasure in these doings was complete,
and nothing that he had desired was left undone, 1605
Zeus crashed with thunder from the earth;[167] the maidens
   shuddered
as they heard it; falling at their father's knees
they kept on weeping, beat incessantly upon
their breasts and drew their lamentions out at length.
And when he heard the sudden bitter sound, he folded 1610
them within his arms and said to them, "Children,
upon this day your father ceases to exist.
All that concerns me has now perished; you'll no longer
have to bear the painful work of nurturing me.
It has been harsh, I know, my children; but one word 1615
alone dissolves all of these anguished toils:[168] no one
has ever given you more love than this man here
has done; but now you'll pass the portion of your life
that still remains deprived of his companionship."
    Thus did they cry together, weeping with great sobs 1620
and clinging to each other. When they reached an end
of making lamentation, and their cries arose
no longer, there was silence; suddenly a voice
of someone shouted out to him,[169] so that for fear
the hair of all stood up on end in sudden dread. 1625
The god called to him many times in many ways:
"You there! You, Oidipous! What is delaying us
from going? You have slowed things down now for too long!"
When he perceived that he was called by god, he said that
Theseus, this land's lord, should come to him. And when 1630
he came he said, "Dear friend, give to my girls the trusty
ancient pledge of your right hand, and, children, yours

---

166 Preparations for burial of the dead included a ritual washing of the corpse and
    dressing it in white funeral garments. No mention is made of where these special
    garments have come from. We may imagine that they are supplied by Theseus,
    but as the story reaches its climax, the poet does not invite us to speculate on such
    practical matters.
167 The "Zeus" who lives under the earth is Hades (Introduction, pp. 23-4). Although
    the same language was used previously for thunder (1456, 1464), it may here signify
    an earthquake, which is more appropriate to the king of the underworld and was
    mentioned by Oidipous as another possible sign of his approaching end (95).
168 The "one word" is "love," as the next sentence implies.
169 The mysterious anonymity of this voice makes it all the more awesome. The god
    may, however, be identified with Hermes (cf. 1547-8), Persephone (cf. 1548 with
    note), or perhaps Hades himself.

to him. Promise you will not willingly betray
them ever, and will fulfill all that you're going to do
to their advantage with good will for evermore."   1635
And like a noble man, without lamenting, he
promised the stranger under oath to do these things.
And after he had done that, Oidipous at once,
touching the children with his blind hands, said to them,
"Children, you must endure with noble minds to leave   1640
this region, and not think that it is just to look
at that which is not lawful, or to hear such speech.
Be gone as quickly as you can. Theseus alone,
who has authority, must stay to learn what's done."
    We heard him say this, all of us, and weeping streams   1645
of tears with them we kept the maidens company
as they departed. After we had left, a short
time later we turned round, and from afar we saw
that man no longer present anywhere, but just
our lord, and he was holding up a hand before   1650
his face to shade his eyes, as if some dread and fearful
thing had been revealed, unbearable to see.
But then, a little later and without a word,
we saw him bowing down in worship to the earth
and at the same time to Olympus of the gods.[170]   1655
But by what doom he perished, there's no mortal man
can tell, except for Theseus. For no fiery bolt
of thunder from the god destroyed him, nor a tempest
stirred up from the sea at just that moment; no,
the gods sent him some escort, or the underworld,   1660
the earth's unlit foundation, being well-disposed
to him, gaped open. For the man was not sent off
with weeping, or distressed by sickness, but in some
amazing way if ever any mortal was.
Perhaps my words seem senseless, but I would not try   1665
to change the minds of those who think I have no sense.

CHORUS

Where are the children and the friends escorting them?

MESSENGER

The girls are not far off; clear sounds of lamentation
indicate that they are on their way back here.

---

[170] "Olympus" here means the sky. Theseus bows down to the earth and then imme-
diately raises his arms to the sky, as he worships both "earth" and "sky" gods.

[Enter Antigone and Ismene, crying aloud, along the side-entrance by which they left. There follow two strophic pairs of lyric dialogue among them and the chorus.]

ANTIGONE   *Strophe A*

> Alas! Woe! It is our lot, it is indeed,
> to weep in full for the cursed blood   1671
> born in us two, ill-fated pair,
> from our father; from him in the past
> we had constant pain, and from him in the end
> we take away things beyond reason,   1675
> which we two saw and suffered.

CHORUS

> What is it?

ANTIGONE

> Friends, we can only surmise!

CHORUS

> He is gone?

ANTIGONE

> In a way you would yearn for most.
> Yes indeed! For neither Ares
> nor the sea confronted him,   1680
> but the unsurveyed plains engulfed him,
> borne off by some unseen doom.
> But for us two—woe is me!—
> deadly night has come on our eyes.
> For how, as vagrants roaming   1685
> some distant land or the swell of the sea,
> shall we obtain the nurture
> of our lives, so hard to bear?

ISMENE

> I don't know! May murderous Hades
> overwhelm me, that I may share the death   1690
> of my old father! Woe is me! For me
> the life to come is not worth living.

CHORUS

> Oh you two best of children,
> bear well what comes from the gods,
> don't burn too much with grief: 1695
> your path is not to be criticized.

ANTIGONE   *Antistrophe A*

> So one can yearn even for evils.
> What was not dear at all, was dear,

while I had him in my arms.[171]
Oh father! Oh dear one! Oh you who are clad   1700
in eternal darkness under the earth!
Not even there will you ever find
yourself unloved by me and her.

CHORUS
He did...

ANTIGONE
      He did what he wanted.

CHORUS
In what way?

ANTIGONE
         He died in the strange   1705
land he desired; he occupies a bed
below well-shaded for evermore,
and has left behind mourning cries.[172]
For these eyes of mine weep tears,
father, for you. And I have no way—   1710
woe is me!—by which I should
erase so much great sorrow for you.
Alas! You wished to die in a strange land,
but you died thus bereft of me.

ISMENE
Oh woe is me! What destiny then   1715
        * * * * * * * * * *

        * * * * * * * * * *

still awaits me and you, dear one,
thus bereft of a father?[173]

CHORUS
Since he resolved his life's end   1720
blessedly, dear friends,
cease from this sorrow: no one
is beyond the reach of evils.

---

[171] Antigone means that the sufferings she endured for Oidipous' sake were outweighed by the pleasure of his company. Note that the word "dear" has the
same root in Greek (*phil-*) as the word translated as "love" in line 1617. It is also
translated elsewhere as "friend" or "dear friend."

[172] Not to be mourned was considered a misfortune, for it showed that one had not
been valued in life.

[173] The asterisks indicate that two lines are missing from the text here or nearby.

ANTIGONE   *Strophe B*
    Back again, dear one, let us speed!
ISMENE
                    To do what?   1725

ANTIGONE
    Longing possesses me...
ISMENE
              What longing?
ANTIGONE
    To see the hearth under the earth.[174]
ISMENE
    Whose hearth?
ANTIGONE
          Our father's—woe is me!
ISMENE
    But how is that lawful? Don't
    you see?
ANTIGONE
       Why rebuke me thus?   1730
ISMENE
    And also...
ANTIGONE
        Why do so again?
ISMENE
    ... he fell without a tomb, apart from all.
ANTIGONE
    Take me there, then slay me!

      * * * * * * * * * *

ISMENE
    Alas! Woe is me! Where then
    bereft, resourceless, shall I live   1735
    the rest of my long-suffering life?
CHORUS   *Antistrophe B*
    Dear friends, don't be terrified!
ANTIGONE
          But to where can I escape?

---

[174] Antigone is not referring literally to a hearth, but to her father's grave, his new
home under the earth. The hearth represents the home, and is also a place where
sacrifices are offered, as they would be at a tomb.

CHORUS
You have both escaped already...

ANTIGONE
What?

CHORUS
...from a lot that falls out evilly.[175]   1740

ANTIGONE
I'm thinking...

CHORUS
What's in your mind?

ANTIGONE
How we shall get home
I cannot say.

CHORUS
Don't seek that!

ANTIGONE
Hardship holds us.

CHORUS
It held you fast before.

ANTIGONE
Ineluctable then, still greater now!   1745

CHORUS
A great sea of troubles is your lot.

ANTIGONE
Woe! Woe! Where shall we go,
oh Zeus? To what remaining hope
does fate from god now drive me?   1750

[Enter Theseus with his attendants, along the side-entrance by which they left.][176]

THESEUS
Cease from your weeping, children; for when the
dark night under the earth is a favor we
must not mourn, or the gods will resent it.

---

[175] The chorus are reminding Antigone that she and her sister may remain safely in Athens. She acknowledges their concern (1741), but remains preoccupied with the coming events at Thebes, which she still regards as "home" (1742). The remote possibility of saving her brothers—her last "remaining hope" (1749)—draws her back to her native city (1769-72).

[176] The conclusion of the play is in anapests (Introduction, p. 15).

ANTIGONE

Child of Aigeus, we fall at your knees!

THESEUS

To attain what desire do you do so, children?   1755

ANTIGONE

What we want is to
see for ourselves our father's grave.

THESEUS

But to go there is not lawful.

ANTIGONE

What did you say, lord, ruler of Athens?

THESEUS

That man himself enjoined me, children, that   1760
no one of mortals should ever approach
close to that region or speak out loud
at the sacred tomb that he occupies.
And he said that if I performed this well,
my land would be free from pain evermore.   1765
A divinity heard me promising this,
and Oath who hears all, servant of Zeus.[177]

ANTIGONE

If this is according to that man's mind,
then it may be sufficient. But send us back
to primordial Thebes, to see if somehow   1770
we may prevent the murder that's coming on
our blood-brothers.

THESEUS

This I shall do, and everything else that I'm
going to do will be for your advantage
and to bring favor to him in the earth who's   1775
newly gone; I must not falter.

CHORUS

Come now, cease your weeping and do not
rouse it further; for
these events have complete authority.

[The chorus and remaining characters all depart in the direction of Colonus and
Athens.]

---

[177] The "divinity" is the mysterious power that spoke to Oidipous. The personified
Oath punishes perjury as a servant of Zeus, who is the guardian of oaths (see
Hesiod, *Theogony* 231, *Works and Days* 803-4).

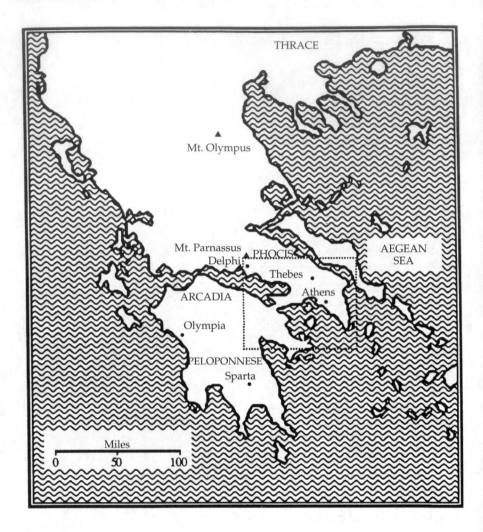

MAP 1
MAINLAND GREECE

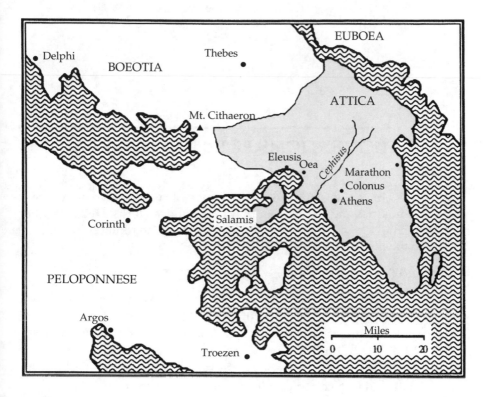

MAP 2
ATTICA AND ENVIRONS

SUGGESTIONS FOR FURTHER READING

This is only a tiny sample of the innumerable works devoted to Greek tragedy, Sophocles and the Theban plays. It includes works cited by author and date in the text, together with others chosen for their interest and accessibility to the English-speaking reader.

CULTURAL AND RELIGIOUS BACKGROUND

Burkert, W. *Greek Religion* (Eng. trans. Cambridge, Mass. 1985) [invaluable concise survey of the gods and their cults]

Buxton, Richard. *Imaginary Greece: The Contexts of Mythology* (Cambridge 1994) [the cultural contexts of myth-telling]

Ehrenberg, V. *From Solon to Socrates* (2nd ed. London 1973) [history of the sixth and fifth centuries with a cultural emphasis]

Fantham, E., H. Foley, N. Kampen, S. Pomeroy and A. Shapiro (edd.). *Women in the Classical World* (Oxford 1994)

Gantz, Timothy. *Early Greek Myth: A Guide to Literary and Artistic Sources* (Johns Hopkins UP 1993) [indispensable for the serious study of Greek myth]

Howatson, M.C. (ed.). *The Concise Oxford Companion to Classical Literature* (Oxford 1993) [a handy reference for looking up names in myth, history, etc.]

Lloyd-Jones, H. *The Justice of Zeus* (2nd ed. Berkeley and Los Angeles 1983)

Parker, Robert. *Miasma: Pollution and Purification in Greek Religion* (Oxford 1983)

Tyrrell, William Blake and Frieda S. Brown. *Athenian Myths and Institutions* (Oxford 1991) [the uses of myth in Athenian culture]

Williams, Bernard. *Shame and Necessity* (Berkeley and Los Angeles 1993) [an important study of Greek values surrounding agency and responsibility]

WORKS ON ATHENIAN TRAGEDY (MOST INCLUDE SOME DISCUSSION OF ONE OR MORE OF SOPHOCLES' THEBAN PLAYS)

Buxton, R.G.A. *Persuasion in Greek Tragedy* (Cambridge 1982) [a useful account of an important aspect of drama]

Csapo, Eric and Slater, William J. *The Context of Ancient Drama* (Ann Arbor 1995) [surveys all the evidence for the ancient theater and production]

Foley, Helene. *Female Acts in Greek Tragedy* (Princeton 2001) [examines problems of female agency in tragedy, in the context of Athenian gender norms]

Goldhill, S. *Reading Greek Tragedy* (Cambridge 1986) [an introduction from the perspective of recent critical theory]

Jones, John. *On Aristotle and Greek Tragedy* (London 1962) [challenges the view that character is central to Greek tragedy]

Kitto, H.D.F. *Greek Tragedy* (3rd ed. London 1961) [a still valuable introduction]

Lesky, A. *Greek Tragic Poetry* (Eng. trans. New Haven 1983) [a thorough survey of tragedy and scholarship]

MacKinnon, Kenneth. *Greek Tragedy into Film* (Cranbury, NJ 1986) [brief survey of many films based on tragedies]

McClure, Laura. *Spoken like a Woman: Speech and Gender in Athenian Drama* (Princeton 1999) [addresses the problem of female "voice"]

Rehm, Rush. *Greek Tragic Theater* (London 1992) [a good introduction from the perspective of performance]

---------------. *Marriage to Death* (Princeton 1994) [a detailed exploration of an important complex of ideas]

Taplin, O. *Greek Tragedy in Action* (London 1978) [a fine introduction to tragedy in performance]

Vernant, Jean-Pierre and Pierre Vidal-Naquet. *Myth and Tragedy in Ancient Greece*, trans. Janet Lloyd (New York 1988) [influential collection of structuralist interpretations]

Vickers, B. *Towards Greek Tragedy* (London 1973) [makes good use of mythic, social and religious background]

Wiles, David. *Tragedy in Athens: Performance Space and Theatrical Meaning* (Cambridge 1997) [an innovative exploration of the use of theatrical space]

---------------. *Greek Theatre Performance: An Introduction* (Cambridge 2000)

Winkler, J. and F. Zeitlin (edd.) *Nothing to Do with Dionysos?* (Princeton 1990) [places Athenian drama in its political context]

Zeitlin, Froma. "Thebes: Theater of Self and Society in Athenian Drama," in *Nothing to Do with Dionysos?* edd. J. Winkler and F. Zeitlin (Princeton 1990) 130-67 [examines the use of Thebes as an "anti-Athens"]

GENERAL BOOKS ON SOPHOCLES (ALL INCLUDE SOME DISCUSSION OF ONE OR MORE OF THE THEBAN PLAYS)

Blundell, M.W. *Helping Friends and Harming Enemies: A Study in Sophocles and Greek Ethics* (Cambridge 1989) [discusses Sophocles in the context of Greek popular morality]

Bowra, C.M. *Sophoclean Tragedy* (Oxford 1944) [old-fashioned but still valuable for its learning]

Burton, R.W.B. *The Chorus in Sophocles' Tragedies* (Oxford 1980) [thorough discussion of the chorus]

Bushnell, Rebecca W. *Prophesying Tragedy: Sign and Voice in Sophocles' Theban Plays* (Ithaca, NY 1988) [a semiotic interpretation using the theme of prophecy]

Ehrenberg, Victor. *Sophocles and Pericles* (Oxford 1954) [relates Sophocles' plays to the political context of his time]

Gardiner: C.P. *The Sophoclean Chorus: A Study of Character and Function* (Iowa City 1987) [looks at the chorus as a character]

Gellie, G.H. *Sophocles: A Reading* (Melbourne 1972) [an accessible introduction]

Kirkwood, G.M. *A Study of Sophoclean Drama* (Ithaca 1958) [good on character and aspects of dramatic technique]

Knox, B.M.W. *The Heroic Temper* (Berkeley 1964) [an influential and readable account of the Sophoclean "hero"]

Ormand, Kirk. *Exchange and the Maiden: Marriage in Sophoclean Tragedy* (Texas 1999) [shows how the plays problematize the Greek ideology of marriage]

Reinhardt, K. *Sophocles* (English trans. Oxford 1979) [demanding but influential]

Scodel, R. *Sophocles* (Boston 1984) [a stimulating introduction]

Seale, D. *Vision and Stagecraft in Sophocles* (London 1982) [explores visual aspects and imagery of sight]

Segal, C.P. *Tragedy and Civilization: An Interpretation of Sophocles* (Cambridge, Mass. 1981) [a detailed structuralist account]

-------------. *Sophocles' Tragic World: Divinity, Nature, Society* (Harvard 1995) [a collection of the author's essays]

Waldock, A.J.A. *Sophocles the Dramatist* (Cambridge 1951) [refreshingly iconoclastic, if often wrong-headed]

Webster, T.B.L. *An Introduction to Sophocles* (Oxford 1936) [old-fashioned but still useful, especially on Sophocles' life]

Whitman, C.H. Sophocles, *A Study in Heroic Humanism* (Cambridge, Mass. 1951) [dated but often stimulating]

Winnington-Ingram, R.P. *Sophocles: An Interpretation* (Cambridge 1980) [an outstanding study by a sensitive scholar]

WORKS ON *ANTIGONE*

Else, G.F. *The Madness of Antigone* (Heidelberg 1976) [detailed study of irrational aspects of character]

Foley, Helene P. "Tragedy and Democratic Ideology," in *History, Tragedy, Theory*, ed. B. Goff (Austin 1995) p. 131-50 [a balanced approach to the Athenian political context]

Goheen, R.F. *The Imagery of Sophocles' Antigone* (Princeton 1951) [a valuable and detailed study of systems of imagery]

Murnaghan, Sheila. "*Antigone* 904-920 and the Institution of Marriage," *American Journal of Philology* 107 (1986) 192-207 [places Antigone's final speech in an anthropological context]

Neuburg, Matt. "How Like a Woman: Antigone's 'Inconsistency'," *Classical Quarterly* 40 (1990) 54-76 [a compelling defense of Antigone's last speech]

Oudemans, Th.C.W. and A.P.M.H. Lardinois. *Tragic Ambiguity: Anthropology, Philosophy and Sophocles' Antigone* (Leiden 1987) [a very detailed structuralist study]

Segal, C.P. "Sophocles' Praise of Man and the Conflicts of the *Antigone*," *Arion* 3 (1964) 46-66 [a subtle account of the play's conceptual ambiguities]

Sourvinou-Inwood, C. "Assumptions and the Creation of Meaning: Reading Sophocles' *Antigone*," *Journal of Hellenic Studies* 109 (1989) 134-48 [a controversial attack on Antigone and defense of Kreon]

Steiner, G. *Antigones* (Oxford 1984) [looks at later treatments of the story]

Tyrell, Wm. Blake and Larry J. Bennet, *Recapturing Sophocles' Antigone* (Lanham, MD 1998) [tries to relocate the play in its original political context]

WORKS ON *KING OIDIPOUS*

Ahl, Frederick. *Sophocles' Oedipus: Evidence and Self-Contradiction* (Ithaca, NY 1991) [revives the provocative view that Oedipus did *not* kill his father or marry his mother]

Burkert, Walter. *Oedipus, Oracles, and Meaning* (Toronto 1991) [a brief and readable introductory essay]

Cameron, Alister. *The Identity of Oedipus the King* (New York 1968) [a straightforward introduction for the general reader]

Dodds, E.R. "On misunderstanding the *Oedipus Rex*," *Greece and Rome* 13

(1966) 37-49; reprinted in E.R. Dodds, *The Ancient Concept of Progress* (Oxford 1973) and E. Segal (ed.) *Greek Tragedy* (New York 1983) [a landmark essay still useful on guilt and pollution]

Edmunds, L. and A. Dundes (edd.). *Oedipus: A Folklore Casebook* (New York 1983) [a wealth of parallels to the Oidipous story from other cultures]

Griffith, R. Drew *The Theatre of Apollo: Divine Justice and Sophocles' Oedipus the King* (McGill-Queens UP 1996) [perverse but sometimes insightful]

Knox, Bernard. *Oedipus at Thebes: Sophocles' Tragic Hero and his Time* (2nd. Ed. New Haven 1998) [a justly famous study identifying Oedipus with the city of Athens]

O'Brien, M.J. (ed.). *Twentieth-Century Interpretations of Oedipus Rex* (Englewood Cliffs, NJ 1968) [a collection of important critical essays]

Pucci, Pietro, *Oedipus and the Fabrication of the Father: Oedipus Tyrannus in Modern Criticism and Philosophy* (Baltimore 1992) [a contemporary psychoanalytic reading]

Segal, Charles. *Oedipus Tyrannus: Tragic Heroism and the Limits of Knowledge* (2nd. edn. Oxford 2001) [an accessible introduction for the general reader]

Van Nortwick, T. *Oedipus: The Meaning of a Masculine Life* (University of Oklahoma Press 1998) [Oidipous as a paradigm for masculine psychological development]

WORKS ON *OIDIPOUS AT COLONUS*

Blundell, M.W. "The Ideal of the *Polis* in *Oedipus at Colonus*," in *Tragedy, Comedy and the Polis*, ed. A.H. Sommerstein, S. Halliwell, J. Henderson and B. Zimmermann (Bari, Italy 1993) 287-306 [on Athenian ideology in this play}

Burian, P. "Suppliant and Saviour," *Phoenix* 28 (1974) 408-29 [treats the play as a suppliant drama]

Easterling, P.E. "Oedipus and Polynices," *Proceedings of the Cambridge Philological Society* 193 (1967) 1-13 [a sensitive study of Oidipous' relationship to his children]

Edmunds, Lowell. *Theatrical Space and Historical Place in Sophocles' Oedipus at Colonus* (Lanham, MD 1996) [locates the play in its historical context]

Hester, D.A. "To Help one's Friends and Harm one's Enemies," *Antichthon* 11 (1977) 22-41

Kirkwood, G.M. "From Melos to Colonus," *Transactions of the American Philological Association* 116 (1986) 99-117 [emphasizes the local religious setting]

Linforth, I.M. "Religion and Drama in *Oedipus at Colonus*," *University of*

California Publications in Classical Philology 14 (1951) 75-191 [downplays religious aspects of the play]

Rosenmeyer, T.G. "The Wrath of Oedipus," *Phoenix* 6 (1952) 92-112 [attacks Oidipous, defends Kreon]

Shields, M.G. "Sight and Blindness Imagery in the *Oedipus Coloneus*," *Phoenix* 15 (1961) 63-73

Van Nortwick, Thomas. "'Do Not Go Gently...' *Oedipus at Colonus* and the Psychology of Aging," in *Old Age in Greek and Latin Literature*, ed. T.M. Falkner and J. de Luce (Albany 1989) 132-56 [views Oidipous as a hero in light of modern studies of aging]

Wilson, Joseph P. *The Hero and the City: An Interpretation of Sophocles' Oedipus at Colonus* (U. Michigan Press 1997) [easy to follow, but should be read critically]